T0072585

WHY I WON'T EAT
SNAILS

WHY I WON'T EAT SNAILS

TRAVEL AND FOOD ADVENTURES

LILA READ DICKEY

iUniverse, Inc.
Bloomington

WHY I WON'T EAT SNAILS
Travel and Food Adventures

Copyright © 2012 by Lila Read Dickey.

All rights reserved. No part of this book may be used or reproduced by any means, graphic, electronic, or mechanical, including photocopying, recording, taping or by any information storage retrieval system without the written permission of the publisher except in the case of brief quotations embodied in critical articles and reviews.

iUniverse books may be ordered through booksellers or by contacting:

iUniverse
1663 Liberty Drive
Bloomington, IN 47403
www.iuniverse.com
1-800-Authors (1-800-288-4677)

Because of the dynamic nature of the Internet, any web addresses or links contained in this book may have changed since publication and may no longer be valid. The views expressed in this work are solely those of the author and do not necessarily reflect the views of the publisher, and the publisher hereby disclaims any responsibility for them.

ISBN: 978-1-4697-8140-2 (sc)
ISBN: 978-1-4697-8141-9 (ebk)

Printed in the United States of America

iUniverse rev. date: 03/05/2012

This book is dedicated with deep love and affection

To our daughter, Alix and to our grandchildren

To give them a glimpse of what came before they did.

This book is also
Dedicated to food and
Thoughts of food
Food I grew up with and loved and
Food I learned to love in remote
As well as familiar corners of the world

TABLE OF CONTENTS

1

BEING BORN FEMALE IN THE ORIENT WORLD WAR II YEARS

BEGINNING AT THE BEGINNING IS always a good thing, so I'm told. Therefore, without further preliminaries, I will start at what I think is the beginning.

My Mother's family history in this country began with the emigration of Abram Claude from French-speaking Neuchatel, Switzerland, at the young age of sixteen. He settled in Annapolis, Maryland, after a sea voyage aboard a ship from Gibraltar. "Sunday, November 13, 1763—leaft Gibraltar for Cape Fair on board of a ship belonging to Neaucap. Commandead by Capt. Robert Auckland." (Quote is from an inscription on the fly leaf of a book he brought with him.) He apprenticed with a local tradesman and became a clockmaker and silversmith. In 1775 he married Nancy Stevens who died in 1784, from whom we are descended. He remarried in 1785. His second wife's name was Elizabeth Quynn.

Annapolis is a small town at the mouth of the Severn River where it empties into the Chesapeake Bay. The city was founded in 1649 and played a significant role in Colonial times, both culturally and politically. Three of the four Maryland signers of the Declaration of Independence had homes in Annapolis. They were Charles Carroll of Carrollton, Samuel Chase and William Paca. These homes are still standing and are still used. The fourth Maryland signer, Thomas Stone, lived in Charles County.

There was also a popular opera house and a very active social life for the upper classes. George Washington resigned his commission in the Continental Army in a room in the State House. In 1784, the Treaty of Paris ending the Revolutionary War was ratified in Annapolis when it was briefly the capital of the new nation. Francis Scott Key wrote his poem *The Star Spangled Banner* in his law office nearby.

*   *   *

My maternal great grandfather, Dr. Abram Claude, named for our original immigrant ancestor, bought a huge home at 58 State Circle in the center of town to house his growing family as he had sired ten children, four boys and seven girls. The building had had a series of prominent owners over the years as it dated from 1695. A few members of the family are shown in the following picture which was taken in the early part of the 19th Century. Some are standing in front of the house. Others are on the porch, while several peer from the upstairs windows.

The house at 58 State Circle with various family members on the porch,
in front or peering from windows, taken in the early part of the 19th Century

The daughters in my maternal great grandfather, Dr. Abram Claude's family, taken in the late 1870s or early 1880s Top: Clara Belle (Clara) Next Row: Isabella Howard (Isabel). Caroline Laurens (Carrie), and Sophia Third Row: Mary Beck (not one of the sisters), Anne Jacob, Lucy Clara Belle (Elsie), and Elizabeth Harwood (Lizzie)

Mary, the one in the lower left corner, was a distant relative who came to visit and didn't want to go home. Apparently she was having too much fun so she stayed until she married. The girl second from right in the bottom row was always called Elsie. She was an elderly lady when my family moved back to Annapolis in 1938 and I remember meeting her. Elsie's real name was Lucy Clara Belle. She was named for three maiden ladies who came to visit for a month and never went home. I guess that they, too, were having fun and didn't want to leave. It seems that Clara was also named for the visitors. Isabel, the first one on the left of the second row, was also still alive when we returned to Annapolis, so I also met her.

Unfortunately I have no picture of the four brothers together. However, their names were: Dennis, Washington Clement (my grandfather), Gordon Handy and William Hallam. I also met Hallam. He was, of course, extremely old and frail by that time.

My great grandfather, Dr. Abram Claude (the one who bought the large house) was a physician, although I don't know where he went to medical school. He was quite versatile as he served several terms as Mayor of Annapolis and was Postmaster at one time. He also taught natural sciences at St. John's College, a liberal arts school located in the center of Annapolis itself. It was originally called King William's School. My grandfather, Washington Clement Claude, (one of his children—see above) was born in 1853. He also became a doctor, graduating from the Maryland University Medical School in 1875. He married Frances Peyton Wilkinson in 1880 (see below) and later served as an Army Medical Officer during the Spanish-American War.

The author's grandfather, Dr. Washington Clement Claude, in his National Guard uniform. The photo was probably taken at the time of the Spanish-American War in 1898.

The author's grandmother, Frances Wilkinson Claude (nee Frances Peyton Wilkinson). The photo was probably taken about the time of their marriage in 1880.

My mother, Anne Howard Claude, was their tenth and last child born in 1902. Her nickname was Nancy or Nan. Family lore is not necessarily gospel, but I should repeat a story Mother told me time and time again about her father. During the influenza epidemic of 1919, he kept my mother out of school to drive him on his medical rounds. The flu was extremely contagious and extremely lethal. Mother claimed that he did not lose a single patient because of the fact that he insisted on caregivers turning over the patients often and regularly to keep fluid from settling in their lungs. I like to think that this is true.

* * *

The Wilkinsons were from Amelia County, Virginia, where they had a large plantation called Woodside. Jesse Wilkinson, my great great grandfather, was appointed a Midshipman in the United States Navy from Virginia on 4 July 1805. He was a Lieutenant during the War of 1812. By 1821, he had risen to the rank of Master Commandant. Later he commanded the frigate *USS United*

States in the Mediterranean. He served in the Navy until 1855 when he retired with the rank of Commodore and later died in 1861 just before the Civil War began. Ironically his wife received a pension from the U.S. Government based on his service in the U.S. Navy even though his sentiments would certainly have been with the South. However, I understand from family records that this small amount of money was of great help after the war.

The author's great great grandfather, Commodore Jesse Wilkinson, USN, from a photo of a family painting.

His son, John Wilkinson, my great grandfather, married Mary Blair Peachy of Virginia. He resigned from the United States Navy at the start of the Civil War, and was immediately commissioned in the Confederate States Navy as a First Lieutenant. John purportedly laid the first maritime smoke screen by burning oil soaked cotton balls in the firebox of his ship. This generated a great deal of smoke and masked his ship's progress through the Yankee blockade. He became a famous blockade runner making twenty-one successful trips. When the war was over, he went to Halifax, Nova Scotia, for a few years and then returned to his Virginia plantation, Woodside. During this period at Woodside, he wrote a book which was published in 1877 called *The Narrative of a Blockade-Runner.* Shortly thereafter he moved to Annapolis where his daughter, Frances Peyton Wilkinson, married my

grandfather in 1880, as I mentioned above. He opened a school in Annapolis preparing young men for entrance to the Naval Academy, which I understand was highly successful.

LIEUTENANT JOHN WILKINSON OF THE "LOUISIANA,"
AFTERWARD IN COMMAND OF THE "R. E. LEE."
(FROM PHOTOGRAPH BY S. W. GAULT.)

The author's great grandfather, First
Lieutenant John Wilkinson, CSN.
(Picture courtesy of the U.S. Naval
Institute)

Curiosity got the better of me and I looked up John Wilkinson on the Internet. I found quite a bit of information about him. To my consternation, however, I discovered that the Internet is not infallible as he was said to have been a lifelong bachelor, which was definitely *not* the case. There are too many descendants—legitimate ones at that.

One of the great problems I have tracing Mother's family is that they were fond of naming children after other members of the family; using surnames and maiden names as first names in the next generation; and then marrying, by coincidence, people whose surnames were already first names in the family. It's *very* confusing and I'm not sure I'll ever get it straight.

*   *   *

My Father's lineage is a bit more difficult for me to sketch as he came from Portland, Maine, which is a long way from Maryland and we didn't visit there very often. His full name was Walton Runnells Read and he was born in 1896. Walton was his mother's maiden name. Other family surnames include Arnold, Stevens and Runnells. His father's name was William Runnells Read and his mother's name was Marion, while his sister was named Helen Louise.

The author's father, Walton, and his sister, Helen, at ages ten and seven,
December 1906.

By accident I discovered that Helen had applied for membership in the
Daughters of the American Revolution and was rejected. When I asked Father
why, he was quite elderly and was so embarrassed that he blushed scarlet. With
much hemming and hawing he confessed that the ancestor she had chosen was
Benedict Arnold. (Although other ancestors had fought in the Revolution and
she could have chosen any one of them.) As a military man and a true patriot,
he had kept this information from my sister and me for decades. I don't think
he would have told me then had I not asked outright why my aunt was denied
membership.

The author's paternal grandparents, William and Marion Read, 4 June 1915.

From left to right: The author's grandfather, William Read; a great grandmother, name unknown; her aunt, Helen, (her father's sister); and her grandmother, Marion, 4 June 1915.

The author's grandfather, William Read, with his son, (her father) Walton Read, 4 June 1915.

The author's grandmother, Marion Read, with her aunt, Helen, later in 1915.

Helen married a man named Howard Robinson, nicknamed Robby. They had three sons, who are now deceased, as are Helen and Howard. The sons were William (Bill), Shepherd (Shep or Brud) and John (Jack). I have no way of tracing the sons' children as we lost touch many years ago. Visiting my aunt and uncle was great fun as they had not only a tennis court, but also a swimming pool. My uncle and the three boys had built the pool in a modern freeform shape, the bottom painted a bright aqua. It was always a special treat to swim in it. Father and Auntie Hearn, as I called Helen, were always playing the piano and singing, so the visits were pleasant in many ways. My grandchildren seem to be interested in where people went to school, so I will mention that Helen attended Smith College, but married before graduating. Robby, Bill, Brud and Jack were all Dartmouth graduates.

The author's Uncle Robby and Aunt Helen at home in Westfield, Massachusetts, sometime during the 1940s or 1950s.

*   *   *

The U.S. Naval Academy was founded in 1845 on land bordering the Severn River immediately adjacent to the city of Annapolis. There was much social interaction between the city and the Academy. Therefore, there will be a considerable number of references to the Navy and the Academy in this book as many local young women, including aunts and cousins and sisters, married

Academy graduates. (For some reason, it always seemed necessary to identify them by their Class at the Academy, so I will also do that.)

Purportedly Commodore Mathew C. Perry, who "opened up" trade with Japan in 1853 and 1854 gave a pair of tall Japanese vases to someone in the family. My sister and I each have one. I'm not sure how the family knew him as he did not go to the Academy. He was appointed a Midshipman in the Navy in 1809 when he was fifteen. The Academy was not founded until 1845. It would be interesting to know if the story of the vases is true and, if so, how the family got to know him.

My cousin, Dennis Claude, made the suggestion that the vases were brought back from Japan when the "Great White Fleet" was sent by President Teddy Roosevelt around the world in 1908-1909. One of our relatives, Rear Admiral Thomas Benton Howard, Naval Academy Class of 1873, was in command of the *USS Ohio*, one of the battleships on that cruise. He had married Anne Jacob, a sister of my grandfather, Dr. W. C. Claude. (See picture of girls in family) He bought an enormous number of Japanese things while on the cruise, which were all later placed in his apartment in the house on State Circle. When he died, it was Dennis's impression that some of the pieces were given to family members. This is a much more logical version of how the vases came into the family. Admiral Howard's brother, Douglas Alexander Howard, who went to West Point, Class of 1878, married Elizabeth Harwood, sister to Anne Jacob and to my grandfather (again, see picture of girls), so you can further understand how the names of the family members become so involved.

The "Great White Fleet" was indeed white, as Teddy Roosevelt had all the ships painted that color for the cruise. It was supposed to make them highly visible and impress people, which I'm sure it did. Later on in 1915, Captain Thomas Benton Howard was appointed Commander of the Pacific Fleet and made the fifth full admiral in the history of the U.S. Navy up to that time. However, when that tour of duty was over, he reverted to his permanent rank of Rear Admiral. His successful career must have affected the family considerably as many of the children born after he married into the family were christened "Howard" as part of their given names. My mother included. As I noted above, her name was Anne Howard Claude. She had a cousin named Anne Claude Howard. I truly mean it when I say that my Mother's family names are completely confusing. Admiral Howard himself compounded the problem by naming his son Abram Claude Howard. Also note that my father's sister, Helen, married a man whose first name was Howard, although totally unrelated to my family.

Dennis also told me that family lore had the two Howard brothers orphaned at an early age but not legally adopted by anyone, although they did have a guardian. He claims that that guardian was none other than General U.S. Grant.

The General apparently took his duties seriously. He made sure that the younger brother, Douglas, went to West Point and the elder, Thomas, to the Naval Academy. He went to Annapolis to see exactly what needed to be done to ensure Thomas's acceptance at the Academy. During that visit, he knocked on the door of what I assume to be my great grandfather's preparatory school to discuss the matter. The door was opened by a black servant who promptly slammed the door in his face. Although a border state, Maryland was still Southern in its convictions and sympathies well after the war ended.

*   *   *

My Mother was one of the young women of the family who married into the Navy. However, she did not meet my Father when he was a Midshipman but later when he was sent to the Naval Academy for postgraduate work and held the lofty rank of Lieutenant.

The author's father, Walton Runnells Read, in the uniform of an Ensign. The photo was probably taken immediately after he graduated from the Naval Academy in June of 1918.

Father had attended Bowdoin College before entering the Naval Academy. At the Academy, because of his sunny disposition and stocky build, he was nicknamed "Tubby." (The name seemed to fit him and I never heard friends call him anything else.) He was a member of the U.S. Naval Academy Class of 1919, which because of the urgency of World War I, graduated a year early in 1918. His first assignment was aboard the *USS Balch*, a destroyer, on convoy duty between the United States and Ireland with the occasional trip to Murmansk in Russia. After that tour, he was ordered to a destroyer, the *USS Overton*, patrolling the Eastern end of the Mediterranean. The ship had a complement of 105 men—according to Father only one was married. Istanbul, or Constantinople as he preferred to call it, became his favorite city. At that time, Istanbul was a city not to be missed. It had everything imaginable, including White Russian émigrés, intrigue, espionage, exquisite food and an incredible night life. The Bolshevik Revolution had turned that part of the world upside down and excitement was there for the asking.

Although he had been trained in the classics, Father preferred popular music and played the piano by ear. He had the uncanny ability to hear a tune, go directly to a piano and play the song note for note, as could his sister, Helen. He also loved to sing and loved people around him singing and having a good time. He played many an evening at Novotny's, a Russian restaurant, as well as in the bar of the Pera Palas Hotel, both of which were in Constantinople. Rumor has it that he had a White Russian girl friend named Natalie, but I never heard much beyond that. At any rate, he led a bachelor's life in a very exciting city at a very exciting time.

(In the preceding paragraphs, I have used the words "White Russian" twice. I should define that term. The Bolsheviks were "Red" or Communist and those opposing them were "White" or sympathetic to the Tzarist regime that had been overthrown. Hence they fled Russia going to many parts of the world, the Far East in particular. There is also a group of people from the area of present day Belarus who are referred to as "White Russians," but they are not the same.)

When the ship was patrolling off the coast of Turkey, the men saw many ancient ruins on the mainland, which tantalized them, but they were unable to get ashore to visit them. Father and my Godfather, Robert Maury (Class of 1914), who was also an officer on the ship, were able to get leave to go to Cairo. Of course they went to Giza to see the Sphinx and the Pyramids. I have a tourist photo of them in full uniform sitting on decrepit camels with the Sphinx and the Pyramids in the immediate background. That was so long ago that the Sphinx's paws were still covered with sand and no other buildings are to be seen. Now there are buildings from Cairo all the way to Giza with scarcely a break.

Officers from left to right: Lieutenant Robert Maury, unknown officer from the ship, and Father all riding camels near the Sphinx in Egypt in about 1920.

Jerusalem was also one of their shore leave destinations. I have three pictures from that trip. One of the Garden of Gethsemane, another of the Sea of Galilee, and the third of the Dome of the Rock, which is a religious building sacred to all three major religions although controlled by Palestinians at the present time. All of the pictures are sepia, beautifully photographed and proudly hang in our entrance hall. However, they are too dark to reproduce for this book. It was interesting to compare those photographs from the early 1920s with our impressions of those sites in both 1960 and later in 2010, when I went to Israel with my husband.

Although the Navy did not pay young naval officers very handsome salaries, Father (perhaps because he was not yet married with a family) managed to buy a number of Oriental rugs. Frankly, I don't think he knew which part of the Middle East the rugs were from or what dyes were used, but he bought them anyway because he loved them. I always loved them, too—especially the ones with lots of red and blue, which I subsequently discovered were from the Caucasus—big, bold designs with the colors becoming luminous when the sun hit them.

Many of the rugs were bought off the dirt floors of restaurants or bars. One in particular, which he gave to my Grandma Read, was a blue, pink and beige fairly large rug made in the city of Isparta. Apparently it was so filthy when he bought it that he had it nailed to a log and dragged behind the ship until at least the top layer of dirt was washed off. (Grandma Read was a complete teetotaler and I wonder if she ever knew that it had come from the floor of a bar.)

*   *   *

As the adage goes—all good things must come to an end, and he was eventually ordered to Annapolis to the Postgraduate School. The family story goes that he was again playing the piano (this time at the Blue Lantern Inn on King George Street, long since gone) when my mother walked in with some friends. He played a grand flourish and announced to the crowd that she was the woman he would marry.

Actually they were married in October of 1924 in a quiet ceremony at her home as her father had died only a month previously. After a year at Columbia University for more postgraduate work, where he earned his Master's Degree in Engineering, Father was ordered to Shanghai aboard the *USS Penguin*, a gunboat on the Yangtze River Patrol.

The author's mother, Anne Howard Claude, as a young single woman about the time she and the author's father met, around 1922 or 1923.

The *USS Penguin* at anchor on the Yangtze River in China sometime during the mid-1920s.

The pilot house of the *USS Penguin* using sandbags before having bullet proof shielding fitted some time during the mid-1920s.

The Patrol was deemed necessary by our government to protect American interests in that part of the world, including oil people, missionaries, travelers, and so on, as the country had no effective central government and was virtually overrun by warlords, each of whom was trying to carve out a lucrative place for himself. (These boats were the ones depicted in the movie, *The Sand Pebbles*. By the way, my husband nominated Father for the job of Technical Advisor when we heard that the movie was going to be filmed. However, the decision was made to go with an enlisted man instead of an officer as the movie was shown from the enlisted point of view.) The Yangtze River is an enormously long waterway, central to the way of life of China and has been for millennia. The river was uncontrolled; if it weren't for high water, low water, and rapids, there was the added problem of the inevitable armed smugglers and gun battles between various warlords. Since the gunboats and commercial vessels did not have sufficient power to overcome the swiftness of the river's current, which was about fourteen knots, the gunboats had to be hauled upstream over some of the rapids by Chinese coolies pulling on heavy, long ropes, walking on narrow, treacherous paths hewn into the sides of the cliff far above the swirling water. The ropes would sometimes snap, hurling the men to their deaths in the river below. They were immediately replaced by other coolies who needed the meager wages to feed themselves and their families.

Coolies walking along the tow path above the Yangtze River in the mid-1920s.

As a newlywed, Mother wasn't about to let her husband go up river without her, so she followed on commercial vessels of every description. One time she was napping and heard gunfire. She got up, went to one of the portholes to see what was happening. When the firing subsided, she went back to her bunk and found a bullet hole in her pillow.

Dr. Corydon M. Wassell while working as a missionary in China in the mid-1920s.

Apparently *Penguin* didn't travel too swiftly going upstream and there was plenty of stopping along the way. Westerners in China were hospitable to other Westerners, so Mother stayed with missionary families, as well as Standard Oil people as she followed the ship up river. She and Father became lifelong friends with an oil man named Jess Poole. She also knew Dr. Corydon M. Wassell, who was working at that time as a physician and missionary. He later became famous for saving the lives of twelve sailors in Java during World War II. This was after the Japanese had invaded Java. He was a physician in the Naval Reserve by that time. The twelve sailors were not permitted to be evacuated aboard one of the ships available because they couldn't walk. Dr. Wassell stayed with them trying to get them to the other coast of Java to be evacuated on a different ship. Eventually he was able to do that after much difficulty and they ultimately made their way to Australia. He received the Navy Cross for his heroism and dedication. His story was made into a movie starring Gary Cooper, *The Story of Dr. Wassell.*

Life was always full of interest of one kind or another. Mother told of getting desperate for meat and asking the houseboy to scour the market for some. When she finished the meal he prepared, although she didn't recognize what had been served, she didn't even flinch when the Chinese houseboy declared that it was "Bow, wow, Missy."

There was also a fairly gruesome story about a time when she was walking through the market area of a small town where a warlord's recruiter was trying to get one particular man to come with him. The man refused and started running. The recruiter threw his sword at the man severing his head. The head rolled on the ground to one side, the mouth opening and closing, while the body kept running another ten steps or so. The head was subsequently displayed on a pole to serve as a reminder for other reluctant recruits.

The severed head of the reluctant recruit, in China in the mid-1920s.

My favorite story about my Mother was the time she somehow acquired a head of fresh lettuce. Don't ask me how she got it, but it represented a great delicacy to her. She asked the cook to wash it and serve it immediately. Finally she got tired of waiting for the lettuce and went to see what was happening. She found the cook kneeling over a bathtub of soapy water, first washing the lettuce in the soapy water and then holding up each leaf and rinsing it by squirting mouthfuls of plain water from between his teeth.

Mother obviously enjoyed every minute of her time in China. She especially loved Shanghai. After all, these were the 1920s—era of flappers, gin, cigarettes, short skirts and endless parties. The Sunday afternoon tea dances at the Astor Hotel were frequented by a mixture of all the nationalities in Shanghai—most of them trying to get something for themselves or their country—French, German, British, Americans, and again, the ubiquitous White Russians. She and Father went to the tea dances often.

Downtown Shanghai, China, around 1927 or 1928.

One time while Mother and Father were in Shanghai, they were guests of honor at a dinner party given by someone fairly senior in the British diplomatic community. I'm not sure why this honor was bestowed upon them. I only know that it was.

Everyone was seated at table and the first course, which consisted of freshly cooked asparagus, was served. Nothing happened. Mother, as guest of honor, was supposed to start. Unfortunately no eating utensils were provided and she had no idea what to do. Her host realized her dilemma and quietly told her that she was to use her fingers. She picked up the first spear and breathed a sigh of relief as the other guests followed suit.

When I first heard this story, I was aghast that ladies and gentlemen in full evening dress would eat with their hands, but I found out it was indeed a fact. However, only if the asparagus had no sauce. If sauce was present then a knife and fork were to be used. How's that for odd.

When she became pregnant with me, the upriver trips were over and Mother settled into a "boarding house." I don't recall hearing too much about it, but I believe Father was on *Penguin* and Mother lived with several other women in a sort of "collective." They had a houseboy named Chang who organized a splendid party with fireworks, firecrackers and all the Chinese trimmings to be held on the day of my birth. I made my appearance 5 October 1928, a Year of the Dragon according to the Chinese zodiac. The Dragon is the Fifth Sign of the Zodiac, so being born on the fifth of the month made it even luckier. Of course, Chang expected me to be male and when I turned out to be female, he cancelled the party, went into a sulk and did not speak to Mother ever again.

I have had a great deal of fun over the years because of the Dragon—great birthday presents in the form of dragon jewelry; lovely jadeite and bronze dragons; and especially, a silk wrap, encrusted with embroidered dragons. I was fortunate to travel throughout China in 2000, which was a special Golden Year of the Dragon. (This trip is mentioned later.) Two thousand twelve (2012) will be another Year of the Dragon, and I expect spectacular things to happen.

Mother, Anne Claude Read (nee Anne Howard Claude), is standing in the street outside the collective holding the newborn author. The *amah* or nursemaid is to the right and several street urchins are in attendance, Shanghai, China, in October 1928.

My *amah* or nursemaid was not as unforgiving as Chang. She presented me with an embroidered silk bag, which contained the soil of China. Because of my twin cowlicks, Mother was told that I belonged to two worlds and that the bag of soil would ensure that I returned to China. (The bag of soil has been lost, but I *have* returned to China and I *do* have an embroidered strip of silk which has been framed and is purported to have come from the sleeve of my *amah's* wedding dress. In some ways I doubt that, as the stitch used is called the Forbidden Stitch because it is very hard on the eyes and is therefore very expensive. I don't think that she could have afforded it. Nonetheless, I enjoy having it hanging in the hallway anyway.)

Mother received another gift. This one was from her favorite *rickshaw* boy. (A rickshaw is a small two-wheeled passenger vehicle pulled by a man.) He gave her a pair of small blue and white ginger-jar shaped vases on graceful little stands. I always liked and admired them. Unfortunately I broke one of them when I was a teenager, but I still have the other. It sits on our mantle with a number of other blue and white porcelains. Shanghai had a number of thieves' markets which really were thieves' markets. You could buy anything there. I believe that the *rickshaw* boy got the vases at one of the markets very reasonably. We have never had the remaining one appraised, but down deep in my heart, I feel that it is a genuine antique of some value.

*　　*　　*

Mother and Father returned to the States in late 1928 or early 1929 after a long voyage aboard a fashionable passenger ship. I don't know about Father, but Mother enjoyed it completely. They then went to Annapolis for a period of leave to see Mother's family.

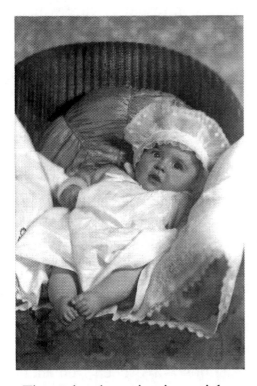

The author lounging in a wicker chair during a visit to meet her Claude Grandmother, probably taken in mid-1929.

During the early 1930s, Father was transferred to the *USS Trenton*, a cruiser, which went up and down the West Coast, staying briefly at various ports. At that time the Navy did not pay for household goods to be shipped. There were many furnished houses for rent, so the procedure was to pack up personal belongings—china, silver, pictures, rugs, clothes, kitchen utensils, and so on—in wooden cruise boxes and place them aboard the ship. The wives and children would drive to the next port, find a furnished rental, and when the ship arrived, the personal belongings would be off loaded and a new home established in Vallejo, San Diego, Long Beach, Bremerton, Coronado, or wherever the ship was assigned.

We were in Coronado and I was five when the big earthquake of 1933 struck. It was a Sunday morning, and I had just stolen into the kitchen to find a banana when the whole house started shaking. Terrified, I raced to my parents' bedroom, jumped on top of Mother, hugged her and quite efficiently stuffed the banana in her ear. For years I associated bananas with earthquakes.

Sometime during this period, probably when we were still living in Coronado, doctors determined that I had a "spot" on my lung. In those days that meant tuberculosis. Mother and I moved immediately to Palm Springs for its warm, dry climate, while Father stayed with the ship.

I wasn't confined to bed. I couldn't go to nursery school. I couldn't play with other children. I couldn't yet read, so in essence I was bored to tears. My imagination conjured up a playmate named Daisy. She had blonde curly hair (my hair at that time was straight and dark) and was somewhat mischievous. I therefore blamed most of my misdemeanors on her which didn't go over too well. Even so, she was great company and we had good times together.

Mother bought me a six-pack of live pansies that I planted and replanted in the sand on the shady side of the house every day. I was very proud of having my own garden. One afternoon I was sitting in the sand playing with the plants, when Mother came rushing up to me. She pointed to the horizon. There was a thick roiling cloud of sand rushing towards us. It contrasted vividly with the azure blue of the sky above it, but was so menacing that I dropped everything and ran quickly into the house after her. We watched as it approached, enveloped the house and threw sand and pebbles against the windows with a great clattering noise scaring us both. It didn't last very long, but was quite intense. Even I helped with the cleanup of the house afterward as sand had gotten into the smallest openings near the windows, under the doors, and dust and grime were everywhere.

At that time Palm Springs was an easy and quick getaway spot for Hollywood movie stars. I was too young to know how it happened, but apparently my parents met some people connected with the movie industry. Mother and Father were invited to a Christmas party at someone's home in Hollywood. Stories of that party enthralled me every time I heard them—trains circling the base of an enormously tall tree; toys, toys and more toys; blinking lights and glittering ornaments. Best of all, to my way of thinking, guests were given BB guns and were urged to shoot at and break all of the big round tree ornaments that they could. I'm sure a lavish prize was given to the one who hit the most. I always thought that, although hideously destructive, it must have been tremendous fun.

Eventually the doctors decided that I did not have tuberculosis after all, so Mother and I moved back to Coronado to be with Father. Evidently my need for my imaginary Daisy ended. I said goodbye to her without regret but with fond memories.

*　　*　　*

We were living in Long Beach in 1934 when my sister, Petra, was born in November of that year. She was named for one of Mother's roommates at the "collective" in Shanghai and was immediately nicknamed Petie. I was totally delighted to have a little blonde "doll" of my own to play with and have adored her ever since. Unfortunately, I have no picture of her as an infant.

The author at the time of her sister, Petie's, birth in Long Beach, California, in November 1934.

The house we lived in was a low one-story affair with a large spreading fig tree in the side yard. It was perfect for a small person to climb and I virtually lived in the tree, especially when the figs were ripe. It was a great place from which to watch the world go by. There was a true "icebox" in the kitchen. A man delivered large blocks of ice, carrying them with lethal looking tongs. The ice was deposited in a certain part of the icebox theoretically to keep the contents cold. Looking back, I can't see where it was particularly efficient or effective. Frankly, I don't see why we weren't all afflicted with food poisoning on a regular basis.

The cat of the moment was named Gilmore as it was a ginger tom and vaguely resembled the "Gilmore the Lion" logo of one of the local gasoline companies. Names for pets do come from unusual places. However, I loved him and that was all that mattered. He was especially amenable to being dressed in doll's clothing and being inserted into wagons and toy carriages.

Fashions were changing. I can remember accompanying Mother to a beauty parlor (they were not called "salons" at that time) that was located on an upper floor of a building in the center of downtown Long Beach. Mother went there to have the long hair she had worn all her life cut off and the remaining hair given a permanent wave. The machine to work this miracle was one of the huge round variety that hovered over the victim with long black wires like snakes going down to be attached to each of the metal curlers that the hair had been wound around. It was a horrendous looking contraption and to me looked exceedingly dangerous. Frankly, I don't doubt that it was. In addition, the solutions that were put on the hair smelled totally vicious. To escape from the monster and to try to breathe, I went over to one of the windows to watch a parade that was taking place in the street below. It was an NRA parade. (The NRA was a government entity, one of President Roosevelt's brain children, that was quite socialistic, and was eventually declared unconstitutional. However the provisions of the

NRA were reestablished in a bill passed later.) So there I was at age six taking in two modern phenomena at the same time. I'm not sure which was worse.

*   *   *

When it was time for the second grade, Father's ship, the *USS Trenton*, was ordered to Panama. We settled down in Balboa, on the Pacific side of the canal, living in a typical, tropical wooden house on stilts with play and storage areas underneath. There were several *iguanas*, which are large, extremely ugly lizards, under the house which fascinated, yet terrified me with their fierce appearance. They didn't last too long as they are edible. The various workmen and gardeners in the neighborhood soon caught them. I'm sure their dinners were good. (In later years, in Mexico, I ate *iguana*. It tastes somewhat like chicken. Of course every type of unusual and exotic meat is said to taste like chicken. At that meal, I also had some roasted *armadillo* (a burrowing mammal from the warm sections of the Americas), which was much tougher and not as tasty.) The yard also had a fruit tree—this time a mango. The succulent flavor and sweet aroma of the fruit was strangely exotic even to a seven year old. I still love them.

Because of the heat, school in Panama was normally over at noon unless you were behind in your studies. Apparently I was *always* behind because I attended the afternoon session every day we were there. However, it helped me in the long run, for when we got back to the States, I was ahead of everyone else in my class.

A few months later, we moved to the other end of the Canal Zone to Colón on the Caribbean. My parents rented an apartment overlooking the city market. A huge red and blue parrot which belonged to the landlord lived on a stand on the large communal balcony. The parrot and I sat side by side watching everything. The market was one of the most colorful, lively things I had ever seen and it never stopped fascinating me. I watched for hours. The fruit and vegetable vendors shouted, the sundries vendors shouted, friends shouted to one another—it was simply spectacular—equivalent to the "greatest show on earth" and wonderfully noisy. It was a special treat when I was allowed to buy a piece of sugar cane and chew the end to suck out the sweet juice. I gladly shared the sugar cane with the parrot. Although I may be romanticizing somewhat as I look back on that experience, I truly feel that it may have been the beginning of my wanderlust and the feeling that the world had much to offer and I needed to see it all.

Occasionally Mother would drive to one of the neighborhood bakeries to buy bread. We always took a stick of butter with us. We bought two loaves—one loaf to take home, and the other to eat in the car while slathering it with the butter.

The loaves were still warm and the butter melted into our hands and down our chins and was heavenly. I still delight in a good loaf of bread.

Living was extremely casual with children allowed almost everywhere, as I recall. We did not have live-in house servants, so Petie and I were taken to the outdoor restaurants and bars or wherever Mother and Father wanted to go in the evenings. It also seems that there were no objections when we were given a pony of beer to drink. Can you imagine the horror and consternation if a two-year old and an eight year-old drank beer in a bar here in the States?

*　　*　　*

We returned to California, this time to San Diego. We traveled aboard a liner which stopped in Haiti. It was in port long enough for us to hire a horse drawn carriage and drive up a road to the top of a big hill overlooking the harbor. Even I, young as I was, thought the view glorious. Father had been ordered to the *USS Maryland*, a battleship, which was more or less permanently stationed in San Diego. The house we rented was a little pink stucco flat roofed building with a mass of yellow climbing roses to the left of the front door and pink ones to the right. To me they were the most beautiful and elegant flowers I had ever seen. The way they cascaded down each side of the porch never failed to enchant me.

Petie standing in the front yard at 2227 Ft. Stockton Drive in San Diego, California, waving a five dollar bill, sometime in late 1936 or 1937.

Years later when I was in the Foreign Service and on a coffee break in the basement restaurant of the Consulate General in Munich, a friend and I were casually reminiscing about things our Mothers made us remember when we were little—phone number, full name and address and so on. I said that I had liked the flow of an address in San Diego—2227 Ft. Stockton Drive. It rather "tripped lightly off the tongue." There were some men sitting at the next table who overheard me. With a gasp, one of them said that his parents had owned that house. Very small world.

The house lot sloped downward toward the backyard. The windows in my room looked out into the upper branches of a peach tree that bore huge fruit. I watched them grow and develop, anticipating the pleasure of eating one. Finally the great day came when I was allowed to open the screen, reach out and pick one. I wasn't disappointed. The peach was so large I had to use both hands to hold it and the flavor was utterly delicious. To this day I find fruit to be one of the sublime blessings of the plant world.

Father had duty nights aboard ship and on those evenings we did one of two things. We either went aboard ship for dinner or Mother took us to San Diego's Old Town to the *tamale* factory for supper. Either one was a treat. Going to the ship was a heart stopping experience. The ship was anchored in the harbor, so to get there we had to go by launch, which would pull up to a dock where we were waiting. The attendant sailors would then carefully help us into the launch and Petie and I would run to take our places on one of the benches that were near the windows. The launch was always immaculate and the windows were hung with white cording knotted in intricate patterns called "lace." The term always amused me. It has a much more formal nautical name (marlinspike seamanship), but I like lace better. The minute we sat down and the engines revved up, an odor of a combination of diesel fuel and salt water would permeate the air. To me that odor has always been a very masculine smell and a typically "Navy" smell. (Later on when I, too, married into the Navy, my husband had that same smell when he came ashore. It clung to his uniform until it was dry cleaned.)

After the exciting ride to the ship with spray flying, Father met us. To keep Petie and me entertained, he would draw (with the ubiquitous red and blue pencils the ship seemed to have by the dozen) flying lamb chops. I'm not sure why flying lamb chops, but that's what they were and we loved them. They were half red and half blue and Father made up wonderful adventures for them as they flew through the air in our imaginations.

The meals weren't that memorable but the wardroom was. The tables were set with white linen, sparkling glassware and silver cutlery. The forks were so big and heavy that I could hardly use them. The meal service itself was as impeccable as the best of restaurants. The officers were all in uniform which was impressive even to someone of my tender years. The formality ensured impeccable behavior by Petie and me. We would have another wild ride in the launch, drive home and I would go to bed one happy little girl.

If we went to the *tamale* factory, I was equally pleased because we usually went with another family from the ship. The seating was outside under a grape arbor with the sunshine making splotchy patterns over everything. We would play with the other children until the tamales appeared. Then run to our table ready for dinner.

The handmade *tamales* or meat stuffed cornmeal rolls, were about the size and shape of a pound package of bulk sausage. They were wrapped in corn husks and tied at each end with cotton butchers twine. As the husks were removed the outer layer of *masa* or corn meal appeared, dense and smelling richly of corn. It was filled with a cubed beef mixture, very thick and dark brown with deep red chili overtones. It wasn't peppery hot but had a pungent richness which made your mouth feel alive. As you came to the middle of the *tamale*, you were rewarded with an enormous black olive.

In spite of constantly checking menus, I have never found that sort of *tamale* served in any other restaurant or in any of the parts of Mexico I subsequently visited. Years later, when I went to San Diego with my husband, we inquired of older people we met in Old Town and they said that the factory had been torn down and, no, they didn't know where we could find that kind of *tamale*—what a shame.

*   *   *

Time was passing and Asia and Europe were beginning to seethe with all sorts of problems. Hitler and Mussolini were in power and the world was deeply concerned about it. Our government decided to send a "show of force" to the South Pacific to impress Asia, so off went the *USS Maryland* to display the flag with Father aboard as the Engineering Officer. They went to Australia and

Hawaii as well as a number of other places I can't recall. I don't remember how long they were gone, but I was extremely happy when they returned. Father brought me back a children's book from Australia, as well as one from Hawaii, and I treasured them both.

*   *   *

In 1938 Father was ordered to the Naval Academy in Annapolis as an instructor in the Engineering Department. One of the first things Mother did when we arrived in town was to pile Petie and me into the car while Father was at work and drive downtown. She pulled up in front of the house she had grown up in and where she and Father were married, and promptly burst into tears. The street was named St. John's Street and formed the western boundary of St. John's College, the liberal arts school located in the center of town near the Naval Academy. My grandfather had died in 1924 just before Mother and Father were married and my grandmother had died in 1932 while we were living in California. Somehow the house was sold to the college and, as I recall, was used to house visitors.

A few years later Mother, Father, Petie and I drove to Mount Vernon, George Washington's estate in Northern Virginia, just outside the District of Columbia. As we walked through the rooms, Mother again burst into tears. This time she was standing in front of a magnificent old secretary. After she calmed down, she said that it had belonged to her father and had been donated to Mount Vernon by one of her siblings when a call was made for furniture of Washington's period to finish furnishing the building properly. It was indeed beautiful and was situated in a perfect place. Mother seemed reconciled to its "new" location.

*   *   *

Although Mother's family had been in Annapolis for many years, the city now became my city, too. I enjoyed meeting all the relatives and learning how to get around. At that time Annapolis was very safe. I was given free rein to go wherever I wanted even though I was only ten years old. People did not even bother to lock their front doors. I never had a key to our house. The stores in town closed on Wednesday afternoon so that people could fish, crab or just relax. Life was simple and uncomplicated.

The large house on State Circle, which had been purchased by my great grandfather, had eventually been left to the unmarried and widowed female members of the family. Believe me, there were a lot of them. Some because they were just old maid material and one because she wouldn't marry a man with a common name like Smith. She somehow failed to recognize that Claude is a very common name in Switzerland. (It is conceivable that the huge number of men killed during the Civil War also affected the marriage opportunities of some of the women. Somewhat similar to the situation of British women after World War I.) Most of the ladies were delightful. Anyway, the interior configuration of the building had been changed years ago to make a number of apartments. One of them had a large dining room where a number of the aunties gathered to have their meals together. Mother once told me that there was so much chit-chat and gossip at lunch and the ladies lingered so long, that the servants had to chase them out in order to ready the dining room for dinner.

I'm also told that Aunt Anna Lovell, one of the delightful aunties, her husband, James Harry (Jack) Lovell and infant daughter, Mary Dulaney (Jimmy), went to Neuchatel, Switzerland, to do some genealogical research quite a number of years ago. They stayed in a comfortable guest house for several weeks. They were hoping to find out more about the Abram Claude who was the first in the family to immigrate to this country. While they were on the train to Neuchatel, Aunt Anna struck up a conversation with a woman who had already been there to do the same thing with her family. This woman discovered that members of her family had owned a number of bordellos. Anna was horrified. To my knowledge she didn't find anything untoward in the Claude family tree, although I don't really know what she *did* find.

There was also a large house across State Circle reserved for the sons and single male members of the family, but it is my understanding that that house was sold many years ago.

There were family picnics every Fourth of July. They were held at various homes in the Annapolis area, but one favorite venue was Aunt Bessie's. Her house was on the water with a small beach, which all the children enjoyed as they could swim and play in the sand. There was also plenty of lawn for the grownups to sprawl on. Each family brought a favorite dish to share and there were many versions of our beloved Maryland crab cakes. There were far too many people for me to ever know which was which and who was who, but I enjoyed them anyway. In 1936 a professional photographer took a group photo, a copy of which was sent to my parents in California. There were forty-five people and two dogs in attendance. In later years the number of attendees dropped off as the older people died and younger ones moved away. Even so, they are held to this day and everyone who comes still has a good time. (I went to one in August of 2010 and discovered to my horror that *I* was one of the "older generation" and there weren't very many of us. However, I had a good time and talked to many people, which was the point of the whole thing anyway.)

In those last few peaceful years before World War II, we all settled down to enjoy life. My parents caught up with old friends, made new ones, and in general had a fine time. Father enjoyed teaching the Midshipmen, Mother enjoyed her family and the social life. They were both great "party people" and liked having friends over for cocktails or dinner. Many of the other military couples in town had also been in China, so there was much swapping of stories of the Orient. The "Old China Hands" thoroughly enjoyed each other. As a young person, I wasn't allowed to be in the room but I heard enough later to realize what incredible experiences some of them had.

My parents got together frequently with Tom and Betty Boyce. They had met the Boyces when we first moved to Annapolis and both families lived in a development in West Annapolis called Dreams Landing. The Boyces had met one another and married in China. Betty was British and Tom was a young Lieutenant on the Yangtze River Patrol at that time. They had a son, Tommy, who was my age and in my class at school, as well as two younger daughters, Betsy and Berta. (Customs become really ingrained, don't they? As I write this I am having difficulty calling the adult Boyces by their first names. They were always Mr. and Mrs. Boyce to me, and they still are.) My parents and the elder Boyces remained friends the rest of their lives. Tommy and I were friends through grammar and high school and still are today. (I spoke with Tommy a few minutes ago on the phone. He said that when he was a Midshipman (he was in the Class of 1951 at the Academy while his father was in the Class of 1923) he was having difficulty with his course in thermodynamics. Father tutored him a bit, straightening out some of Tommy's difficulties. It amused me as later on my husband also had difficulties with thermodynamics at the Academy, and Father had helped him, too. That must be a terrible course.) On weekends the two houses in Dreams Landing were always filled with people and laughter, and in the winter with lots of oysters, too.

*　　*　　*

Although he was not a naval officer, another Annapolitan who spent time in China was our family doctor, George C. Basil, M.D. He and his wife, Maud, went to China in the twenties sometime so that he could assume the position of Superintendent of a hospital in Chungking, which is a large city fairly far up the Yangtze River. The climate there is very hot and debilitating. His first person account of his years there is set forth in his book *Test Tubes and Dragon Scales,* which was written in collaboration with Elizabeth Foreman Lewis and published by The John C. Winston Company. The book is great reading and is full of exciting personal stories, including how he taught himself Chinese and his struggles to make the Chinese orderlies keep up a decent standard of sanitation—in other words, no spitting on the floor and other things even worse.

The experience that completely fascinated me was his story of having the most powerful of the local warlords bring his fifth wife to the hospital to be checked over as she was pregnant. His other wives had given him only girls and he was desperate for a son. He and Dr. Basil seemed to get along well and they bantered back and forth about how the doctor would ensure that the baby was a boy.

As the weeks and months went by and the bantering continued at each checkup, Dr. Basil began to realize that the situation was becoming extremely serious and his position increasingly precarious should the child be a girl. The warlord was all powerful.

The day his wife began labor finally arrived. Needless to say Dr. Basil was somewhat tense. Things took their natural course, and as the baby emerged, Dr. Basil gave an enormous sigh of relief when he saw that the baby was indeed a boy. An exceedingly nasty situation had been averted. (I suppose I was rather taken with this story as my own arrival rather upset Mother's houseboy, Chang, when I was born a female.)

A few days later when Dr. Basil returned home after work, his entire front yard was filled with boxes containing innumerable exotic and expensive gifts from the grateful warlord. To add to Dr. Basil's problems during the incident with the warlord, his own wife, Maud, was pregnant and was due to deliver at the same time as the warlord's wife. She proceeded to do this without untoward incident, but without the comfort of her husband's presence. Their child was a girl whom they named Betty. Betty was about my age and we ended up in the same high school class in Annapolis.

Mrs. Basil's health was adversely affected by the miserably hot climate of Chungking, so she returned to Annapolis with Betty before Dr. Basil did. He opted to go north, ultimately catching the Trans-Siberian railway to Moscow and then on to the States. His account of that journey also makes exotic and exciting reading. All of his adventures took place before World War II, so there was virtually no infrastructure as we know it in that part of the world. Large stretches of the journey were by sedan chair or just simply by walking, hiking and climbing.

Although Mother and Father did not socialize frequently with the Basils, they knew one another well. Dr. Basil was the doctor who came to the house when Petie and I were ill. I remember finding him extremely pleasant and comforting. I wish I had been older and could have known him better. Had I known him today, I would have pulled every bit of information possible from him. What an utterly fascinating time he must have had in Chungking.

*   *   *

Mother and Father were also friendly with another couple who shared the same Read surname although unrelated. They lived outside of Annapolis in the St. Margaret's area in a large rambling house with many rooms and lots of space outdoors. There were two children in the family, a girl named Nancy who was about my age, and a boy, Lance, whose nickname was Tickie, and who was just a little older than Petie. Nancy was also born in China, so I assumed that the "Old China Hand" syndrome kicked in with our parents and made the bond between them even stronger. (Captain Read was from the Class of 1924.)

Nancy and Tickie, with a great deal of imagination and help on the part of their mother, held the most wonderful Halloween parties ever. The attic was spooky and dusty—just perfect as the location for the witch who stirred a huge cauldron of evil ingredients while muttering all sorts of imprecations and spells which made the hair on our necks stand up. We loved every minute of it, squealing with pleasure. The house was also conducive to lengthy games of hide-and-seek of the variety where you don't acknowledge that you have found the "it" person, but squeeze into the hiding place with him until only one or two timid souls are left wandering around absolutely terrified that something in the dark will catch *them*.

There was also a large vegetable garden where all sorts of things were grown. The house had an old wood burning cook stove which I think Mrs. Read really preferred to the more modern one. She certainly prepared some memorable meals using it. The yard was also blessed with a number of large shade tree that we sat under while playing board games or just chatting. It was a charming old house, the family who lived there was hospitable and loving. It was a pleasure for all of us to visit.

*   *   *

I enjoyed the freedom I was given and the new friends from school. I learned how to use the public bus system (two routes), to go to the movies (35 cents plus 4 cents tax) on Saturday afternoon (choice of two theatres). The city waterfront was a working area then as opposed to the tourist area it would become. The watermen pulled their boats in and unloaded the crab, oysters and fish right there. They were always interesting to watch. You could not get a fresher oyster than the one shucked and handed to you at the dock.

Another activity I loved was visiting my favorite aunt, the one for whom I was named. She operated a women's dress shop on Maryland Avenue, which in those days was the poshest of the three business streets in town. Most of the stores were tailor shops as naval uniforms in those days were made to order. However, there were a few other businesses including one of the two grocery stores downtown. I don't remember the name of it, but it was always referred to as "Bloody Mary's" because the butcher, Mary, always wore an apron covered with blood. The Little Campus Inn was on Maryland Avenue, as well as the soda fountain where I met my future husband. There were also a book store and several antique shops.

Auntie Lila was about seventeen years older than my mother, and had had two husbands, both of whom were Academy graduates of the Class of 1908. She was extremely stylish and had a keen sense of humor. She was great fun to visit after school and of course her dress shop was exciting to a young girl. Her apartment was on the top floor of the building on State Circle dedicated to single ladies, and she furnished it with great flair. She and her first husband, who had been commissioned in the Army instead of the Navy, had been in the Philippines for a while, as well as other parts of the Orient, so her furnishings were interesting as well as being very attractive. She died later while I was in Germany. Annapolis was never quite the same and I still miss her.

*   *   *

Of course, Mother and Father plunged right into the Maryland food scene, eating all the things that they had done without for so long, especially the crabs and oysters. As I have mentioned, Annapolis is located on the Chesapeake Bay, about thirty miles south of Baltimore. The Bay is famous for its seafood—crab, clams, oysters, shad, shad roe and any number of other delicacies. There is no crab in the world that produces the sweet, succulent meat of a blue crab. It is prepared in dozens of different ways, but my favorites are crab salad and crab cakes.

Crab salad is delicious because it has so few ingredients to mask the subtle taste of the crab. You carefully pick through a container of fresh crab meat to remove any of the shell. Place the crab in a medium size bowl, add finely chopped celery, a little pepper and some good quality mayonnaise. Mix very gently to avoid breaking up the crab and serve with lettuce and a few tomato slices on the side. Parker House rolls and fresh iced tea with lemon complete a perfect summer meal.

We used to have that meal frequently during hot weather. I was always amused by the tug of war that went on between my parents over the salad. It was made early in the day so that the flavors would blend and at about five o'clock Mother would take it out of the refrigerator to allow it to come closer to room temperature to further enhance the flavor. If Father saw the bowl sitting on the counter, he would immediately put it back in the refrigerator because he was afraid of the bacteria count. If Mother discovered this, she would put it back on the counter. Finally the dinner hour arrived and we ate the salad with much gusto no matter what temperature the salad had reached.

*   *   *

Every now and again, I was sent alone by train to Portland, Maine, to visit Father's parents, Grandma and Grandpa Read. Visiting them was a great trial. They weren't fun to visit because they had, as far as I could see, absolutely no sense of humor and were rigidly strict. This was probably a wrong assumption on my part because Father and Auntie Hearn were certainly humorous, pleasant people. Nevertheless, Grandma and Grandpa Read were old before their time and a chore for a young girl to be with.

One mitigating factor was that Grandma Read was an excellent cook of the heavy, fried food variety. Every Saturday morning she fried cake doughnuts. They were absolutely splendid. Even though fried, they were light and airy, and smelled enticingly of nutmeg—great with cold milk or, for the adults, hot coffee. Helping her roll out the dough and cut it into the traditional doughnut shape was very rewarding as she fried the holes just for me.

Everyone tried to get the recipe from her, but no one ever succeeded in getting it in its entirety—something was always left out. Everyone in the kitchen would watch her like a hawk, but never caught her adding that last essential ingredient. Even so, the memory of the doughnuts is bright and clear and tasty.

Another of her recipes, which we did manage to get, was for deep fried clams. The clams were shucked, drained and roughly chopped. Then flour, beaten egg, and other ingredients were added. The coarse batter was dropped by the spoonful into hot bubbling lard and a light, golden brown morsel emerged, full of calories, cholesterol, clams and fat but tasting utterly delicious.

My most memorable and upsetting visit to Portland occurred in 1940 when I was almost thirteen. I had just gotten a new pair of saddle shoes and was carefully allowing them to acquire the requisite delicate coating of dirt necessary to make them "cool" or whatever the word was in those days. Grandma Read took offense to the dirt and made me polish the white part of the shoes, thereby ruining them in my eyes and lowering my image of her. She never quite regained her former position in my youthful estimation.

One of her favorite entertainments was taking me to the cemetery for an afternoon out. There were aboveground graves, huge mausoleums, crosses, angels and weeping female statues in abundance—not to mention lakes with white swans, huge trees, and winding gravel pathways. It was not a particularly festive place, although lovely in its own way. I'm afraid that I didn't respond as she would have wished.

There were also trips to Old Orchard Beach, which was on the ocean. There is no way for me to guess the temperature of the water, but it was painfully cold. I was expected to cavort in the waves and generally enjoy myself freezing to death while she sat in a chair wrapped in blankets also freezing to death.

I really should be more charitable to her. After all, she and my grandfather had lived alone for twenty-three or four years after their children had left home and had had plenty of time to become set in their ways. However, I was always happy to return home again.

*   *   *

When I was ready for high school the State of Maryland was still on a "depression budget" and had only eleven years of school—seven grammar school years and four high school years. I was quite immature for my age and not ready for high school, so I was sent to the local Catholic school for the eighth grade. My parents had not made provisions for me over the years to go to church or to learn very much about religion. They allowed me to take the religion courses at St. Mary's and then wondered why I couldn't make up my mind what church I wanted to belong to. I still can't.

Years later Sister Roseanna, who taught the eighth grade, came back to Annapolis on a visit. One of the classmates arranged for us to see her. She had terrified me. When she stood over my desk to check my work, I literally quaked in my boots for fear of having her rap my knuckles with the ruler she always carried with her. As she stood there, she seemed at least eight feet tall in her black habit with the white wimple around her face. I was also positive that she had eyes in the back of her head, just underneath the wimple and saw everything I did. When we met again on her visit, I chuckled to myself. She was a tiny very pleasant woman. It was only my vivid imagination that made her seem so formidable.

*   *   *

After Dreams Landing, we lived in a variety of rented houses around Annapolis, including some months in officer's quarters in the Naval Academy and in a big, rambling house on Spa Creek, which I liked because we could go swimming from our own dock and my room had lots of space for my beloved books. The threat of war prompted my parents to buy their first house. Father wanted Mother to have a home of her own in case something happened to him. Frankly, I also think he wanted to be able to visualize her at home with us in a place he knew. They purchased a house on South Cherry Grove Avenue on the outskirts of town outside the city limits. My life was intertwined with that house for forty-one years.

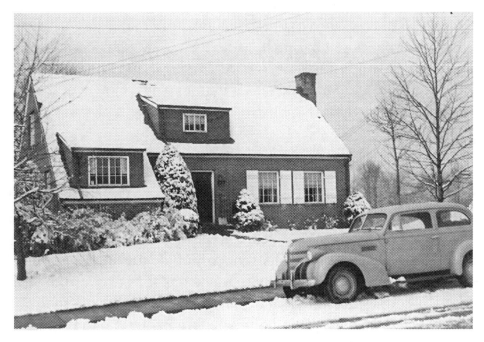

Our house on Cherry Grove Avenue, Annapolis, Maryland, sometime in 1942.

My mother's health was never robust, so we always had cooks and cleaning people about. I'm not sure how they found her, but before Father went overseas, they located a country woman named Dorothy Suit from South County to come and live at the house. She prepared the meals and served at table. She made excellent mashed potatoes. I ultimately found out why. Not only were the potatoes mashed with an entire stick of butter, but an additional stick was placed in the center of the serving dish when she passed it. No wonder the potatoes were so good.

*   *   *

Eventually our idyllic life in Annapolis came to perhaps not an abrupt halt, but a definite slow down. On 7 December 1941, the Japanese bombed Pearl

Harbor and Father, as well as the fathers of most of my friends, went to war to be gone for several years. A number of my friends lost their fathers. Annapolis, as a Navy town, was very hard hit.

For part of my freshman year in high school, which would have been 1942, I attended a school in Palo Alto, California. We were living there as it was close to Moffat Field where Father was involved in work with military units that were going to establish advanced bases in the Pacific. The work was closely connected with the Navy construction battalions, known as the Seabees. It was all very hush-hush and I never knew very much about it. We had spent four nights crossing the country by train to get there, sleeping in berths and playing board games with other passengers. Looking back, I realize that I was a typical obnoxious teenager as I wanted to be in Annapolis with my friends and definitely not in a new school with new people to contend with. I was really horrible. We returned to Annapolis after a few months because Father and his unit had gone on to do their jobs and were no longer in Palo Alto. It rather served me right that I had to go to a Latin tutor to catch up as I had been so lax in California. The worst part was that the tutor's house reeked of stale boiled cabbage and was grossly overheated. The atmosphere was not exactly conducive to learning Latin verbs.

My high school years were the war years except for my senior year, which was still austere in a way because of continued rationing. Because of the war there was little or no gasoline so the temptation or ability to "cruise" wasn't there. Also we had no football team. There was no drinking to speak of and absolutely no drugs. It was very much like an idealistic old television show. The most trouble any of us got into was when one of my classmates put some vanilla extract with high alcohol content in the fruit punch at one of our parties. As far as my friends and I are concerned, life was almost perfect and we all look back on that time as one of the best parts of our lives even though our fathers were at war. Because of those fond memories, most of us attend every class reunion and hope they never stop.

The mother of my best friend, Rosemary Rutt, owned a car that we all coveted. I don't remember the make but it was a little coupe of some sort. Big enough for only two people in the front with an open rumble seat for two in the back. In spite of the gasoline rationing, Mrs. Rutt would sometimes come to the high school at the end of the day to pick us up and take us to their house which was on Hanover Street just outside what was then the Main Gate of the Naval Academy. Since Rosemary had a sister, Tink, the three of us would practically fight over who had to sit in the covered front and who was lucky enough to sit in the open rumble seat.

Some of my other close girlfriends during high school were Nancy Lee Fox, Nancy Herring, Lola Steele, Betty Hopkins and Charlene Halpine. Not surprisingly all of us married Academy graduates. I guess you could say that it was one of the perks of growing up in Annapolis. A favorite male friend was David Jalbert. Although his father had gone to the Naval Academy and David grew up in Annapolis, he elected to go to the Coast Guard Academy instead. A number of other male high school classmates went to the Naval Academy, so the lure of the uniform is not necessarily confined to the female.

Even though we were still in our teens, we tried to contribute what we could to the war effort. I volunteered to "spot airplanes" which meant that on Saturdays I went to the roof of the Maryland Hotel which was the tallest building in downtown Annapolis, stood in a little cupola on top and with the aid of binoculars kept my eye out for airplanes. As I recall, our shifts were about two hours long. I never spotted anything of importance, thank heaven, but I felt that I was helping the war effort in my own way.

The summer I was sixteen I got a job at what locals called the Experiment Station. It was located across the Severn River from the Naval Academy. I had to take a bus to the middle of town, then walk through the Academy, and finally take a launch across the river. I'm not sure of the precise name of the facility, but it had to do with all sorts of engineering projects. It was terribly noisy and not a little smelly. However, I was thrilled that I had gotten the job which basically was to run errands for people in the office and on the hour make the rounds of the station picking up and delivering small sample bottles of engine oil that people analyzed. I felt that I not only had a job, but that in some inscrutable way it was helping the war effort.

By the next summer the war was over and the old law of not allowing anyone below the age of eighteen to work had been put back in place. That precluded my getting any kind of job that summer. I was devastated. However, there wasn't much that I could do about it. I do believe that was the longest summer of my life although there was still sailing, swimming and, as modern young people would say, "hanging out" with my friends.

The Naval Academy celebrated the centennial of its founding in 1945 and I was invited to the gala ball. I was totally ecstatic. It had been talked about for weeks and was to be very formal and quite elegant, which indeed it was. My dress had a full, long apricot taffeta skirt, a sleeveless striped multicolored top in gold and apricot and was visually held together by a lovely wide gold mesh belt. My hair, which was long at that time, had been done professionally and I felt quite swish. The Centennial Ball was a huge success much to everyone's satisfaction—especially mine.

Eventually the war was over and the world returned to something resembling normality. Father came home unscathed, thank heaven, but the stories over cocktails weren't as amusing as they had been when he and his "Old China Hands" swapped their sea stories. There was much talk of invasions, battles, strafing and, as Father was in the Pacific area, Japanese *kamakazi* or suicide planes. After his duty with the Seabees, he was in command of the *USS Mendocino*, an attack transport, which carried troops, landing craft and supplies. The *Mendocino* participated in the invasion of Okinawa on 1 April 1945. He never spoke much about his experiences, so I don't imagine they were too pleasant.

Father aboard the *USS Mendocino* before the landings on Okinawa, probably in November, 1944.

Father's command, the *USS Mendocino,* an attack transport, probably in November, 1944.

Father had remained in the Pacific area for a time after the war ended as he was made Commanding Office of Subic Bay Naval Base in the Philippines. He was there long enough to have instituted some changes and helped the people in the area. He was given a great testimonial not only by the officers on his staff, but by the local dignitaries, too.

Many of the war experiences were ghastly. Tommy Boyce's uncle, Adam Kalkowski, was under contract as a civilian to fly bombers to the Dutch in Indonesia after the Japanese invaded. As he was trying to make his way back to the States after delivering a plane, he was caught in Manila and interned there at the infamous Santo Tomas prison camp and then transferred later to Los Baños. He broke out several times to secure medical supplies. He was apprehended and severely beaten each time. Once he was brutally struck in the head by the butt of a Japanese rifle. Tommy believes that the blow was the cause of his later demise from a brain tumor. Whatever the cause of his death, he had a wretched experience while in the prison camps.

Mother told another story of a friend who had been a prisoner. I don't remember his name or his relationship to the family, but the story has stayed with me to this day. He returned after the war with many scars from the claws of a cat that had wandered into the prison camp. He was able to catch the cat and tried to strangle it. However, he was so weak it took him several hours to do this, hence the scars. The cat was then stewed for dinner which he shared with some of the children who were interned with him, which was his real reason for wanting to kill the cat.

Our next door neighbor, CDR James W. Coe, was in command of the *USS Cisco*, a submarine. He had already had a tour as Commanding Officer of the *USS Skipjack*, also a submarine, and had sunk several Japanese ships. When he assumed command of *Cisco* right after it was commissioned, it went immediately to Asian waters. It developed a hydraulic oil leak and put into Adelaide, Australia, for repairs. Then it set out again, but returned to port to have further repairs done before heading toward the Philippines. Some people believe that the leak developed a third time thereby enabling the Japanese to trace the boat. Anyway, it was discovered and sunk by the enemy in the South China Sea in Philippine waters. Two ships participated in the sinking. Ironically one of them was the former *USS Luzon*, which had been on the Yangtze River Patrol at the time Father was there. It had been taken over by the Japanese at the outbreak of the war.

My sister, Petie, was only nine years old at this time and, of course, heard that CDR Coe had been killed. She was a playmate of his daughter's and it upset her dreadfully. The only problem was that she did not vocalize any of this to anyone, but kept it all to herself. There were trees in our backyard that she could see from her bedroom window. She thought that the Japanese would be coming through them at any minute to "get" her. She also developed a fear of Asian people in general that has diminished through the years, but not completely disappeared. To think that Asian people were after her father was almost too much for a nine year old to bear.

* * *

Father retired from the Navy shortly after he came back from the Philippines and, as I said earlier, life returned to something resembling normality. He joined the faculty at the University of Maryland's Engineering School and enjoyed being back in the academic field. Birthdays were noted and Thanksgivings and Christmases were celebrated in the normal manner, which pleased all of us.

For Christmas, in addition to our standard creamed onions and candied sweet potatoes, we also had a dessert we called Wine Jelly. It was a gelatin concoction that was wonderful after a heavy meal. Among the ingredients was a large amount of sherry which wasn't cooked to evaporate the alcohol, but incorporated right into the gelatin, sugar and lemon mixture. For some unknown reason, Petie and I were allowed to eat it and promptly had cases of the giggles induced wholly by the large amount of alcohol we had just consumed. Naturally we thought it pretty tricky.

*   *   *

After high school, I went on to college. My first year was at Mary Washington College of the University of Virginia. It sounds impressive, but it was an all-girls school at that time, very strict with a prurient attitude toward everything. I loathed it. There was a walkway bordered by bushes which young "ladies" were not allowed to use in the company of a male. All dates had to report to the Dean's office and give their names to see if they were on the list of young men approved by parents. If on the list, they could then go to your dorm to pick you up. If not, they were sent away. You were not allowed to hold hands with your date plus any number of other ridiculous rules to keep the sexes physically separated. The administration did indeed have a prurient attitude. After a miserable year, I transferred to the University of Maryland in College Park which was much more to my liking.

Maryland's campus was inundated by returning veterans wanting to use the GI bill to further their education. The classes for some of the 101 level courses were huge and sometimes held in temporary buildings hastily erected to accommodate the large numbers of students. One chemistry lecture I was attending was briefly interrupted by a crash, some falling debris and a human leg poking through the ceiling where some hapless worker had stepped in the wrong place while repairing something in the crawl space.

Some of my class credits were lost in transferring from Virginia, so I had to spend a full four years at Maryland. I majored in European history and minored in German, graduating with the class of 1951. My common sense told me that one day I would have to be gainfully employed, so with a few extra credit hours available during my senior year, I took intensive typing and shorthand courses, enjoying them both. Unfortunately in those days, nursing, teaching or secretarial work were the usual jobs women had available to them.

The author toward the end of the time she attended the University of Maryland, approximately 1950.

Speaking of teaching, I just discovered as I write this book, that my favorite professor at Maryland, Wilhelmina F. Jashemski, became a prominent archaeologist specializing in ancient gardens and the plants grown in them. She worked for many years at Pompeii and Herculaneum as well as other towns destroyed when Vesuvius erupted in 79 AD. I always looked forward to her classes and particularly remember going to her house for a "Roman Banquet," which we as students had to research and cook. I don't remember the menu except that the dessert used a great deal of honey and poppy seeds. I also remember being extremely impressed by her home. It was furnished with outstanding antiques blended with comfortable furniture and was impeccably maintained. I always chuckled about that because she was always "fly away." By that I mean that her hair was always windblown, her hems uneven and her scarves awry. However, that didn't seem to make any difference to her or to her great teaching abilities. She was always enjoyable and I took every class she offered.

There had been much bomb damage to libraries and museums during World War II. Professor Jashemski was offered some pages from mediaeval illuminated manuscripts taken from damaged books. She acquired a number of pages and offered her students the opportunity to buy some of them. I bought a page from an illuminated English Psalter (a collection of psalms) from 1285 AD on vellum. The initial letter has an odd face looking at you out of half-closed eyes. You wonder what he is thinking. In addition, I splurged on two pages from a Book of the Hours and a printed page on "The Lyfe of Saynt Pelagyen" which I have always enjoyed. The font is strange, and yet it is readable.

*   *   *

I was determined to find some sort of job that would enable me to travel—especially to Europe and preferably Germany. With Father's help, we decided that the Foreign Service would be the ideal place. I took the exams—typing, shorthand, psychological, physical, and mental and passed them. However, I did not have enough actual working experience to suit them, so I worked in Annapolis as a secretary for the State of Maryland Board of Natural Resources for a year, living at home and trying to make the time pass. Eventually the big day came and I reported in to the Department of State. I lived in Washington for about two months attending the Foreign Service Institute, which gives newcomers a certain amount of indoctrination and a chance to discuss and learn about things like body language that is different from ours; customs different from ours; things that we do as a matter of course that are offensive to other cultures, and any number of other obscure but fascinating facts. I know it sounds somewhat peculiar, but it was incredibly interesting and well worth the time.

The day finally came when we "graduated" and were given our orders. The luck gods were in the right place because I had orders to Bonn, Germany, to what was called the Office of the High Commissioner. Incredible. I had studied German, was actually being sent to Germany and it was my first choice.

2

FOREIGN SERVICE ADVENTURES IN POST-WORLD WAR II EUROPE

THE ACTUAL FLIGHT TO GERMANY was an exotic adventure. I left on 22 October 1952. The plane was a big Pan American Stratocruiser with a bar downstairs in its belly with windows all around. There were numerous attendants and anything you wanted was immediately brought to you. My ticket cost $900 one way, which was an astronomical amount of money considering that a loaf of bread was 12 cents. (The ticket was paid for by our government in Swedish Kronor, which I thought was strange. However, I was told that it was in an odd pot of money left over from the war.) The best part of the trip was that at bedtime, you changed into your pajamas and crawled into bunks that were lowered from the side walls. Rather the equivalent of having today's overhead luggage bins come down fully made up into beds with sheets, blankets and pillows. Because of having to refuel, the route was from New York to Gander, Newfoundland to Shannon, Ireland to London, England, and then on to Frankfurt. The trip took twenty-two hours and was the most exciting thing I had ever done.

As we landed in Frankfurt, the plane flew through a series of dirty brown clouds that I now know were smog, rain and mist in equal measures. I did not see the sun again until April, five months of bleak, dreary overcast skies. I didn't care. I was almost sick with excitement at actually being in Germany so that the brown clouds were the least of my worries. I gaped wide eyed at everything, noting the bomb damage, the strange store fronts with signs in German, the cobbled streets, the old cars and the hunched over people hurrying through the rain—everything was different from Annapolis. I reveled in it.

The treaties ending World War II had not yet been signed so the office where I was to work could not be an actual Embassy until that happened, nor could the office be in Berlin, the old capital of Germany. That was because, although the city was divided so that each of the four powers had an area of the city, the city itself was deep in the Russian Zone. Germany was divided into French, British, American and Russian Zones, with each of those countries unilaterally controlling their zone of Germany. At that time, Bonn *was* the capital of Germany and the center of negotiations between the German government and the three Allied countries.

My particular niche was in the Office of the American Secretary of the Allied General Secretariat—the other two Secretaries being French and British. The whole effort was tripartite with each of the three nations chairing every third month. The work was fascinating and my typing and shorthand skills were such that I was good at my job, which gave me a certain amount of confidence.

Our office, as well as the High Commissioner's, were concerned with arranging matters for the eventual signing of the treaties. Therefore, we corresponded directly with Chancellor Konrad Adenauer's office. Those were the days well before computers and even electric typewriters, so the letters had to be written on a Royal upright manual machine. I was in complete awe of the woman who typed them. There could not be a single error—no erasures, no misspellings, correct spacing—nothing that wasn't absolutely perfect. She would insert the letterhead into the typewriter, pace the room for a few minutes, ask for quiet, crack her knuckles and then proceed to type at the most incredible speed imaginable. She usually succeeded in getting a perfect copy on the first try. But then, that's why she had that job. No doubt about it, she was not only excellent but extraordinary.

Occasionally I went to the French or British areas on business and was always amused by what I found. The French wing had the windows tightly closed. The air was hot, redolent of strong perfume and *Gauloise* cigarettes with distinct overtones of garlic. On the other hand, the British had turned off the heat, wore heavy sweaters and the windows were wide open with the wind whipping through at gale force.

The city of Bonn is on the Rhine River, but the building where we worked was further upstream at a little village called Bad Godesberg. Looking across the Rhine you could see the ruins of a mediaeval castle called *Drachenfels* or Dragonrock, which, of course, conjured up all sorts of images of dragons and mysterious maidens and knights in shining armor. However, I understand that it was actually a place where river traffic was stopped so that the owner of the castle could extract a hefty toll before allowing boats to proceed. However, imagination is powerful and to me it was an exceedingly romantic ruin.

The ruins of *Drachenfels* or Dragonrock taken in 1953.

Every once in a while my boss, Dick Geppert, the American Secretary, would take me to lunch. On one particular day he decided on a restaurant across the river. Just getting into his car was a treat. It was a silver Jaguar sports car with an interior which smelled of leather and money. The whole experience was of luxury. We crossed the Rhine by ferry and went to a restaurant that specialized in fresh caught trout. I am not a particular fan of small fish with many bones, but as I was his guest, I went along with it. The first trout appeared and surprising myself, I ate it with great relish. Perhaps it was because the waiter boned it for me and I didn't have to worry about choking. Then another trout appeared hot out of the pan. That, too, was consumed. Then the final trout came to the table, also hot and delicious. Bringing them hot one at a time from the kitchen and having someone bone them were inspired ideas and to be emulated.

The modern office complex where we worked had been added to a huge old rambling mansion referred to as the *Schloss* or castle. At lunch time you could go to the cafeteria in the office building or to the dining room in the *Schloss*. I elected to go to the *Schloss* every chance I got. The food was excellent, but more important, the atmosphere was so calm and elegant I couldn't stay away. Fresh flowers, silver, crystal and glistening white linen with many waiters attending to your every need.

The luck gods were still with me as I drew two wonderful roommates, Melita Schmidt and Laurette Speer. We were assigned a three bedroom apartment in a little village nearby with the improbable name of Plittersdorf. The apartment was completely furnished with everything—linens, china, furniture, appliances and so on. The color scheme was moss green and mahogany. It was quite lovely.

From left to right: The author and roommates, Laurette Speer and Melita Schmidt celebrating Melita's birthday 1953.

We even found a maid named Emme we shared for $10 a month each. Emme prepared breakfast and dinner but wouldn't let us come home for lunch—we interrupted her cleaning. Not only that, she also did the shopping and our washing and ironing.

Emme, our maid, 1953

It seems rather crass to keep mentioning money, but I find it interesting to compare prices in those days to prices today. I don't recall my gross salary, but I do remember that I received $107 after deductions every two weeks. It certainly couldn't be called extravagant, but it enabled me to do virtually everything I wanted.

My time in Europe was an engrossing period in my life. I was interested in everything. I went to as many places as I could; I saw as many things as I could; I talked with as many people as I could; and, naturally I ate as many new foods as I could. There was a club available to all French, British and Americans working in Bad Godesberg. It was run along the lines of a typical officer's club with a bar, lounge, reading room and dining room. In the dining room I was introduced to what were to me exotic foods—snails, *paté de foié gras*, excellent wines, typical German dishes and all kinds of desserts I had never even heard of much less eaten. It sounds as though I should have gained weight, but strangely enough, not only did I not gain weight, but I actually lost it. I attribute it to the lack of hormones in the European meat and to the fact that I was always on the move doing something that interested me.

On weekends when we didn't go away, there were thousands of things to do locally—exploring the cities on the Rhine like Cologne, visiting old castles and the German equivalent of stately homes, or just going to wine cellars and wonderful restaurants. Everything was new, different and, to me, well worth looking at.

By the way, I read something recently about the dreadful Allied bombing of the Cologne Cathedral and how we virtually demolished it. That is entirely untrue. The cathedral is adjacent to the railroad station in Cologne and that was the target. It was a masterpiece of precision bombing as the *railway station* was demolished and only a few incendiary bombs hit the roof of the cathedral, which were quickly extinguished. I was there in 1952, after the war and the cathedral was well and happy. I saw it for myself. The reports of its destruction and damage were wrong.

The young, single people all knew one another (secretaries, code clerks, administrative assistants and so on) and we had some wonderful times together. The Mosel and the Ahr are tributaries of the Rhine. Both rivers meander between slate banks reaching steeply up to the sun. They are thickly planted with grape vines and yield some outstanding wines. On Sunday afternoons when we were not going away, groups of us would head for one or another of the restaurants along the banks of one of the rivers. We would then have a wonderful time swapping stories of the Europe we lived in and of previous duty stations the others had experienced.

Of course we were drinking wine from the area as we talked and invariably played a German game we had learned that determined who bought the next bottle or who got a kiss from a favored attendee. After a bottle was emptied, the person pouring called for numbers. You guessed the number of additional drops of wine still in the bottle that would eventually fall into a glass when the bottle was held upside down. The person furthest off the correct number bought the next bottle. The person closest to the correct number of drops got to give a quick kiss to his chosen one. It may sound like rather a silly game, but the viscosity of wine is different from water and a surprisingly large number of drops were left in the bottle. Besides we *had* been drinking and it was an excellent way to select the next wine buyer. Or kissee for that matter.

Usually we stayed on into the dinner hour and invariably ordered *Wienerschnitzel*, a piece of veal cutlet, breaded and fried. The meat was so tender it "melted in your mouth" and the serving was so large it lapped over both sides of a huge plate. However, we were young and healthy and didn't think of the consequences of eating that much. In fact we usually cleaned our plates. It was always more than delicious.

Through a young girl who came to the apartment to tutor me in German, we met a number of university students. They were fun, but I certainly didn't learn much German from them—they wanted to learn English. They weren't quite sure how long the Americans were going to be in their country so they wanted to learn as much English as possible. Besides English was becoming the *lingua franca* of the world and speaking it would help them in the future. Meeting them introduced another slant on my stay in Germany, and for the most part I enjoyed and liked them. Attending *Fasching* or Carnival with Germans made the experience that much more fun. Believe me, they do party.

The work week was Monday to Friday, so we had two days plus Friday evening for travel. By that I mean that there were trains leaving for all sorts of destinations right after work. There were also night trains that arrived early enough Monday morning to allow time to go to the apartment, take a shower and be at work on time. It couldn't have worked out better.

My roommates and I took our first long weekend in January of 1953 choosing to go to Bruges and Ghent in Belgium. The two cities are mediaeval gems with old wooden and brick houses leaning into the canals and romantic bridges strategically placed here and there. It is somewhat reminiscent of an old European Venice. The famous Ghent altarpiece was spectacular and lived up to everything I had ever heard about it. However, we were so cold we had to sit on the radiator in our room to keep even a little bit warm. Heat was at a premium in postwar Europe and virtually non-existent in our room.

In April my roommates and I made a trip to Paris. The hotel was small, old fashioned and utterly charming. There was an iron cage elevator that shook, groaned and muttered every time you tried to work it, and the bed was so high I had to use steps to get into it. The next morning I found *café au lait* (or very strong coffee with much whole milk), *croissants* (rolls formed into many layers with butter between each layer) and sweet butter (unsalted) on the breakfast tray. All are commonplace now, but in 1953 to a person from a small town, they were incredible discoveries. The amazing part was that I found three new things in one meal. Truthfully I never had *croissants* as delicious as those until my husband and I went to a French bakery on St. Martin's in the Caribbean and got them just out of the oven very early one morning. They had been made with an extravagant amount of butter and were so delicate that the layers crumbled if you even dared to try to spread more butter on them. A really good *croissant* is a treasure.

My roommates went back to Bonn before I did, so I had a few days in Paris to myself. Chartres Cathedral was high on my list of things I wanted to see. In some miraculous fashion (I don't speak any French), I found myself aboard a bus going to Chartres. As we came over a small crest in the road, there it was—rising out of the flat fields like something from another world, growing larger and larger as we approached. Pale morning sunlight made the new growth in the fields glisten. The sky was pale, too, and I felt as though I were in a dream.

The dream continued as I walked through the building. The rose window was as exquisite as I had been led to believe. The colors were rich and gleaming as if the glass had been installed last week. The soaring ceiling was almost like a staircase to heaven. The experience was made more memorable by the fact that I had the entire place to myself except for a very quiet and respectful troop of French Girl Scouts. It was unique in every way.

Finally I went outside to sit for a few minutes to gather my wits about me before looking for a place for lunch. I didn't have to look far. The Scout troop came outside, sat down, opened hampers and promptly asked me to join them for lunch. I can't recall what we ate, but whatever it was, it was welcome. Their generosity enhanced what was already an unforgettable day.

During a separate trip to France, my roommates and I had a flat tire. For some reason we had driven rather than going by train. I don't remember which part of the country we were in, but the countryside was flat and lush. Grain of some sort was ripening in the fields giving everything a golden cast. The sky was sea blue with small clouds floating here and there. Near the site of our breakdown was a local store. While the tire was being repaired, we feasted on a lunch of *brie* (a soft cheese), bread, fresh tomatoes and red wine which we bought at the store, all the while sitting at the side of the road near the ripening grain. The warmth of the sun softened the *brie* so that it spread easily over the yeasty, crusty bread. The richness was cut by the tomatoes. The wine was heavenly. Never did anything taste so good.

Another trip we made was to Switzerland. I had been raised knowing about Chinese food, Maryland food and the occasional curry, but nothing about regional European cuisine. One of my roommates, Laurette, was a sophisticated girl a few years older than I from New York City. My other roommate, Melita, was from Minneapolis and knew as little about European food as I did. The weather was frigid so the first evening Laurette suggested that we have a cheese *fondue*. Melita and I trusted her judgment so off we went—another revelation.

The restaurant was warm and cozy with a fire blazing in an enormous fireplace. We were icy cold. The *maître d'* showed us to some low chairs placed around a coffee table near the fireplace. Laurette ordered a typical cheese *fondue.* By the time it arrived, we were sufficiently thawed out to listen to her explain about the dipping, twirling and eating of this marvelous dish of melted, gooey flavorful cheese. We had only bread to dip that evening, but it was enough to make Melita and me lifetime converts. Later I learned to dip pieces of cooked sausage, ham and other things to vary the taste a little. There was some terrible consequence of losing your bread in the cheese, but I can't recall what it was. I'm sure it had to do with kissing the male sitting to your right or something of the sort. Europeans seem to be big on that sort of thing.

Just as an aside, cheese *fondue* is not a good cheese *fondue* unless it is made with genuine imported cheese from Switzerland. Somehow our American Swiss-type cheeses are great for sandwiches but they do not have the texture and the flavor necessary to do justice to a proper *fondue.* Somehow the taste and consistency are off. Don't try domestic cheese—it just doesn't work.

Another time we went to Amsterdam. I had long been a curry fancier and to think about having one of such huge dimensions as a *riijstafel,* which means rice table in Dutch, was beyond imagining. It is a magnificent array of rice, curry and many, many condiments. We went to the best restaurant we could locate and I immediately became an addict. *Riijstafel* is a dish served in Indonesia, which I mention later on, but this was my first encounter with it. Indonesia was controlled by the Dutch for a very long time, so there were many *riijstafel* restaurants in Holland just as there are Indian restaurants in the United Kingdom. I only know that it was one of the tastiest, most stimulating meals I had ever eaten. Each bite was an adventure.

My birthday is in October. That first year two of my platonic male friends invited me to go to Munich with them to attend what must be the biggest beer party in the world. *Oktoberfest* lived up to its reputation, and we had a grand and glorious time drinking beer, singing and celebrating with the best of them. The beer that is especially brewed for *Oktoberfest* is heavier and darker than usual and infinitely palatable. The only problem is that German beer, and *Oktoberfest* beer in particular, has higher alcohol content than American beer so we couldn't drink as much as we would have liked. However, we tried valiantly.

The *Lowenbrau* tent was our favorite. There were gigantic communal tables, lots of good company, much singing and much laughter, not to mention the buxom waitresses able to carry huge numbers of overflowing *steins* or beer mugs at one time in each hand, and best of all, the oompah, oompah of the band in the background. It was immense fun.

The midway outside the big tents where the beer was served offered not only rides and games, but burnt sugar peanuts, spun sugar and any number of other treats. The most prominent vendor was the *wurst* or sausage man grilling them right in front of you. There were long ones, short ones, fat ones, thin ones, brown ones, tan ones and every combination thereof. If ever a cooking aroma enticed, that was it. I devoured them all except the *blutwurst* or blood sausage. That one brought me up short as it oozed blood when you cut into it. But heaven knows there was enough to choose from so that you could go nearly the whole week of the celebration without repeating and still avoid the *blutwurst*.

There was another sausage that I liked but it had to be well browned to give it some color. Before cooking, the pale *weisswurst* or white sausage was just plain horrid looking. One of the evenings we were at the festivities, my friends had had quite enough beer. As we passed that sausage vendor, one of them took a quick look at the big pile of as yet uncooked *weisswurst*, excused himself hastily and promptly threw up. I must admit that on second glance it *did* look like a huge pile of white, nasty, wriggling worms.

Another short trip was to Austria. The Cellini salt cellar was among my list of "Things to See in Vienna." We went to the museum where it was on view. It was utterly sublime. The workmanship proved to be even more delicate and beautiful than I had imagined. I was thrilled to have been able to see it.

Equally noteworthy was the Viennese food. We made a point of going to the Sacher Hotel and eating Sacher Torte, a many-layered dessert of intimidating proportions. There was also the restaurant or coffee house known as Demel's that had been in existence since the time Emperor Franz Josef and the Austro-Hungarian Empire. It was paneled in dark, gleaming wood that matched in color the chocolate for which they were famous. Bonbons, candies and confections of every description were available with each one tastier than the last. It was impossible not to overeat and we did it with great enthusiasm.

There were other trips we took and enjoyed—one to Holland to see the tulips and other bulbs in full bloom at Keukenhof Gardens, a beautiful area with lakes, trees, grass and bulb gardens laid out like a park. On the way we had Russian Eggs for lunch. I always liked that dish very much, but somehow American bottled mayonnaise doesn't quite match the European fresh mayonnaise and I am ordinarily too lazy to make my own. To prepare the dish, you hard boil an egg, peel it, cut it in half lengthwise and put it cut side down on a plate. Then you assemble diced cooked carrots, a few cooked peas, some kernels of cooked corn, some diced cooked string beans and a bit of diced celery. These are incorporated into about a half a cup of superbly seasoned mayonnaise and poured over the egg. You then use a heavy hand to garnish the eggs with black caviar. Then, along with some crusty bread, you settle down to a fine luncheon.

We visited Trier with its Roman ruins; went to Rothenburg and Dinkelsbuhl, utterly charming mediaeval towns; saw innumerable castles, including Neuschwanstein, mad King Ludwig's masterpiece. We also visited Hitler's mountain retreat, Berchtesgaden, located near Salzburg, as well as Salzburg itself, which was a strange combination of things both German and French. We also skied in Garmisch-Partenkirchen, which was an entirely new experience for someone from the Chesapeake Bay area. Great fun.

From left to right: Laurette Speer, Melita Schmidt and the author in rented sking outfits at Garmisch-Partenkirchen, probably late 1953.

We went to Lichtenstein and Luxembourg and found them to be entrancing, like something out of a fairy tale. But then again, so many towns and buildings in that part of the world are indeed like something out of a fairy tale.

Heidelberg was extremely interesting. It is Germany's equivalent of Oxford or Cambridge. It was founded in 1386 AD. Admission there is somewhat difficult to attain, but once attained will ensure a bright future, also like Oxford and Cambridge. I used to laugh to myself when I heard that years ago most young male students fenced and it was thought extremely manly to have a sabre scar on the cheek. To my way of thinking you were a better fencer if you did *not* have a sabre scar on the cheek. However, I am a mere female, and a foreign one at that, so how am I to know.

One of our last trips was both scary and exceedingly interesting. We took the night military train to Berlin through the Russian Zone. Special military orders had to be cut for us to do this. The passenger part of the train was like any other ordinary train except that it ran at night. We were told *very* emphatically that we were not to open the curtains under any circumstances. Of course it was dark and you couldn't see anything of the countryside, so we didn't bother until the train came into a station. Then, of course, we turned off the compartment lights and surreptitiously pulled aside a bit of the curtain and peered out hoping to see something extremely exciting. There was nothing to see but the occasional guard or sentry, rifle in hand, trying desperately not to yawn. One of the biggest disappointments of my life.

Berlin, on the other hand, was quite startling. We had been used to a certain amount of bomb damage in the American, British and French Zones of Germany itself, but Berlin was different. There was damage everywhere. In some areas there was not a building standing. As this was some years after the end of the war, it seemed incredible to us that so little had been done to rebuild. The other thing that bothered us was the fact that the little cleaning and hauling away of debris that was being done, was undertaken by women, and older women at that.

Berlin itself was also divided into four sectors—American, British, French and Russian. I don't remember how it was managed, but we were taken on a tour of the Russian Sector and found it even more depressing than the rest of the city. One street in particular was pointed out by the Russians as being totally restored. The "restoration" was a two block long area with buildings erected on each side of the street that were one, or at the most, two rooms deep. The back side of the buildings was still nothing but rubble. It was almost like a movie set.

*   *   *

After seventeen months in Bonn, the treaties were about to be signed and my job, as well as that of my boss, were abolished. I was in limbo for a time and then was sent to the Consulate General in Munich to work for the Special Assistant to the Consul General, otherwise known as the "spook." It was interesting but solitary work and I was too gregarious to enjoy it for long. However, the diversion of a new and large city in a different part of the country made it acceptable.

Toward the end of my time in Bonn, I had bought a second hand car from the High Commissioner's chauffeur. It was a 1948 four-door Ford, painted a medium very shiny blue with as much chrome as was possible to put on one automobile, including such things as wind deflectors and searchlights. The crowning touch was a hood ornament in the shape of a bull's head. The nostrils lighted up (one red, one green), when the headlights were turned on. For some reason I never took a picture of that car and I still regret it. It was one-of-a-kind that could never happen again. Sometimes I didn't know whether to be embarrassed to be seen driving it, or thank my lucky stars I had a car at all.

Driving from Bonn to Munich was a road trip of near misses. The *autobahn* or freeway had no speed limit so people drove as fast as they felt they could handle and then some. At that time autos did not have turn signals built into their tail lights, so people either used hand signals or had little sticks that lighted up and stuck out from the side of the car when the driver activated them. We called them "idiot sticks" because half the time no one activated them and the other half of the time they activated them incorrectly.

Also somewhat intimidating were the big German trucks that were in two sections. By that I mean that the front section was directly behind the cab the way our large trucks are built, but much shorter in length. However, they made up for that lack of cargo space by adding another truck section just as long as the first one. It was hooked to the rear of the first truck section by what looked like merely a chain to me. That back section flailed about with a life of its own whenever the driver passed another vehicle, turned or just hit a bump in the road. Those trucks were to be avoided at all costs.

In spite of all the difficulties, I made it to Munich in one piece, found the Consulate and reported in for duty. The building was a huge square, three stories high, surrounding a courtyard which had been used for carriages and horses in the days when it was first built. It was rather like the Pentagon, but had only four sides. It had been bombed as had many buildings in Munich, which made going from one section to another somewhat tricky. If you were on the second floor and needed to go to another office on that floor, you may or may not have to go up a floor or down a floor to get there. Repairs were often made simply by closing off the damaged area and hoping for the best. It was a dark and somewhat nasty place to work and, as I said earlier, I was too gregarious to enjoy the type of work I did, which was basically clerical and totally uninteresting. My boss, who spoke a number of Eastern European languages, spent most of his time interviewing *emigres* or refugees from behind the Iron Curtain to glean bits and pieces of information. However, Munich, in spite of the damage, was and is a magnificent city. It was great to explore.

Again, I drew two roommates who were easy to live with. However, we had different attitudes toward life and they didn't want to be bothered with maids, definite meal times and routine in general, so we went our separate ways. The apartment was in an older building that was directly across the street from the theatre that was used as an opera house. The main opera house had been destroyed by bombing with the ruins left as a monument to the evils of war.

Since the opera house was so close, I decided that I needed to take advantage of it. One week I subjected myself to all four of Wagner's Ring operas in five days, with Wednesday off for good behavior. It was all extremely "edifying," but I would never do it again. However, there was one marvelous moment in *Siegfried* when he comes across Brunhilde laid out on her shield and covered with her cloak that I will never forget. He approaches her cautiously wondering who this person is. She is lying there very still with the mound of her too-ample bosom thrust into the air. He finally catches on and sings "*Ach, das ist kein mann*," which means "Ach, that is no man" in a very loud voice. He was right on.

While on the subject of the theatre across the street, ballets were also presented there. We went to a number of them, enjoyed them, but always had to remember that we were in post-war Germany. By that I mean that the Germans had had a shortage of food during the war, especially sweets and luxury items. Now that the war was over, they had begun eating everything in sight. The women especially showed the results—even ballet dancers. Therefore the corps de ballet, even in *Les Sylphides* was not very sylph-like. The floor of the stage trembled and the male dancers really had their work cut out for them when it came to lifts.

Another unusual feature of attending public gatherings or performances of any kind that entailed large numbers of the local population was that most of them had not yet discovered that miraculous bathroom accessory, the deodorant. Sometimes it got a bit ripe.

Because of this universal and all-pervading consumption of sweets, the German coffee houses were absolute dreams, if you kept your appetite in check. Cakes, cookies, puddings, tortes, and every other dessert imaginable were available served with huge portions of fresh whipped cream so thick it had to be literally thrown off the spoon onto the dessert. The coffee was excellent and would put Starbucks to shame. Relatively speaking, it was hideously expensive, costing more than some of the desserts, but worth it. My favorite pairing was English tea cake (a pound cake stuffed with dried and candied fruit of all sorts) with a cup of black coffee. It was so good that I even omitted the whipped cream. It was also interesting to see that the coffee houses performed the function of a gathering place for friends and neighbors, as well as a place to read the daily newspapers that were attached to rods hanging on the wall and available to everyone. If computers had been in existence, there would have been people using them, too. The pace was leisurely and comfortable. You could stay there as long as you liked.

* * *

I did meet a wonderful Irish American girl from the Chicago area who also worked at the Consulate and lived next door. Her name was Eileen O'Loughlin and we became very good friends. We took a trip together in my fabulous blue car over the Alps and into Italy. We both loved the warmth, the color, the food, and the wine—all were good.

Our route took us to Bologna, Florence, Rome and on down to Naples, Capri and Pompeii. We also saw Juliet's balcony in Verona plus a number of other ancient towns that made us want to go back in time. (If only one could.) Florence was an incredible experience. Ghiberti's doors to the Baptistery were as magnificent as I thought they would be. In those days, you could get quite close to them so the detail was staggering to examine. Each figure stood out in perfect relief. (After I married, my husband and I toured Italy and he found the doors as remarkable as I had even though we were looking at a reproduction.)

Our *pensione* wasn't quite that perfect. Eileen was bitten by bedbugs which marred her perfect Irish complexion and put her in a temper, for which I don't blame her. Years later, in San Francisco, I was also bitten by bedbugs. The bites are nasty, itch ferociously and take a long time to heal. Rome was a wonderful dream, too. We saw the most famous ruins and sights, and threw some coins into the Trevi Fountain. We enjoyed every minute, and there were no bed bugs.

In Pompeii we had a guide who was under the impression that unmarried young women should not be allowed to go into the ruins of the brothels. We, on the other hand, felt that we had every right to view the squalid rooms. Therefore, the expected bit of bargaining took place and with the exchange of a certain number of *lira* or Italian currency before the Euro, we were given entrance. It was worth it. The wall paintings were explicit, and at that point I was extremely pleased that I lived in the twentieth century and could earn my living by other means.

Having the car serviced at an Italian station was an interesting procedure. One time I pulled in, not only to get gas, but also to have the windshield cleaned. Since my Italian was nonexistent, I rolled down my window, reached out around the door and pointed to the windshield covered with squashed bugs. The attendant responded instantly by kissing my fingers, then my wrist, and then my elbow before I had time to pull my arm back. As if that weren't enough, we needed something in the trunk of the car. As I was leaning over to rearrange the items, he promptly reached around and pinched me on the bosom, grinning all the while. Ah, *Italia*.

Mount Vesuvius was fun. We hired a guide although I drove my car. We proceeded up the mountain. The higher we went the warmer it became and the more little steam holes and bubbling lava we saw. There was absolutely no sign of anything green. The landscape was stark and ugly. It must have made Eileen nervous because she insisted to the guide that all Italian men sang and she not only wanted, but needed, a song to accompany us on our drive up the slope of the volcano. He was a wizened old man, but the minute music was needed, he broke into song with a resounding rendition of *O Sole Mio* which brought a huge grin to Eileen's face.

When we arrived at the top, we couldn't have had a more Italian welcome. Three men were sitting under the shade of a tarp that had been stretched between poles. They were drinking and selling wine. The wine was *Lacryma Christi del Vesuvio* or the Tears of Christ of Vesuvius, which is a beautiful white. They had even chilled it. Of course we bought some, sat drinking and singing with them for a while and then wended our way back down the mountain.

Capri was another special place. We both thought that it was one of the most beautiful places we had ever seen. In later years when I read about some of the vicious and terrible things the emperor Tiberius did to people who visited him on the island, I wasn't too sure. However, at that time I was totally ignorant of his nasty nature and simply enjoyed what I saw of the island at that time.

Since we had driven south on the coast road, we decided to take a more inland route back to Rome. I had just recently met Eileen and I didn't know much about her family. I wish that I had known more because as we came to the part of Italy where the monastery of Monte Cassino is located, she broke into terrible sobs. When she recovered, she told me that her brother had been killed there during the war. The battle had been an important one and quite bloody. From what I can gather, it was imperative that Monte Cassino be wrested from the Germans in order for the Allies to continue their march north to Rome and thus to eventually be in a position to invade Germany itself. At any rate the Germans held on tenaciously and many, many men on both sides were killed until the Allies finally prevailed.

My Bonn roommate, Melita, had also lost a brother during the war. He was aboard the *USS Arizona* and was killed at Pearl Harbor. Few American families escaped having close relatives or friends killed during the war. I dated a young man in college whose brother had also been killed in what to me was a truly grisly manner. He was an army courier and was to take some documents from one place to another. The road went through enemy territory. He was decapitated by driving his motorcycle at high speed on a roadway where the Germans had stretched a heavy wire from one side of the road to the other.

I would be remiss if I didn't mention that Melita was posted to Mexico City after her tour in Bonn was finished. There she met a young German man whom she married. In the course of time she became pregnant. I don't know the details, but either her doctor did not watch her properly or something else happened. Anyway, she developed a lethal blood problem and died in Mexico before the baby was born. It was my first experience of the death of someone my own age and of someone I had been very close to. I still think about her and regret the waste of such a fine person.

We made it back to Munich with only one other mishap. The brakes on my beautiful blue car failed as we were going down the far side of the Brenner Pass. I used gears to control the speed all the while listening to Eileen shouting Hail Marys loud enough for them to reach heaven and definitely secure the Virgin's attention. We spent two nights at the village at the bottom of the pass while the brakes were repaired. We called the Consulate to report the incident and tell them that we would be late in returning. They were not too pleased with us, but by the time we got back, everything had simmered down and we were welcomed.

*   *   *

Eileen and I made another trip together, this time to Spain. Again we drove my blue car, which behaved very well this time, I might add. We went through southern France, crossed the Pyrenees and on to Barcelona. The city is beautiful, situated right on the Mediterranean and the weather was glorious—everything sparkled. We were fortunate in finding a waterfront restaurant that served truly tasty *paella*, that incredible mixture of sausage, chicken, seafood, rice, tomatoes and seasonings—the best of which is saffron. We happily gorged ourselves.

After Barcelona, we drove to Madrid via Saragossa through what to me were dry, arid areas that now remind me of the New Mexico I live in at the present time. Madrid lived up to its reputation. We had a grand time visiting the sights and especially the Prado, that museum to end all museums. The only thing that bothered us about Madrid, and it seems to bother most people, other than Spaniards, is the fact that you cannot get an evening meal much earlier than nine o'clock. Ten or eleven are the preferred hours and I'm afraid we didn't like the late dinners very much. Dining that late seems to upset all the rhythms of the body, or at least our American bodies.

I forgot to mention that while in Barcelona, we saw the famous *Church of the Sagrada Familia* being built under the direction of a man named Gaudi. It is an utterly incredible and wild building and occupied the man for forty years after he began until his death. It is still under construction. (My husband and I saw it in the mid-2000s still only half finished. However, we were more impressed by the apartment complexes and other secular buildings he designed. They were immediately identifiable as his. The designs are really quite rhythmic and lovely.)

Toledo was a delightful place. The little side streets, quaint buildings and squares all appealed to us. Flowers were everywhere. We decided to attend a bull fight and I really wish we hadn't. I hated it and have never been to another. However, I guess that the only consolation is that I probably would have attended one at some time in my life, and this way I got it over with and never had to do it again.

We returned to the coast driving toward France via Valencia, which was indeed one enormous orange orchard. We loved the drive. Everything was green and fresh. It invigorated us and we returned to Munich ready for work.

*   *   *

Since I had already spent seventeen months in Bonn and seven months in Munich, my two year tour was up in late October of 1954. I received "Home Leave and Return" orders which meant I had two months in the States and then was to return to Munich for another two years. So off I went to Annapolis with a short stop in London. Annapolis hadn't changed and I was very pleased to be there for both Thanksgiving and Christmas.

The author's future husband, James Allen Dickey, as a Second Class Midshipman, 1955.

During the Naval Academy's Christmas leave period, a friend and I went into town to attend a movie. Afterward she and I went to a local soda fountain. Lo and behold, there was no one in the place but the two of us and two Midshipmen. Oddly enough, we began talking to them. They were Second Class Midshipmen or juniors at the Academy and had not gone home for Christmas for one reason or another. One of them, Jim Dickey, had sparkling eyes, a great sense of humor and was fun to be with. We started dating and that was it—I didn't go back to Munich, but stayed in Annapolis working, living at home and waiting for him to graduate so that we could be married.

3

TWO WEDDINGS AND MORE TRAVEL

D URING MY TIME IN EUROPE, my sister, Petie, who inherited her Grandfather Claude's interest in medicine, was attending the University of Virginia's School of Nursing in Charlottesville. She graduated with honors returning to Annapolis to work at a mental institution (which upset Mother considerably) while waiting for her fiancé, James Allen Evans, a classmate of Jim Dickey's, to graduate from the Naval Academy. She shared an apartment in downtown Annapolis with two other girls who were also waiting for the big Academy graduation day.

The author's sister, Petie, in her nurse's uniform, 1952.

However, Jim Dickey, (James Allen Dickey), had gone to Kansas State University (where he belonged to the Kappa Sigma Fraternity) for two years before entering the Academy and I was an old lady three years his senior. We were somewhat old fuds to the others, so on the whole we stayed pretty much to ourselves. In addition Jim wanted to get away from the Academy atmosphere when he could.

The author's future husband, Jim, at the time he attended Kansas State University, 1951.

Jim's admission to the Academy had been marked by good news and bad news. The good news was that he came in first in a competitive examination given by his Senator to determine who would be awarded the one remaining appointment to the Academy from Kansas. After passing his physical, he was then given that appointment. At the time, however, he was also an enlisted man in the Naval Reserve with an F-8 fighter squadron based at Olathe, Kansas.

One day his commanding officer, who had received news of Jim's appointment, called him into his office and somewhat facetiously offered him the choice of going to Korea to a combat zone with the squadron as it had been called to active duty, or going to the Academy. Jim describes his decision as taking at least three nanoseconds to make. Obviously, he selected the Academy.

The decision to leave his enlisted status to go to the Academy was the first event in the bad news category. In order for him to go to the Academy, he had to be discharged from the Navy as an enlisted man, and then re-inducted into the Navy as a midshipman. In 1952 there was still a draft because of the Korean War. Therefore, the minute he was discharged from the Navy, his draft board was notified and he became eligible to be drafted as he did not have enough service credit to be excluded from additional military service. Since there was an interval of time between his discharge and re-induction, the local draft board notified the authorities that he had not reported for his physical for induction and they, in turn, issued a federal warrant for his arrest.

About a month into plebe summer at the Academy, Jim was called to his Company Officer's office and informed that a Federal Marshal was waiting at the main office to serve him an arrest warrant. Fortunately the Academy's Legal Officer convinced the Marshal that Jim's service as a Midshipman satisfied his military obligation and therefore voided the arrest.

When Jim's mother heard of the arrest warrant, she visited the members of the local draft board with fire in her eyes. She left little doubt that the members, who had all known Jim since he was a youngster, had not had the common sense to realize that Jim was in fact in the military by being a Midshipman at the Academy. She emphasized her point by presenting them with a front page article from the local paper about Jim's appointment. From what Jim heard it was some time before members of the local draft board could look her in the face.

*   *   *

Jim has always said that he had a reverse dowry. I can see why he feels that way. When I left the States to work in Germany, Father had told me that I didn't have to pay income tax as I would be out of the country. Unfortunately, he was wrong, very wrong. When I came back the Internal Revenue Service informed me what I owed. I nearly fainted. I don't remember how much it was, but I certainly didn't have anything close to the amount of money necessary. My "Knight in Shining Armor" came to the rescue and paid it for me and has held it over my head ever since.

Mother and Father both liked Jim very much. He and Mother used to trade off-color jokes (as Jim did with *his* mother), and he and Father traded sea stories. It was probably more that Jim listened while Father told the sea stories. One afternoon they were chatting about World War II and Father's experiences in the waters around Vanuatu and Noumea with the Seabees. Father mentioned that he had met the French planter, on whom the part of Emile DeBecque was based and who was featured in the Rodgers and Hammerstein musical *South Pacific* which in turn was based on the James Michener book, *Tales of the South Pacific*. Jim sat up straight and said that through his cousin, Roy Dickey, he had met Oscar Hammerstein II when he was taken to Hammerstein's home in Doylestown, Pennsylvania by some of Roy's friends. There Hammerstein had played music from *South Pacific* for which he had written the lyrics. Small world.

*   *   *

Since I had not packed any of my belongings when I left Munich as I expected to return, Eileen, who was still there, very kindly assumed the task. A German woman sold wine to the people at the Consulate at extremely inexpensive prices. I sent Eileen one hundred dollars to buy wine from that woman to be included in the shipment. That amount of money went a long way and it seemed to me that thousands of bottles arrived in the States. Neither she nor I realized that we probably should not have included alcohol in the shipment, nor apparently did the commercial packers, but it arrived intact and Jim and I were very pleased. At that point in my life I was a white wine drinker. These were all whites from the Mosel, Rhine and Ahr River valleys. Most of them I was familiar with from my weekend jaunts, so I was exceedingly happy when the shipment arrived, especially since the selection was varied, but included some good vintages.

When the huge wooden crate arrived, it was put in the garage and Jim undertook the task of taking the boards off, disposing of the nails and straps and getting the wine to the basement. Unfortunately the basement wasn't air conditioned so during the following hot summer a few of the bottles spoiled. However, most were palatable, so we had the occasional glass on weekends.

Jim was a Second Class Midshipman or junior at the Academy when we met. He and his classmates were not allowed to ride in cars. If they were caught there were demerits and marching and all that nasty sort of thing. However, my house was a good long hike from the Academy, so during the spring semester I would drive Father's car to the corner of Hanover Street near Gate Two. Jim would jump into the back seat, hunker way down so as not to be seen and I would drive off to the house as fast as was prudent. Fortunately it worked. During his first class or senior year, I could pick him up openly as by that time First Class Midshipmen were of high enough rank to ride in cars. (Father always laughed and said that the two best ranks in the Navy were First Class Midshipman and Admiral. I'm somewhat inclined to agree with him.)

Some of the regulations at the Academy over the years were extremely strict. During Father's time (1915 to 1918), one of his classmates was dismissed because tobacco crumbs were found in his coat pocket when his uniform was sent to the dry cleaners. Mother had an experience along those lines, too. I'm not sure of the exact year, but I imagine that it was in the early 1920s. She had an operation on her feet and was out walking on Maryland Avenue near the Academy for exercise. She met some Midshipmen friends and wanted to show them how well she was doing without her cane. One of the Midshipmen held the cane for her. An officer walked by and put him on report for "Being Out of Uniform." Can't imagine how many demerits he received for the heinous offense of holding a cane.

Jim had scooped wheat by hand during harvests before he entered the Academy and had developed quite a physique. He was on the gym team which only added to his collection of muscles. Mother's washing machine was in the basement and was in its usual state of disrepair, so Jim volunteered to fix it. Since he was in uniform, he removed his white shirt and tie, going to the basement clad only in his trousers. The lighting in the basement was bad. When Mother poked her head around the door at the top of the stairs, I thought she was going to fall down the entire flight as the single light bulb was directly above Jim and etched his muscles making them stand out like Charles Atlas.

During various Midshipman cruises and summer leave, Jim had been to Rio de Janeiro and also to Barcelona, Madrid, Paris, Rome and England, so we had a lot to talk about when we first met and much in common. We had each attended operas at the Baths of Caracalla in Rome. He had seen *Aida* with Beniamino Gigli singing the part of Radames, while I had attended *Nabucco* Both of them were filled with parades, marches, elephants, camels, horses and ballet, not to mention loud music and a good deal of audience participation in the form of cheers and boos. Going to an Italian opera in Italy is like nothing else on earth.

Eileen and I had attended a performance of *La Boheme* in a small town outside of Rome. The audience was totally uninhibited and booed some of the singers, cheered others and wept when Mimi died. The entire audience was completely engrossed in the presentation. It seemed to me that it must have resembled a performance by an ancient bard in the days when minstrels went from town to town giving their performances from memory with complete audience attention and participation.

Jim liked European food, especially snails. One time when he had a weekend leave from the Academy and Mother invited him to stay at the house, we drove to the Italian section of Baltimore and bought some live snails. After all, if canned snails are acceptable and tasty, then live ones should be even that much better, right? Wrong. We brought the snails back to the house, put them in the kitchen sink, sprinkled them with oatmeal so that they could cleanse themselves internally during the night and left them alone. The next morning we found that they had crawled all over the kitchen—walls, ceiling, floor, counters—leaving the typical nasty, slimy, shiny snail track that you see in the garden. Both of us gagged and threw them out. I have never eaten another snail to this day, but after a few years Jim got over it, and likes them again. I try not to look at him while he is eating them.

Jim and the author before the Ring Dance, Annapolis, June 1955.

In June at the end of Jim's junior or second class year, the Ring Dance was held at the Academy. This was the time for the Midshipmen to begin wearing their class rings. Each graduating class has a ring of a different design. Some of the rings are smaller than others, but most of them follow the general rule of having the Academy crest on one side and the class crest (which shows the year of graduation) on the other. The stone of choice is in the center with the words "United States Naval Academy" surrounding it. Father's ring has no stone as he broke too many of them. The center of his ring is a gold plug with his monogram on it. Jim's roommate broke his stone right away and immediately carved another one from a clear plastic toothbrush handle. Ingenious.

If you are in Annapolis, you can visit the Naval Academy Museum which has an eye catching display of all the class rings in chronological order. Some of the early classes did not have rings as we know them today. They almost look as though each graduate designed his own. Some of them are almost flamboyant by military standards.

This is also the time for the female half of any engaged couple to receive her "miniature." The miniature is exactly what it sounds like—a smaller and more feminine version of the class ring. It is worn as an engagement ring. It, of course, has curved sides so that the wedding ring and any subsequent anniversary rings have to be made to order to fit next to the curved contours of the miniature. This is not a problem if you go to a jeweler in the Annapolis area as they are used to it. If a graduate decides he wants to wear a wedding ring, his band also has to be curved around the class ring

The Ring Dance is very special to the Midshipmen as it signifies that when classes reconvene in the fall they will be the seniors or First Class Midshipmen and virtually on the downhill path to graduation. A replica of the class ring is made (I certainly don't know how they make it) large enough for a couple to walk through. It is painted bright gold and has a navy blue "stone" in the center of the "roof." The couples walk through the ring one couple at a time. She removes his ring from where it has been hanging on a ribbon around her neck. She then dips it in a bowl that holds water from each of the Seven Seas. This water has been collected and sent from ships actually in that body of water. It is done every year. If they are engaged, she then receives her miniature. At that point they are supposed to kiss, hold hands and exit the ring to make room for the next couple.

Some of the embraces had embarrassed me beyond belief, so when our turn came Jim and I barely touched lips. We heard someone say "She must be a blind date." Of course, by that time we *were* engaged. However I had elected to have white gold rather than yellow, which caused some complications. In addition there had been several other mixups on the order, so there was no ring for Jim to give me.

Jim as a First Class Midshipman, Annapolis, spring of 1956.

(Although I haven't as yet mentioned meeting Jim's parents, the diamond in the center of my miniature was given to Jim by his mother to give to me. I always thought that was a generous and lovely thing for her to do. She had inherited the stone from her Aunt Lottie Grage. My wedding ring was a plain white gold band. On our tenth anniversary Jim gave me a diamond band to add to the collection, and on our thirtieth he gave me a third one quite lavishly set with diamonds.)

*   *   *

During his August leave of 1955, we went to his home in Medicine Lodge, Kansas, a small town (population 3,000) south and west of Wichita, so that I could meet his parents. Kansas at that time was extremely conservative. Jim really shocked his mother when we got off the plane in Wichita. Tailored walking shorts were all the rage for men on the East Coast. He had bought a good looking pair and wore them on the trip with a white shirt, a tie and sports jacket, as well as knee high socks. To top it all off, he was carrying his furled British umbrella. We had changed planes in St. Louis and found out that the people there also were not up to East Coast styles. As we got off the plane to walk to the terminal, the crowd parted like the waters of the Red Sea before Moses. When we arrived in Wichita it happened again. When his mother saw him, she viewed Jim's "outlandish" clothes as some sort of disease. She gasped and quickly hustled us to the car for the drive to Medicine Lodge. His father was at work and she actually made Jim go to the house and change his clothes *before* seeing his father. Medicine Lodge certainly was not up to such *avant-garde* men's outfits. What fun.

His parents seemed to accept me readily enough, (although his Father always thought me rather extravagant.), and I certainly liked them. His mother's name was Irene and his father's Ralph. Irene's maiden name was Parker. They owned an appliance business where Jim had worked while growing up and Irene worked in the office of the store. I also met his mother's great friend, Mary, who also worked in the store, and other ladies with whom they both played bridge. Irene's sister, Pearle, was visiting at the same time and was a big help in "breaking the ice," since Pearle's son, Ralph Freese, had also gone to the Academy and was in the Class of 1953.

*   *   *

The State of Kansas has always had a love-hate relationship with all things alcoholic. The whole conflict has been compounded by "gross hypocrisy as well as gross stupidity." (Jim's words, not mine.) For years there had been state-wide prohibition. Then they decided to allow voting for county option and even township option. The negative impact of the vote of township option was graphically illustrated when Coldwater, a small town about twenty-five miles west of Medicine Lodge, voted "dry" and Medicine Lodge voted "wet." Within two years Coldwater was a ghost town. All but one or two businesses had closed because on Saturday, when all of the farmers shopped for groceries and farm supplies, they came to Medicine Lodge for the added benefit of obtaining some "booze."

In some jurisdictions you could buy alcohol from a liquor store but not in a restaurant, unless that restaurant has been designated a "private club" and then you had to buy a temporary membership. On top of that, at some of the "clubs" you paid for your liquor on one bar tab and any mix you might want on another tab. The clubs then had to maintain totally separate accounting documents for each individual serving to present monthly to the idiotic liquor review board. Of course, you could also buy your liquor from a bootlegger if you were "tall enough to reach his window," as Jim would say. The most ridiculous part of all is that the bootleggers had federal liquor licenses and therefore were to some extent "legal." But not completely. The local option then kicked in.

The most incredible fact in all this confusing mishmash is that Carrie Nation, the notorious hatchet wielding demon of saloons, lived in Medicine Lodge. Her house is now something of a shrine and is open to the public for a fee. However, she died in 1911, so we cannot blame her for most of the modern day illogical liquor bans. (Jim claims that her first husband drank heavily because she was so ugly. There might be something to that after seeing her picture.)

The town had a very active WCTU (Women's Christian Temperance Union). One of Irene's dearest friends made her liquor purchases at the three liquor stores in Medicine Lodge in rotation on different weeks to avoid the WCTU ladies' scrutiny. In a small town, criticism would certainly have followed had she been less circumspect. However, she cannot be faulted as her husband had died an alcoholic and she did not want that label.

Jim tells a wonderful story about when he was ten or eleven. He and a friend named George Stewart were out tramping in the wild area south of town between Elm Creek and the Medicine River. They found a hoard of liquor hidden there by the Swinton brothers, who were well known local bootleggers. The Swinton's name was even on the shipping label glued to the boxes. Jim and George took the case of whiskey and transported it on a red Radio Flyer wagon to Main Street. There they offered a fifth of Canadian Club for $1.50, which was normally priced at $12 from the bootleggers. This was 1941 and $12 was a lot of money. Their price of $1.50 per bottle was such a bargain that their business immediately flourished.

After they had sold two or three bottles at that low price, their business started picking up even more. Unfortunately, the Sheriff heard about what was going on and went to see Jim's dad. He told Ralph that he should go check things out. Ralph found the two young businessmen sitting on the curb on Main Street with their remaining supply of merchandise. Unfortunately for Jim and George, Ralph confiscated the remaining bottles. That was the end of Jim's bootlegging career.

However, there is one more story that is worth telling. While in high school, Jim played football and was excused from working for Ralph after school and on Saturdays during the fall. He did not play any other sports, including basketball because by his own admission he was too short, too slow and a lousy shot. (That pretty well covers it.) Therefore, during the rest of the school year, he had to work after school and on Saturdays. One evening when he had finished working, Jim was driving one of Ralph's trucks home when he decided to stop at Charlie Blackwell's beer joint for a bottle of his 3.2 beer. (Yes, he was underage but was served there anyway.) It was indeed a "joint." The saloon was an old shingled frame building of indeterminate age, with a few parking spaces directly in front.

On this fateful evening, Jim managed to get one of those parking spaces. Unfortunately the space did not have a barrier to stop vehicles from driving directly into the building. Jim's luck that evening was not too good. When he applied the brakes, the brake pedal went to the floor, and the truck proceeded in slow motion to ram the building, shearing off numerous wall studs and lifting the entire front of the building up over the top of the truck, that finally came to rest in the middle of the saloon. In so doing, he scattered tables and chairs all over the room, but fortunately did not hurt anyone.

Charlie, the owner, did say rather facetiously that had he known that Jim was coming in, he would have opened the door. Jim's luck still had not improved. Within about ten minutes, who should appear but Ralph, Jim's dad. Fortunately, by that time Charlie and a few of the patrons had discovered that one of the hydraulic brake lines had broken, eliminating any and all of the braking capabilities of the truck. After the truck was removed, Charlie then had the first and only drive-in beer joint in town. (Jim laughs over this story, but I shudder to think what might have happened had he tried to brake on the open highway with "no brakes."

The alcohol or no alcohol question and who will or will not be served in Kansas is even more confusing than Mother's family names, so I am just going to have a glass of wine and drop the subject.

*   *   *

Another of Jim's high school escapades (that had nothing to do with alcohol) involved the "borrowing" of a "two-seater" outhouse from a public park, using Ralph's A-frame power winch truck to lift it and wedging it tightly in the front door of the high school. Anyone entering or leaving the premises had to climb over the seats thereby losing what little dignity they had.

All of this took place on Halloween with about ten of Jim's friends taking part. I have been to some of Jim's high school reunions with him and have heard other people's reactions—they loved it and thought it an outstanding prank. However, they were students, too, at the time of the prank. I'm not sure how much the school administrators admired it when it happened.

Another questionable activity Jim participated in, along with some of his buddies, was to drive to Pratt, a town about thirty miles north, to date some of the young ladies. Of course there were many available girls in Medicine Lodge. However, the grass is always greener on the other side of the fence, or in this case, the other town. Naturally the local boys of Pratt found out about these overtures and proceeded to chase the Medicine Lodge Lotharios out of town on a regular basis.

As it turned out, one of the leaders of the Pratt ruffians was a fellow by the name of Jim Goodloe. It was ironic that later when Jim walked into the Kappa Sigma fraternity house at Kansas State, who was there to greet him but Jim Goodloe. Admittedly it took some time before the animosity subsided, but as fate would have it, Jim Goodloe and Jim Dickey became very good friends.

Their friendship led to Jim Dickey being Jim Goodloe's best man at his wedding. Again, life gave events a few twists because while the two Jims were waiting for the ceremony to begin, Jim Goodloe had a mild panic attack and offered Jim Dickey one hundred and fifty dollars to help him slip out the back door. Even though the amount offered was a lot of money in those days, Jim Dickey laughed, declined the offer and the wedding proceeded on schedule. In retrospect, it probably would have been better to have helped Jim Goodloe out the back door as the marriage didn't survive. However, good things do happen and he is now married to a delightful lady named Juanita.

Even though the two Jims went their separate ways for over sixty years, their friendship has survived the test of time. From what I hear, they still laugh about the dating games and the young lovelies of Pratt.

*   *   *

During the trip to Medicine Lodge for me to meet his family, we also went to other equally small towns in the area so that I could meet his Grandmother Dickey, his uncles, aunts, cousins and other relatives. While in Ashland, another small Kansas town, we went to Ralph's brother, Orville's house. We were invited to stay for lunch. This was a typical summer "harvest" meal with large serving dishes brimming with everything tasty and fattening. The food was served at an enormous kitchen table seating about twelve people. On this occasion there were many young girls from the family and also a number of neighborhood girls who had been invited over to see the "Lady from the East Coast" who had brightly painted fingernails. Not a single other female at the table used nail polish of any kind, much less red nor did they use lipstick. While in Kansas I was always being stared at because of my nails. The little girls were especially entranced. Some of them were unable to take their eyes off the fingernails long enough to put their forks in their mouths. They usually stabbed their cheeks with the tines of the forks instead.

We went on to Meade, another small town, to meet his Grandmother Dickey. Her maiden name was Hattie Lemmon. She was from Iowa. She was a spritely woman who moved quickly and seemed to enjoy her new house. She had had it built approximately three blocks closer to the Post Office than her previous house so that she could collect her mail more easily. I don't know how many grandchildren she had, but there were many, and the trip to pick up the letters from them was the highlight of her day. I don't remember what she served us for lunch but Jim and I were chuckling to ourselves at the china and glassware. Nothing matched and it was all chipped and cracked. However, it didn't matter to her as she had better things to do with her money. One of the truly wonderful things she did was to have a large swimming pool built which she donated to the city so that the children would have a place to cool off and play during the scorching Kansas summers.

One day Grandmother Dickey scared the family badly by completely disappearing. Even though she was in her nineties and a widow, she obviously felt no obligation to tell anyone that she was going out of town. The Grand Ole Opry was extremely popular in the Midwest and she was an avid fan. She simply took a bus to Nashville, saw the Opry show and went blithely backstage without permission or invitation. There she introduced herself, chatted with Minnie Pearl, Roy Clark, and other regulars, who apparently enjoyed her so much that they gave her a private tour of the theatre and the back stage area normally closed to non-performers. She then re-boarded her bus and returned to Meade just in time to avoid having the police called to report her as a "missing person"—a very independent lady.

Before moving into town, she and her husband had lived on a ranch about eighteen miles south of Meade. She was the postmistress there working out of a very small wooden building about the size of a single car garage. That was the Post Office. It had one small safe and a bench for the local ranchers to sit on while exchanging the latest news. It was more like a gathering spot than a post office. It was listed as "Nye, Kansas" and was shown on maps of the state. Later when the post office was closed "Nye" disappeared. She had obviously enjoyed her position. Looking at it from my perspective, I'm sure she also enjoyed the contact with the people who came to utilize the postal services. All of those ranches were exceedingly isolated, not only from town but from one another.

Although the Jesse James outlaw gang may be better known than the Dalton Brothers gang, there is nothing like personally knowing a man with a price on his head. Apparently Jim's grandmother and grandfather knew the Dalton Brothers. A Dalton sister was married to a man named Whipple. They lived in

Meade and never mentioned the outlaw members of their family. No one else did either as the Daltons seemed to have been liked by the people of the town. Also, the brothers liked the people in Meade and never robbed anyone or any institution there. In other words, there was no "squealing" when the Daltons came to town even though the Daltons had to escape through a tunnel from the Whipple house to a barn down the hill several times when the law was after them.

*　*　*

Ranching and the raising of cattle seem to generate a slightly different attitude toward the law from that of the East Coast. Jim told me that when he was in high school he went down to the Court House to be a spectator at the trial of a rancher who was being tried for killing three men.

The judge asked the defendant what had happened. The reply was that he had caught the three men loading some of his cattle onto a truck, took umbrage to the situation and admitted shooting them dead on the spot. The judge paused briefly, then announced, "Case dismissed." Rustling is obviously frowned on in ranching circles.

*　*　*

The Dickey clan was descended from one of five Dickey brothers who came to the United States from Scotland in the 1850s. Each one went to a different part of the country, Jim's ancestor going to the Ames County, Iowa, area. Ralph's father, Roy, who was born in 1877, came to Kansas with his wife, Hattie Lemmon. He secured a large ranch on the Cimarron River, part of the ranch in Kansas and part in Oklahoma. Roy and Hattie had four sons: Ralph, (Jim's father), Orville, Clarence and Lloyd.

Grandmother Dickey with her four sons, from left to right: Lloyd, Orville, Grandmother Dickey, Ralph, and Clarence, date unknown.

On my visit to the ranch, we walked to a particular part of one field where Indians had camped. I actually found a small arrowhead. I was told it was the size and shape for shooting birds.

Coincidentally, when we were living in Annapolis many years later, a neighbor inherited some handmade quilts from a maiden aunt who had been a schoolteacher and lived in the Ames, Iowa, area. One of them was a "friendship" quilt with quite a few of the squares signed by children with the last name of Dickey.

Irene's father's name was Lee Seth Parker while her mother's name was Edna Traver Parker. They had a large farm in Stevens County, Kansas. Unfortunately, Irene lost her father when she was quite young, only four. He was riding a horse along a barbed wire fence. For some reason the horse went berserk and rubbed her father up against the fence while running rapidly. This, of course, damaged his leg and thigh severely. We do not know whether he died from loss of blood or from a subsequent infection.

Jim's mother, Irene, and her extended family. Irene is the little girl in the lower right corner. The picture was taken sometime in 1912 in Kansas.

Irene was quite athletic and truly loved basketball. She played all during high school, as well as on the town team after graduating. While she was still in high school and the team was playing on a warm day, the girls rolled down their knee socks. One of the fathers took great exception to this and walked out onto the court insisting that his daughter roll up her socks immediately and keep them that way.

Jim's mother, Irene, with fellow basketball enthusiasts. Note that she is on the far left and has her socks UP. The picture was probably taken in Kansas in the mid-1920s.

Oil and natural gas were discovered in Stevens County and Jim still receives royalty checks from a natural gas lease previously owned by his mother. The gas is extracted from acreage where the old homestead stood.

In 1929 when Irene and Ralph were married, they lived in Hugoton, Kansas, a small town in the southwest part of the state. Ralph had $100 of his own money and borrowed another $150 from an uncle of Irene's. With this money he opened an appliance business. One of his main appliance lines was the Maytag washing machine. At that time, Ralph would completely overhaul a washer for the tidy sum of $1.50. At Christmas, Ralph always received a five pound wheel of the famous Maytag cheese, which was wonderful present, as well as delicious treat.

Jim's father, Ralph, as a young man. The picture was probably taken about the time of his marriage in Kansas in 1929.

Jim's mother, Irene, as a young woman. The picture was probably taken about the time of her marriage in Kansas in 1929.

Money was so scarce that Ralph sometimes had to resort to barter to make a living. One of his best trades was a washing machine for a pair of Percheron horses. He subsequently sold the horses for a nice profit. The other great trade was another washing machine for ten one-gallon jugs of white lightning. Even during the Depression and the Dust Bowl, people somehow came up with money to buy booze.

Things were so tight financially that when Jim was born in 1931 and was found to be healthy, his parents had to have the phone removed from the house since they could not afford the fifty cents a month that it cost. The Dust Bowl and the Great Depression took their toll in the Midwest.

Jim as child of eight months in Kansas in 1932.

When Jim was about four years old, Ralph and Irene moved to Medicine Lodge where they opened another appliance business and worked and lived for many years.

*   *   *

Finally THE DAY came. The two Jims graduated on Friday, 1 June 1956, in the morning amid all the usual military fanfare—marching, music, flyovers, smiling and weeping parents and the final wondrous toss of Midshipmen caps into the air. (By the way, the reason the caps are thrown is that they are obsolete since the officer's caps are different. Besides it makes an exciting show.) It was marvelous and everyone enjoyed it to the hilt.

The two Jims as First Class Midshipmen in June 1956, Jim Evans to the left, Jim Dickey to the right.

Petie and Jim were married that afternoon at St. Anne's Episcopal Church and I was her maid of honor. Jim and I were married the next day and she was my matron of honor. The two Jims ushered for one another, so everything was "all in the family." Petie's reception was at the Naval Academy Alumni House, which is a beautiful colonial residence, furnished with period furniture. It is gracious and elegant and was built by a member of one of the prominent early families in Annapolis.

Petie and Jim Evans walking down the aisle after their wedding ceremony in
Annapolis on 1 June 1956.
(Photo courtesy M.E. Warren Photography, LLC.)

We were married June 2nd at 7:30 in the evening also at St. Anne's Episcopal Church in a military wedding with all the bells and whistles except the arch of swords, which the church would not permit. The ceremony itself went well. However, I had decided not to wear my glasses. In addition, I was wearing my usual four-inch heels. After Jim and I exchanged our vows and were pronounced "man and wife," I turned to go back down the aisle determined not to trip over the small step near the altar or any other step for that matter. In other words, I was so intent on not falling over anything that I totally forgot to kiss Jim. He forgave me.

Jim Dickey and the author walking down the aisle after their wedding ceremony in Annapolis on 2 June 1956. (Photo courtesy M.E. Warren Photography, LLC.)

Our reception was held at the Officers Club and was splendid. The alcohol served was a Claude family recipe called "Tea Punch." I must say that it did indeed have a punch. It is an extremely strong mixture of alcohol and other ingredients and it really does include tea. This combination is, unfortunately, as smooth as silk—which can cause problems. It is placed in a punch bowl and ladled into small punch cups filled with cracked ice, thereby diluting the alcohol a bit. I'm afraid my young flower girl drank a tad too much for a little girl and felt the effects. She had obviously eluded adult observation.

Jim's parents came from Kansas. Rosemary Rutt, my great friend from high school was a bridesmaid. Eileen was able to come plus several other people from Germany, including my roommate, Laurette, college friends, family and neighbors, plus Father's sister and brother-in-law, Helen and Robby.

The author's father, Walton Runnells Read, and his sister, Helen Read Robinson, at the author's wedding reception 2 June 1956. (Photo courtesy M.E. Warren Photography, LLC)

One particularly honored guest was my Great Aunt Sophie who was the widow of one of my grandfather's brothers. She was ninety-two and had seen much Annapolis history pass before her, including the return of John Paul Jones's body from France to be placed in the Naval Academy Chapel Crypt in 1913. She lived to be one hundred and one and was deeply mourned when she died.

The wedding presents were lovely as people had been very generous. I think our favorite was a gallon of homemade dandelion wine given to us by Florence, one of the old black cleaning women who had worked for the family for years. It was tasty, a little sweet and reminded us of some of the wines that had been shipped from Germany. We truly appreciated it and enjoyed every drop.

All in all, the wedding was a great celebration and to our eyes a complete success.

*   *   *

Since there were two weddings on two successive days, Mother and Father had a large number of guests of their own who arrived in town to attend both ceremonies. Because of this, Petie and I decided to do each wedding differently. In other words, she wore a long gown, I wore a short one; she was married in the afternoon, I in the evening; her reception was at one venue, mine at another; her menu was one thing, mine another; her color scheme was red and white, mine pale yellow, and so on. It was somewhat difficult, but we managed it. Besides that, it was great fun and challenging to do. Every woman loves planning a wedding, and we had two.

One small thing that did jar Jim and me slightly was that when we drove to Washington, D.C. for the first night of our honeymoon, we arrived in the hotel room to find a bottle of champagne chilling in a tub with a note from one of Jim's friends. However, the startling part was that there were *four* glasses. We expected guests any minute. To preclude such a surprise we looked in the closet, under the bed, behind the curtains and any and all spaces large enough for a person to hide. Guests were definitely *not* welcome.

Next morning we cancelled some plans we had made and drove quietly back to the little guest house we had rented on Weems Creek not letting anyone know that we had returned. It was much less nerve wracking.

However, we were in for a rude surprise as the house was completely trashed. All of the food and beer were gone. There were wet towels everywhere, along with dirty glasses, plates and silverware. Every counter and tabletop was covered with debris and sand crunched underfoot. We couldn't imagine who created the mess, but assumed it was Jim's parents letting off steam after the strain of the week of wedding festivities. We were young and healthy, so we set to cleaning it up and did not mention it to Ralph and Irene until many years later. That was another surprise—they said that they had not done any such thing. It had not occurred to us to question our landlord, but apparently he, or someone he allowed in, had had one hell of a party.

*   *   *

Jim's eyesight had deteriorated during the last part of his first class year, so he went into the Navy Supply Corps rather than becoming a line officer. He blames it on the installation of fluorescent lights in the dorm rooms which made it difficult to see when studying. However, after the fact, he has claimed that going into the Supply Corps was the best thing that happened to him. The Supply Corps is the business side of the Navy which gave him hands-on practical experience that helped him immensely after retirement.

Jim had two months leave before he had to report to the Supply Corps School in Athens, Georgia. We lived in our tiny guest house. He, believe it or not, got a job as a pipefitter at the Maryland Shipbuilding and Drydock Company in Baltimore through David Jalbert, an old friend of mine. I continued the job I already had working for Charles and Edward Lee at their real estate and insurance office. One particular morning Jim forgot his wallet and therefore had no money with which to buy lunch. When he came home and told me what he had done, I was very proud of him and thought his a fitting solution for one just recently trained in using his brain and learning leadership at the Academy. He found an old gunny sack and collected all the empty soda bottles he could find (which were worth two cents each at that time), turned them in at the food wagon and bought lunch with the resulting cash. Not bad for a new Ensign.

Anyone renting the little house had the use of a dock which projected into Weems Creek. In his off time, Jim liked to try his hand at crabbing. One afternoon he caught a huge crab that was just beginning to shed its shell in order to grow larger. He put it in a bucket and watched the crab finish the process. Then he brought the crab to me. I cleaned and fried it. It was so large we each had a thick, wonderful soft shell crab sandwich. It was the best one I had ever tasted.

*   *   *

At the end of leave and Jim's very successful tour of duty as a pipefitter at the shipyard, we loaded up the 1956 Chevrolet Del Rey Club Coupe, which Jim's parents had given him as a graduation present, in preparation for our drive to Athens.

While the 1956 Chevy has become a "classic" due to its great engine, this car was a real gem in other ways. It had the V-8 power pac engine, was loaded with extras too numerous to mention, and even had air conditioning, which at that time was an optional, extra cost luxury. It was painted blue and white, and in our eyes was gorgeous. The addition of the extras, plus the air-conditioning, drove the cost up to a staggering $2005 which included taxes, tags and all of the unknown charges added by the dealer. Wish car prices were like that today.

We drove to Athens and found an apartment on Lumpkin Street. (One of my cousins addressed our Christmas card to "The Bumpkins on Lumpkin Street"—and we actually received it.) There were six small apartments on our floor and we became friendly with all the other tenants, who were young married couples. It was somewhat like a legal co-ed dorm. We made friends with Marty and Jack Binns who lived directly next door. He was another classmate of Jim's who got out of the Navy later on, went into the Foreign Service and ultimately became our Ambassador to Honduras.

We also were very friendly with Ed and Helene Cooke. Ed had attended college in Pennsylvania where the school had a Naval ROTC unit. He also resigned from the Navy after completing his obligated service and went into the CIA. Jim caught up with him in Vietnam in later years and heard some really hair raising stories. As a matter of fact, *all* of Ed's stories were hair raising. Even after retirement, he couldn't sit still and did a lot of volunteer work in the Balkans during the Kosovo conflict. He had an old VW bus which he used to evacuate people from the areas where there was fighting going on.

Marcia and Larry Arnold, who were Jewish, lived down the hall and were lots of fun. One evening Marcia pounded on our door and quickly thrust a pound of bacon into my hands asking me to keep it for a few days as her Orthodox aunt was coming to visit and she didn't want it to be found in *her* refrigerator. Unfortunately, we ultimately lost touch with them.

Athens was incredibly small and incredibly provincial, especially in the area of food that was not Southern. When we wanted rye bread, we had to call Leb's Deli in Atlanta and have it put on a Greyhound bus. Then we would go to the bus depot and pick it up. Our diet while in Athens was exceedingly bland. Just recently we met a couple from Atlanta. We were pleased and surprised that Leb's was still in business after all these years.

There weren't many jobs available for the wives of the students at the Navy school as their time in Athens was so brief. I was lucky and secured one with an insurance adjusting firm. It wasn't much of a job, merely transcribing the tapes that the adjustors dictated about accidents they had investigated, and so on. The adjustors were all men, big time male chauvinists with the additional problems Southern men have. They were semi-literate, although college graduates. Even with their higher level of education, one of them dictated a long report on an accident that had happened in a "parking lot 150 feet square in diameter." Statements like that gave me the opportunity to clean up their texts and grammar to a certain extent.

One of them came up to me one morning and asked if I knew the difference between a Yankee and a damned Yankee. I replied that I didn't. He then proceeded to tell me that "Yankees live in the north, but damned Yankees come down here." (All spoken in a ripe full blown Georgia accent.) After that I typed his reports exactly as he dictated them. They were astonishingly bad and I left them that way. Sweet revenge.

I also had a good bit of fun keeping a list of expressions and sayings that I heard from the people in the office, which were provincial, regional and utterly delightful. I kept the list under my typewriter and added to it each time I heard a new one. Unfortunately I was so happy to leave on my last day that I left the list behind. However, I do remember one which was quite graphic and simple and explained the situation precisely. One of the young women employees rushed into the office a bit late one morning and loudly complained that she had been "bus left." That does indeed describe the situation of missing your bus, does it not?

On numerous occasions Jim's classes would be over before I quit work for the day. As we had only one car, he came to pick me up and if he had to wait for me, usually went to a small corner news kiosk which also housed an older black man and his shoe shine stand. It soon became obvious that the old bootblack was also the "Dear Abby" of some of the patrons who frequented the news stand. One day when Jim was waiting for me, he overheard a very attractive young black woman confiding in her "Dear Abby" counselor.

The comments went like this: "I don't know what I'm goin' to do with that man of mine. Every time I go out with my girlfriends or even just shoppin', he 'cuses me of 'doin' it.' I'm fed up. Tonight I'm goin' out and 'do it'."

Even though Jim waited for me on other afternoons, he never found out if she 'did it'.

* * *

As newlyweds, we had a few pieces of furniture, but lacked a coffee table. Between Jim and the lumber yard, they came up with an attractive round walnut table that was just perfect with our 1950s Knoll furniture. Jim finished it with a "French Polish" all done by hand in the middle of the living room. We still have it and use it today although at one point Father caused a huge cigarette burn on one side of the table. We have never repaired the burn. I just put a potted plant over it, and salute Father when I dust the table.

In February of 1957, Jim graduated from the Supply Corps School. He received orders to the *USS Columbus,* a heavy cruiser stationed in Long Beach, California. We started our cross country journey in the 1956 Chevrolet club coupe. It was a great car and we both enjoyed driving it. We drove the southern route and spent one night in Albuquerque. We had dinner in a restaurant along the Route 66 part of Central Avenue. Naturally we ordered a southwest meal, but found to our horror that it was too hot and spicy for either of us to eat. How I wish we had that meal in front of us now that we live in Albuquerque to see just how hot it *really* was.

*   *   *

We found a small apartment on Third Street in Long Beach just a few blocks from the beach and settled down to "old married life." I got a job in the Trust Department of a bank, which I liked and Jim enjoyed his work aboard ship. Inevitably the Navy broke into our lives and *Columbus*, with Jim aboard, left for West Pac (Western Pacific) for an eight month cruise.

The Navy was still relatively formal at that time with junior officers and their wives calling on their seniors. We made our required call on Captain and Mrs. Uehling (he was the Commanding Officer of *Columbus*) never expecting for one moment that they would return the call. One Sunday we had donned old clothes and gone to the building's parking lot to wash our car. We returned to our apartment and plopped down on the rug because our clothes were wet. We had opened the wooden door so only the screen door was in place. One thing led to another. However, before anything too serious occurred, there was a knock at the door and some stifled giggles. We looked up and there were the Uehlings standing in the doorway, quite formally dressed and prepared to make their return call on us. They laughed with us and not at us, came in and we had a fine visit with them.

*   *   *

The ship first stopped in Hawaii where Jim met Rosemary Rutt, my old high school friend who had been a bridesmaid and was now a Pan American Airline flight attendant on their South American runs with the occasional run to Hawaii. Of course they went bar hopping. (Rosie had fared better than I in Spanish class. She had also had the good fortune to have her father ordered to Madrid as Naval Attaché right after high school, so her Spanish was fluent and she was able to get a great job with PanAm.)

Then the ship went on to Fiji where the men were entertained royally at an afternoon tea dance. One of the Fijian naval officers, very tall with huge muscles, grabbed Jim by the arm, lifted him off his feet and escorted him on tippy toes across the room to meet his sister. She was also tall and black and towered over him. Jim guessed she outweighed him by a hundred pounds. She had a typical Fijian "fuzzy wuzzy" hairdo that was at least ten inches high. However, he said she was "as light as a feather" and a pleasure to dance with.

The ship then proceeded to Melbourne, Australia, to commemorate the Battle of the Coral Sea. They stopped in Subic Bay where Jim saw Father's picture and name on a plaque in the entrance foyer of the administration building as the first Commanding Officer of the base after the war.

After Guam, they went to Hong Kong, the shopping mecca of the world at that time. Unfortunately I had had some dental work done, so Jim was greeted with a message that we were broke and he couldn't spend any money. This was especially infuriating as I found out later on that the dental work was unnecessary.

Speaking of money, I am reminded of the story that Jim told about what happened quite early in the cruise. He was sitting in the disbursing office talking with another Ensign by the name of Hank McNamara, who was the disbursing officer. In this office were two safes which contained the cash for the coming paydays. The lower safe was referred to as the "bulk" safe as it contained approximately two hundred fifty thousand dollars in cash in relatively small bills.

Jim was sitting next to that safe, and while talking, reached over and without thinking casually spun the combination dial. Normally this would have had no consequence as far as a workable combination was concerned. However, this time the dial stopping spinning. Dead silence. Hank reached over, moved the handle on the front of the safe and the door opened. You should know that money, which belongs to the government, is the disbursing officer's *personal* responsibility. He is accountable for every penny. If he comes up short, he must replace it. That, of course, is something that is hard to do on the pay of a new Ensign.

Since there was no way to determine how long the combination had been broken or stuck, there was no alternative but to fix the combination and count all of the money to make sure all was in order. Without the mechanical counting machines which are available today, Hank and Jim spent the better part of the night counting that huge pile of bills manually. As they both agreed, money under the wrong circumstances is no fun. Fortunately, it was all there.

Looking back, the money counting incident and their daily association during the cruise cemented a friendship that lasted from February of 1957 to 18 August 2011 when Hank "crossed the bar" and Jim lost a dear friend.

*   *   *

Hong Kong was and is unique. One person who made it so, at least in my eyes, was a Chinese woman named Mary Sue. She owned a fleet of *sampans* (small boats) manned by young women. It was rumored that she also owned the young women. Of course there was no way of proving that even though at the time one could easily buy a young girl for whatever purpose one desired. Mary Sue would agree to scrape and paint the outside of the naval vessels in trade for access to the garbage generated by the mess hall. The *sampans* would surround the ships and the painting would be accomplished, hopefully without the stealing of too many brass nozzles or other portable items within reach of the painters. After that the garbage cans were brought out and the real business began. The women would go through the cans using chopsticks to separate the contents into "boy chow" or people food, "pig chow" and lastly, true trash. There would be great gnashing of teeth and cursing when a choice item of food had had a cigarette stubbed out in it. To me Mary Sue exhibited true enterprise.

After Hong Kong they went on to Taiwan, where Jim again went bar hopping. This time with one of my colleagues from the Foreign Service. When the ship reached Okinawa, he and his cousin got together. Roy Dickey, who was also an Academy graduate, was there with the Air Force flying jets. Roy wanted to show off and Jim wanted to fly in a fighter jet, so off they went into the wild blue yonder buzzing *Columbus* about fifty feet above the bridge. I am told it was a very exhilarating flight. When Jim returned to his ship, the officers could talk about nothing else. Jim didn't say a word. Luckily the plane could not be identified as Roy put it into a continuous vertical spin after the flyover.

Osaka and Yokohama, Japan, followed. Then Kwangiu, Korea, where the men on the ship were entertained by orphans from a nearby home to which the men from the ship had donated useful items.

While on cruise, Jim couldn't resist the typical Navy custom of growing a moustache. He sent me a picture of himself with the waxed ends of the moustache curled up magnificently, a la Hercule Poirot. I was looking forward to seeing the moustache in person, but, alas, he shaved it off before returning to Long Beach. Unfortunately, the picture has disappeared.

There are certain Navy traditions which have been in place for years. When a ship returns to its home port after an extended cruise, the entire ship's company is on deck and at attention in formation as the ship approaches the dock. After the fore and aft lines are secured to the dock, the order to "Man the Rails" is passed over the ship's loudspeaker system. At this point, the crew breaks formation, goes to the rails, and looks for wives, girlfriends or family.

Jim was very much amused by two very young enlisted men who were standing behind him on the deck directly above the main deck. Their conversation was limited to describing the various physical attributes of a gorgeous young woman on the pier who was wearing a fashionable green knit dress. It appeared to have been applied with a paint spray gun. Form fitting was an understatement. The closer the ship came to the pier, the more enthusiastic the descriptions of her features became until one of the young sailors abruptly stopped the discussion by proclaiming that "She's an old bag. She must be twenty-three."

*   *   *

For some reason Jim received orders to a ship going back to West Pac for another eight months leaving just seven days after returning to Long Beach. However, some compassionate soul intervened, and he was ordered to the *USS Goss*, a destroyer escort, instead. The *Goss* was assigned the job of taking reserve officers out on their two week annual training cruises. It was odd duty in the sense that the ship was gone for two weeks at a time and then in port for two weeks. The middle weekend of the time they were gone was spent in some delightful destination—Mazatlan, Acapulco, Hawaii, Ketchikan, and so on. I'm not sure why. Maybe it was to keep the reserves happy and interested in the Navy. All I know is that I was exceedingly annoyed for several reasons. One, I wanted to see those places myself. Two, we had no money for me to meet Jim in any of the ports. Three, I missed him as he had already been gone for eight months.

Another reason the *Goss* irritated me was that the steward, Godwin, was an excellent cook and presented the Officer's Wardroom with outstanding meals. He had always been on an Admiral's staff and did things perfectly. Jim never could figure out what Godwin had done to demote him to a mere destroyer escort with only five officers to please. Anyway I disliked Godwin even though I had never met him. The crowning touch came when Jim asked me why I didn't make broiled grapefruit for him for breakfast like Godwin did.

The *Goss* had outlived its usefulness to the Navy and was scheduled to be put out of commission in Astoria, Oregon. By this time I was pregnant and a bit queasy, so the drive up the coast was a real trial. We eventually got there and were assigned small furnished quarters on the base. The back side of the quarters faced a heavily wooded area filled with ripening blackberry bushes. The first thing that was said to us was not to go into the woods because there were a number of bears who were also interested in the berries and might take offense if we got there first. I was quite content to let them have first choice.

Salmon were running and I must admit that that is one of my favorite foods. Jim doesn't care for salmon, so my treats are few and far between. However, one "dark and stormy night" there was a knock on the door. When Jim opened it, Mr. Fladaboe, a Chief Warrant Officer, was standing there in an apron covered with fish scales. In his hands was a platter of tier after tier of salmon steaks from fish he had just caught and cleaned. He presented them to me with a bow and I nearly wept with delight. I had salmon at every meal for a week and each bite was better than the last.

Half way through the de-commissioning my doctors insisted that I leave Astoria and go to Annapolis to stay with my parents as Jim's next orders were to take him to the Navy Retail School in Brooklyn, New York, and there was no place for me there. Since Annapolis had a Naval Hospital and Mother and Father were willing, I went along with it.

Apparently Jim enjoyed the school, the nearby Jewish delicatessen and his trips to the old Metropolitan Opera House and other theaters. He always tried to get tickets at the theater itself at the last minute. He would go into the lobby, hold up his hand and loudly proclaim "Looking for one". It never failed. He never missed getting a ticket—and at the regular price instead of a scalper's price.

One particular evening he secured a ticket in the front row of the first balcony of the old Metropolitan Opera House next to a lovely elderly lady. They talked and chatted and had a splendid time. After the performance she asked him if she could give him a lift home. He declined, but escorted her out to the front of the building. A huge Rolls Royce pulled up and a liveried chauffeur got out to assist her into the car. Again she asked him about the ride but manners dictated that he decline again and take the subway home. Too bad.

*   *   *

On 17 October 1958, I gave birth to a son we named Mark Wilkinson at the Naval Academy Hospital under less than ideal conditions. Although his birth had been difficult, he was a healthy infant and quite beautiful.

Our son, Mark, as a baby. The picture was taken in Sanford, Florida, in early spring of 1959.

Jim came down from New York and stayed a few days. Then went back to finish his course. (I subsequently discovered that Jim was AWOL when he came to Annapolis. His roommate had simply driven him to the airport and must have covered for him as Jim never heard anything official about it.) Mark was a big handsome healthy baby. Jim had finished his course, so when Mark was six weeks old, we got into our trusty Chevy and drove to the Naval Air Station in Sanford, Florida. Jim was to be the Navy Exchange Officer. We bought a little house, moved in and spent the next two years snorkeling, gardening, partying and generally having a good time.

The best parties were held after one or two of the officers who had to keep up their flying proficiency would route themselves to Rhode Island. They would return with the plane loaded with Maine lobsters. We would all chip in to cover the cost of the lobsters. Everyone loved those parties, believe me.

Another flying proficiency destination was Cuba. If you took your own empty gallon Coke syrup bottles, you could have them filled with dark rum for virtually nothing. The men did this frequently. The drink that was usually made from the rum was a wonderful tall concoction of rum and some other ingredients I can't remember. It was tall and cool and topped off with a liberal sprinkling of nutmeg. They were exceedingly tasty and I wish I still knew how to make them.

The St. John's River, a fresh water stream, flowed through the area. We discovered by accident that our favorite blue crabs thrived in its depths. One afternoon we caught fifty jumbo crabs, some of them thirteen inches from point to point, and one small one. The large ones were so big that I could eat only three, believe it or not.

That same afternoon while Jim was snorkeling, he saw a manatee which attracted his attention as it had a long nylon fishing line wrapped around its body. The fish hook was caught in its flesh and the poor animal had no way to disentangle itself. Jim approached the manatee and began cutting the line away.

The manatee did not swim away from him. Eventually, he came to the hook and with a quick jerk pulled it out. The manatee gave a start, swam around a little and then came up to Jim and gave him the manatee equivalent of a hug. Then he swam off almost jauntily. Jim had certainly done his good deed of the day. He will never forget that experience. A gentle one-ton water animal saying "Thank You."

Our house was in a brand new area so there were no mature trees. We planted a few spindly little things here and there. One of them was near the line where I had to hang the clothes to dry as we had no mechanical dryer. One afternoon I put Mark, who was still an infant, in his carriage and wheeled him near the clothes line so that he could watch what I was doing. Then I went to the washer to retrieve the wet wash. As I was coming around the corner of the house with the wash, I heard the most awful buzzing noise. It was loud and intense and seemed to come from the depths of hell. I soon discovered its source. A huge swarm of bees was circling the house, diving and banking. It absolutely terrified me for Mark's sake. I ran to the carriage, grabbed him and fled toward the back door of the house. I managed to get inside with no bees accompanying us. When I finally calmed down, I looked out of the window and saw that the swarm had alighted on one of the little trees, bending it over with its weight. They did not move. However, their proximity to the house frightened me. We finally had to have a bee keeper come to the house a day or two later. He performed what seemed to be voodoo rites by finding the queen bee, putting her into a hive and taking the entire colony away with him. Fortunately, they never returned. However, once is enough.

In spite of the bees, Sanford was a very pleasant interlude and we enjoyed our time there immensely.

4

EXOTIC THAILAND

I N THE FALL OF 1960 Jim received orders to Bangkok, Thailand. We were ecstatic. He would be attached to the Joint U.S. Military Advisory Group (JUSMAG) and run the Navy Exchange, and ultimately several other retail and food service operations. Later he also provided support throughout the country for our troops well before the Vietnam conflict started in earnest.

By this time I was pregnant with our second child and was concerned that the Navy doctors might not let me accompany Jim on the trip to Bangkok. I solved that problem by fudging the due date. Had I not done so, I would have had to wait in the States until the new baby was six months old and was found to be healthy. Then I would have had to make that long journey with two children alone with no one to help me, and miss all the fun en route to Thailand that we could have had together. So I lied.

We packed up the house in Sanford with great glee, keeping out only the clothes and other small items we could take with us or that the Navy would ship to us once we arrived in Thailand. The rest would go into storage awaiting our return in two years.

We were to travel in an easterly direction. As Jim had a month's leave to make the trip, we decided to bypass Western Europe and visit some of the (to us) more exotic cities along the Mediterranean Coast. I was familiar with Europe and Jim had also visited on summer cruises as a Midshipman. We elected to stop in Athens, Istanbul, Cairo, Luxor, Jerusalem and Beirut. How I was looking forward to that journey.

However, our first stop was in the opposite direction to say goodbye to Jim's parents in Kansas. Afterwards, on our way back to Annapolis to say goodbye to my parents, we met a Lebanese man while we were changing planes in St. Louis. When we told him we would be stopping in Beirut, he entrusted us with a letter to deliver to his family when we eventually arrived.

And so we set off. Two excited adults, one of them "quite" pregnant and two year old Mark. He had learned to talk very young and continually asked us when we were going to meet Asia, as we had been talking about going there and he wanted to know who she was.

Our first stop was Athens, Greece. We toured with a guide named Constantine and a very patient driver who watched Mark while Jim and I were climbing the Acropolis and doing other tourist things. Athens was miraculous. It seems to me that I had known about the Acropolis and the Parthenon all my life. To actually see them and stand on the ground near them was unbelievable. It couldn't be happening to me.

When Constantine discovered that we were on our way to Bangkok, he told us that he had just guided a Thai princess, gave us her name and said that he thought we would like one another. We did look up Princess Chumphot when we arrived in Bangkok and formed a nice relationship with her and her protégé, Montlee, who was closer to us in age. They were both instrumental in helping us find and buy some truly outstanding pieces of Thai art.

There was a friend from my Foreign Service days on duty at our Embassy in Athens. Her name was Genevieve Konkol. She made our visit nicer by taking us to Sunion, a temple on the coast, and to Piraeus for seafood. I had not been able to eat much of the food thus far. It was (to my pregnant palate) too heavy and reeked of questionable olive oil. They even put olive oil on mashed potatoes. In other words—to me it was just plain nasty.

We sat at a table in the restaurant watching an enormous fish being cooked on a vertical grill over glowing coals. The aroma was indescribably delicious and I was almost drooling. The waiter came in, checked the fish, pronounced it done, detached it and placed it on a huge platter. Before anyone could stop him, he picked up a carafe and poured quantities of poor quality olive oil over the fish and presented it to us with a flourish. I nearly cried.

We flew to Istanbul the next day via KLM, the Dutch airline. The little sandwiches they brought me looked like manna from heaven. It may have been airline food, but it was sublime airline food. No olive oil.

In Istanbul we made a point of trying to find Novotny's restaurant, Father's favorite when he was there. With the help of an illegal taxi driver, we located the building. The restaurant was long closed, but the brass name plate was still near the door. The windows were not covered so we wiped off the dirt and grime and peered in. The view was eerie—tables and chairs still in place, everything covered with cobwebs and dust. You could almost see the people. It was like an old movie set. I expected to hear Father's music any minute.

We also went to the famous Pera Palas Hotel where Father had also played the piano (and, incidentally, Agatha Christie had written *Murder on the Orient Express*). The hotel had seen better days, but it was still marvelous—an iron cage elevator, wide staircases with worn maroon carpeting, heavy drapes you wouldn't dare draw for fear they would collapse—I loved it all. The piano was in the bar and judging by the rest of the furnishings, it must have been the very one Father played.

Our faithful taxi driver took us around the city to some of the more unusual places—one of them being a gypsy encampment at the inner base of one of the huge thick city walls dating from heaven knows when. He warned Jim not to take any photos. However, when two of the gypsy women got into a fight and started pulling hair, he couldn't resist. He took several shots without raising the camera to his eye. What great pictures.

(Jim and I were negligent about the proper storage of our boxes of slides. When I was nearing the completion of this book, we began to hunt for the slides to do a little preliminary sorting. To our consternation we found that a huge percentage of the slides were completely ruined. Therefore many of the pictures I talk about are no longer in existence. It really upset us both. However, there is no way to bring back a completely black slide. Fortunately, a few survived. We also have many black and white pictures, as well as photos of places revisited on later trips.)

Beneath one end of a high bridge was a flea market area which was great to walk through. In addition to typical flea market offerings, stalls where people sold enormous baked potatoes right out of a huge, hot oven were set up. They offered dozens of toppings for the potatoes—chopped meats, vegetables of all sorts mixed with sour cream, yoghurt or mayonnaise, cheeses, butter and almost anything else that could possibly go with the flavor of a potato. They were appetizing, colorful and very tempting. However, with no refrigeration for the toppings, we felt we would be asking for trouble to try one. So we didn't, much to my annoyance. I'm sure they were as tasty to eat as they were appealing to the eye. They certainly were popular with the locals.

The *souk* or Grand Bazaar is another of the Seven Wonders of the World as far as I am concerned. It is roofed, many parts of it are housed in ancient buildings, it sells some of the most fascinating things known to man (or woman, for that matter), the passages meander about and you can browse for hours and rarely see the same thing twice. There are rugs, antiques, perfume, spices, food, copperware, gold, jewelry, silver, coins and almost anything else imaginable. The dealers are pleasant and many of them speak English. It is an absolute paradise.

Part of the antiques section of the Grand Bazaar in Istanbul taken on a later trip.

Jim and the author in part of the spice section of the Grand Bazaar in Istanbul taken on a later trip.

In the Bazaar we met Melinda, a sleek ginger and white cat. She was sleeping blissfully outside one of the antique shops with her head cradled on a tiny pillow made especially for her. People love their pets the world over.

Melinda the cat having her nap outside a shop in the Grand Bazaar in Istanbul, December 1960.

Istanbul was very smoggy—even in 1960—and Mark developed a deep chest cough. Cairo was our next stop, so when we arrived there, Jim took him to the doctor at the American Embassy. Between medication and the warm, dry climate, he perked up immediately.

We toured Cairo lapping up everything as though it were an incredible banquet just for us. Of course we went to the Cairo Museum. It was a huge, rambling building that was virtually nothing but a storehouse of antiquities. There were very few people visiting the museum, so we had it to ourselves. However, the curators had set aside a separate area for the display of artifacts from King Tutankhamen's tomb. Remember this is 1960. King Tut had not made his famous tour around the world to numerous museums. Not many people except those truly interested in Egyptology were on a first name basis with him.

At that time they allowed pictures to be taken in the museum. Jim got out his trusty Leica, but the reflection on the glass cases was so bad that a decent photo could have been impossible. However, the cavalry came to the rescue in the form of the two watchmen. In halting English, they asked if Jim would like them to open the cases for him so that the pictures would be better.

We were both dumbfounded—the items on display were the incredible gold and lapis mummy cases and masks belonging to Tutankhamen that everyone is now familiar with, plus innumerable other things of immense value.

Speechless, Jim just nodded. Off came the covers. Jim snapped happily away grinning like the proverbial Cheshire cat and then, equally happy, doled out the expected *baksheesh* or tip to the watchmen.

The picture of King Tut's gold mask included in this book is one slide that did survive the poor storage conditions.

King Tut's mask out of its display case, taken at the Cairo Museum in December 1960.

Soon afterward, we flew to Luxor. As the decrepit old DC-3 took off from Cairo, I felt a draft on my right foot and looked down. There, through a hole at least eight inches long by an inch and a half wide, were the lights of Cairo twinkling at me. Fortunately nothing untoward happened during the flight, but it was a mighty uncomfortable trip.

At that time even poor Lieutenants could afford to stay at the Winter Palace in Luxor. It was a pleasure to return to the hotel after a long, hot day exploring, take a shower and descend to the dining room and be presented with such good food. They were incredible meals. Nothing exotic but just well prepared, excellent quality three to four course meals served in a beautiful dining room with white linen and candlelight by attentive waiters. Then we escaped to our room—the bed so high we had to use a three-step stool to reach the mattress. Then the huge mosquito net tumbled down from the ceiling and we were snug for the night.

This was still during the years when you left your shoes outside the door at night and got them back in the morning shined and cleaned. After the dust of Luxor, that was a real plus.

Jim, Mark and the author in front of the Winter Palace Hotel steps in Luxor, Egypt, taken in December 1960.

About the only thing I really did *not* enjoy in Luxor was a visit to a perfume shop. The Egyptians love scents and perfumes and use them lavishly—the heavier the better. The proprietor of one of them invited us in to the shop to try samples. I innocently agreed, got just over the threshold, took a deep breath, nearly fainted and ran outside. Being pregnant had its real disadvantages.

After Egypt, we flew to Jerusalem which, at that time, was part of Jordan rather than Israel. We were impressed by everything. It was impossible not to be impressed when set down in a city one has heard about all one's life. Father had also been there, and had been equally impressed. Something other than the religious factor that struck us was the quality of the air—it was clear, crisp and soothing—like fine white wine.

The Dome of the Rock was extremely interesting. Until then I had not been aware that it was holy to all three major faiths. We entered with no problem. The interior was dim and quiet. The rock where Abraham was supposed to have almost slain Isaac was the central feature. I understand that the rock is also where Mohammed is supposed to have ascended to heaven.

We went also to Jericho, Bethlehem and the Sea of Galilee. On the way to one of them we passed, fairly well set back from the road, huge encampments of people living in tents and hovels with tin roofs. Heaven knows what the sanitation was like. We asked who these people were. The answer was that they were Palestinians. Very little was being done by Muslim countries to alleviate this dreadful situation. I have never been able to figure out why they were not assimilated into Jordanian society at that time, thereby solving some of the problems of that part of the world. After all, both Palestinians and Jordanians are Muslims as well as fellow Arabs. It is still a mystery to me.

The Western Wall at that time was called the Wailing Wall and was hemmed in by shops and houses of all kinds. One could almost touch the Wall with one hand and the houses with the other at the same time. When Israel took control, they demolished these buildings so that now there is a huge empty courtyard in front. Near the Wall itself, we passed a bakery where aromatic pretzel-like bread was being baked in a wood fired oven. The baker gave Mark one. Here we were walking down a narrow street in Jerusalem with a little boy eating a pretzel almost as big as he was.

After Jordan, our next and final stop was Beirut, one of the handsomest cities I have ever seen. Situated directly on the Mediterranean, its *corniche* or beachfront was breathtaking. Spotlessly clean, with benches and walkways, statues and swimming areas—it was truly enticing. After we arrived in Thailand, we were appalled to see a picture of the hotel where we had stayed in ruins after hostilities began in Lebanon. The front of the hotel had been blown off by a bomb.

Again a wonderful taxi driver came to our rescue. He spoke a little English, knew the city well and was willing to drive us to the outskirts of the city where the letter we had been given in St. Louis was to be delivered. We knocked on the door, handed over the letter and were immediately smothered by their hospitality. The family was delighted to hear from their relative and we were delighted by their enthusiasm.

They sat us down, took note of my pregnant state, and plied us with all kinds of delicious and unfamiliar food—watching as we ate each bite. The *feta* or goat milk cheese was especially tasty. I was glad that I didn't realize that the goat skins (fur, feet and all) I had seen men carrying around the city had *feta* cheese aging inside them. Another item happened to be walnuts treated in some fashion to render them jet black, sweet, tender and perfectly delicious. Even the shell was good. I never thought that I would bite into a walnut, shell and all, and like it, but I certainly did.

Soon many more relatives and neighbors arrived until the house was overflowing. Finally someone arrived who spoke English and it made a big difference. The taxi driver was so interested that he had turned off his meter and stayed for the fun. After the "party," he drove us back to the hotel. What a day.

* * *

After Lebanon, we flew directly to Bangkok arriving on 20 December 1960. Although it was "winter," Jim and I were completely prostrated by the heat and humidity. Every Westerner we met, however, was bundled up in sweaters and coats and couldn't keep from shivering. Needless to say, Jim and I secretly laughed to ourselves, but *we* were shivering the following December.

During our first weeks in Bangkok, I really didn't see much of the city. We were both tired from the trip and since the baby was due in mid-February, I was somewhat cumbersome. I had gained only thirteen pounds, so I wasn't too big, but my center of gravity was off somewhat. However, what I did see of the city made me realize that it was quite beautiful. Tall graceful rain trees lined the streets and there were a number of handsome old houses. The *klongs* or canals cut through the city in various places and the water had a somewhat cooling effect. They were tidal at that time and helped clean the city. The *klongs* which opened to the sea have since been filled in and the remnants are now just stagnant pools of water. Bangkok was also filled with *wats* or temples that were colorful, calm and beautiful and lent an exotic and charming air. The one really bad situation was the traffic. It was horrendous and still is, and I don't see that much can be done about it.

We found a small white house to rent in the Bangkapi area of the city. We then spent time getting settled and living quietly until Alix, our daughter, was born 2 March 1961 at the Bangkok Nursing Home, a typical tropical wooden structure on stilts. My room was on a corner of the building. It had a high pointed ceiling, no screens and the birds flew in and out nesting in the rafters. There was a rigid metal frame around the mosquito net that was lowered from the rafters in the evenings. The frame had a door and was large enough to cover the bed and a small table on either side. I was enchanted. Hot water for washing was brought by a Chinese woman with a bucket suspended from each end of a bamboo pole over her shoulder. And I certainly mustn't forget the Australian nurse who would pop in periodically and ask, "How's your arse?" in a loud booming voice.

Jim got a surprise when he was asked if he would like to see the baby. He thought he would be taken to a big window and a wrinkled up little bundle would be pointed out to him. *Au contraire*, the little bundle was placed in his arms and he met his new daughter up close and personal.

My doctor was a Thai who had been educated at Johns Hopkins University Medical School in Baltimore and married a lovely blonde American woman. Between Dr. Sermsakdi and the nursing home staff, primitive as it might sound, I had excellent care and enjoyed my stay.

The author sitting on a couch holding her newborn daughter, Alix,
taken in Bangkok, Thailand, in March 1961.

Alix was born with red hair. (Irene had red hair.) One of my most cherished
gifts was an orchid plant in bloom. The flowers were the size of my little
fingernail clustered on stems about six inches long. They were the exact color
of her hair. When we left Thailand, I gave it to an American friend, Ken Dilks.
Several years later we returned for a visit and there it was in Ken's orchid house
in full bloom.

By the way, Alix's Thai birth certificate was written in that language. It was
about twenty inches wide by six or eight inches high and was folded vertically
into several sections. At the bottom right hand side there was a phrase which
ended with a flourish. I am told that the translation was "Lots of Luck."

One evening I heard two car doors slam after Jim's car pulled up in the
driveway. I hurried to the door to see who was with him. He entered with an
old friend of mine whom I was extremely surprised to see. Then the two of
them proceeded to tell me the story. It seems that during the afternoon, Jim's
secretary informed him that a man wanted to see him who had no papers or other
identification, but wanted to buy a few things at the Exchange. Jim and the man
sat down and began discussing things such as: What outfit are you with? Where
have you come from? and so on. It eventually emerged that he had gone to the
Naval Academy, spoke French, and had been in Laos on an undercover mission.
Jim also discovered that he was raised in Annapolis, had gone to Annapolis
High School and was actually one my classmates named Ron Shaw. No wonder

Jim brought him home to dinner. It was wonderful to see him, and I need not tell you that he was allowed to buy whatever he wanted at the Exchange.

Life in our little white house was odd. Mark's *aya* or nursemaid found him playing in the yard with a cobra. Since Buddhists do not take life, she grabbed the snake and threw it over the garden wall. I was horrified. We were told that if we had a pair of geese there would be no cobras because they do not like goose droppings. Unfortunately or fortunately, we could find only one goose. He arrived and immediately began to do his job in a very professional manner.

A week or two later the General's wife came to call on me to welcome the new baby. Her driver pulled the car into the driveway and ran around to open the door for her. She alighted, stood immobile for a moment, lifted her skirts and tiptoed between the droppings to the front door with a very peculiar expression on her face. Needless to say the goose left the next day.

Our servant's name was Chileo. Her duties were primarily to look after Mark and to keep the house clean. Almost all the houses in Bangkok had quarters where the servants lived. That was part of their wages. One evening after we had retired to the upper floor, we heard a great racket with much thumping and screaming downstairs. Suddenly Chileo burst into our bedroom a few steps ahead of a man, who turned out to be her husband, brandishing a knife following in hot pursuit. Jim jumped up, got the knife from him and ordered him out of the house—all in his undershorts and with great dignity and authority.

We felt that with cobras in the area, the fact that we were paying too much rent and we didn't know when Chileo's husband would come back, it would be prudent to find another house. Jim had met a Thai man named Sangob who was a contractor working on the renovation of the Navy Exchange. He spoke excellent English (although he had trouble with my name because of the two Ls and preferred to call me Mem). He had a great sense of humor and was willing to help us locate another house, which he did. It was brand new, made of wood and painted an acceptable shade of blue. There were three bedrooms, a living room, dining room, servants' quarters, kitchen and bath. There was no air conditioning, but the ceiling fans kept us comfortable. After the first few months of getting used to the climate, we did not use them much. There was no television and no phone. If you needed to send a message to someone, you wrote a note, gave it to your driver and he delivered it to the proper person, waiting for a reply to take back to you if one was required.

The author standing in front of the second house we rented in Bangkok
taken on a later trip to Thailand.

The kitchen was separated from the rest of the house by a corridor which kept the cooking heat in that part of the building. The equipment was Western. We had brought our own refrigerator with us and everything else was fine. We just had to remember that the water coming out of the single tap was not safe and to work around it. Everything that was eaten raw had to be washed in a solution of sodium permanganate (which turned a livid purple when wet) and boiled cooled water, then rinsed in pure water. Also Alix had to be bathed in pure water. (We dispensed with the sodium permanganate in her case.) We also drank pure water and cooked with it. As you can see, we used a tremendous amount of water, which was obtained by boiling buckets of tap water over charcoal in the paved back yard.

Alix having a bath in the kitchen, in Bangkok, taken in the fall of 1961.

A number of Americans bought water delivered to the house in glass bottles. However, the bottles were recycled and were, I'm sure, washed in contaminated water before they were filled with the "pure water." We made it a point not to drink water at American homes. However, I'm not sure where the germs came from, but the few times we were sick, we had eaten in an American home.

The servants' quarters also opened onto the back yard, the clothes lines were there, the huge *klong* jars, their equivalent of an old fashioned rain barrel, stood to catch the water for plant watering, laundry, and so forth. Some of the children's toys were also there. It was a very busy place.

The bathroom had no tub. However, it was entirely tiled in white with a shower stall in one corner. No shower curtain—just tile walls about four feet high that kept the water from splashing all over everything. There was only one water faucet, which was cold and a shower head, also cold. The faucet was waist high and the water came out in one solid stream. Again the water was not pure and you didn't want to get any in your mouth. The procedure, in warm weather, was to soap all over, and then stand under the shower head rinsing in the normal fashion.

In cold weather, one of the servants would bring a bucket of hot water she had heated over the remains of the charcoal from her breakfast fire up to the bathroom. Then the bath routine got tricky. There was a tin bowl in the shower stall which held about three cups of liquid. You dipped the bowl into the hot water, filling it half full. Then you filled it completely with cold water from the tap. This was used for the scrubbing, soapy part of your shower. Then it was dip, fill, rinse; dip, fill, rinse until you were squeaky clean but your teeth were chattering from the cold. Primitive but effective.

The shower was used often. I showered at 5:30 in the morning so that I would be ready for the bus to my office to pick me up at 6:15. (I'll tell you about my job later.) I took another shower when I got home in the afternoon, and another before bed. If I had come home early and we were going to a party, there was another shower before going out. The weather was just plain hot and sticky.

Several years later when we were ready to leave Thailand, we stayed in a hotel for a night or two after our household items were packed up. Our room had a *real* bathtub with hot and cold running water. Mark and Alix had never seen anything like that so they were in awe of it at first. Then they got used to the idea and had a great time making the biggest mess ever. For a while it was easy to get them to take a bath.

The bathroom in our house had frosted glass windows. *Chinchooks* are little gecko-like lizards that you want to have in your house because they eat insects including vast numbers of mosquitoes. One of them had laid three eggs, each one about the size of a kidney bean, on the inside of the glass window over the shower. Sunlight coming through made the eggs somewhat transparent. It was incredibly interesting to watch them develop into baby lizards. It took about three weeks. One day they were gone. However, I had the comforting feeling that they were inside, not outside, and were doing their best to keep the insect population down.

At the house there was space in the front driveway to park the Mercedes Benz that the Thai government provided us in lieu of allowing us to bring over our own car. However, it was not air conditioned so driving in traffic was sometimes extremely uncomfortable. Even so, it was fine with me that someone else drove as the traffic was horrendous and they drove on the left. The Thais also supplied a Thai enlisted man to drive the car. His name was Charoen and he was one of the kindest most patient people I have ever known.

In addition, Jim also had the use of a VW beetle. He learned to drive on the left without too much trouble. I got my driver's license in case there was an emergency and I had to take one of the children to the hospital, but never had to drive, thank heaven. In addition to securing a driver's license, I also had to keep a small suitcase packed with essentials such as diapers, powdered milk, medications, changes of clothing and so on for a possible emergency evacuation.

At that time planes were not allowed to fly over the city of Bangkok. Early one Sunday morning we were in the living room playing with the children when we heard the unaccustomed drone of several planes. Jim and I looked at one another. Immediately visions of another Pearl Harbor type attack popped into our heads. We later found out that they were AT-6 planes flying low in a practice formation over the city. You may think we were being somewhat sensitive and alarmist. However, bear in mind that we had to keep emergency supplies ready as I said, and don't forget that the real Pearl Harbor had happened only twenty years earlier and we both still remembered the attack and its aftermath—World War II and all its misery.

The house and neighborhood had some interesting features. Across the street was a water buffalo wallow. It was about four to five feet deep, filled with water and when the buffalo moved they generated sticky, black mud just the color of their hides. They liked it there and never put up much of a fuss. In fact they were rather fun to watch. On one occasion, Mark went to our front gate, which had vertical openings in it, and came face to face with one of the buffalo which outweighed him by a thousand pounds. I don't know which one was more surprised.

The front gate was also where Mark learned the art of sticking up for himself and watching out so as not to be cheated. This was later when he became quite worldly about life at the age of four. Vendors would pull up at the gate riding bicycles with all sorts of wares displayed on a contraption hooked to the front of the bicycle. One of Mark's favorites was a man who sold fresh water chestnuts on a stick which were then dipped in salt. Mark gave the vendor the very devil one day because he reduced the number of chestnuts on the stick, but kept the same price. I understand that Mark's language was colloquial Thai of the most adult male type. By the way, he got the proper number of chestnuts at the right price after that.

To our left was a large house occupied by a Chinese family. Virtually all properties in Bangkok are separated by fences. The fence also divided the back yards as well as the front. In the back they had four or five mango trees whose branches hung over into our yard. With my passion for mangoes unabated, I watched them develop. One evening I thought the fruit on our side of the fence was about ready for picking. The next morning I got up early, went to the back yard and nearly wept. Someone had come over and picked every one of those hanging so temptingly in our yard. I guess it served me right for my greediness.

To the right, several buildings down the street, was a foundry, behind the foundry a duck farm, and behind us a stable for horses. Interspersed among all this were other houses and dwellings. It really didn't bother Jim and me about the wallow and the foundry, but if the wind was wrong, the duck farm was pretty odoriferous.

With Sangob's additional help, we also acquired two wonderful house servants, Soh, the number one, who spoke English, and Daeng, a Laotian country girl, who did not. (We left Chileo at the first house.) The new servants turned out to be treasures. They were bright, intelligent and seemed to love Mark and Alix.

Soh and Charoen in the front yard of the new house, taken in Bangkok about September of 1961.

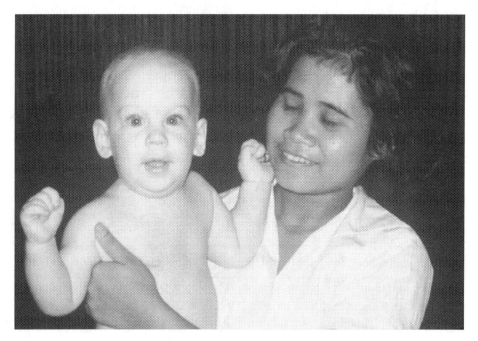

Daeng holding Alix, taken in about September of 1961.

There was also a gardener who came in once a week to cut the grass sitting on a very low wooden stool using hand held hedge clippers to cut the entire front yard. The yard boasted a poinsettia in one corner that eventually grew to about ten feet and bloomed its heart out at just the right time—Christmas.

Speaking of Christmas, and I'm jumping ahead a bit here. Soh and Daeng joined us early one Christmas morning for the present opening bit. As a joke, I had bought Jim a *pakama*, which is a wide tube of fabric that Thai men step into, then draw the fabric close to the waist in folds and tie the material itself to hold the *pakama* securely in place. It is used for informal wear around the house, to take a modest bath in public, an after-swimming cover up, and so on. I had chosen a slimy synthetic fabric in the most bilious shade of lavenderish purple I could find. Jim took the joke in stride and then raced upstairs to try it on. Apparently he didn't tie it properly and the slimy fabric was too much for his amateur knots. As he was coming back down the stairs, in full view of Soh, Daeng, Alix, Mark and me, the *pakama* slipped and fell to the floor. In his haste he had removed not only his trousers but also his undershorts, so there he was in all his glory. Everyone burst into peals of laughter, the two girls falling to the floor and rolling about holding their sides. Mark, Alix and I weren't too far behind them.

*   *   *

Through Peggy Smith, the wife of another Navy Supply Corps Officer with JUSMAG, I acquired a job as an administrator at the American University Association Language Center (AUA). Peggy insisted that I take the job as she had seen the effects of too much idle time on some of the other officers' wives. One of the best things I have ever done was to take her advice and the job.

I worked from seven in the morning until noon juggling the number of available classrooms with the number of instructors and textbooks, plus other mundane tasks that nevertheless turned out to be interesting. Instructors had to be native speakers of English, so most of them came from the ranks of the American wives whose husbands were stationed in Bangkok. An extremely large percentage of these women were married to Air America pilots. (Air America was a covert operation of the Central Intelligence Agency in Southeast Asia from 1950 to 1976. It ceased operating after the fall of Saigon.) The basic mission of AUA was to teach English as a second language to young Thais who wanted to go to the States to college. I liked my job and it kept me busy and also out of the servant's way while they did the house work, which was even better.

Thai is a difficult language for Americans to learn as there are five tones (high, mid, low, rising and falling) and the same syllable can be repeated in each of those five tones and mean five different things. A young American man fresh from the States joined the staff and everyone, including the Thai students, was asked to assemble in an amphitheater-type classroom to meet him. He was introduced by the Thai director in Thai. Then the young man rose and started speaking in flawless colloquial Thai. You could have heard the proverbial pin drop. When he finished there was thunderous applause. From that day forward he was almost idolized by the Thai students.

*   *   *

Charoen would pick me up at noon after work and take me wherever I wanted to go—sometimes sightseeing and sometimes straight home, but most of the time shopping of the most delightful sort.

My salary at AUA was the *baht* or the Thai currency equivalent of $50 per week, which doesn't seem like much, but actually was a good amount as things were very inexpensive. A dressmaker charged $5 to make a dress, shoes covered in matching fabric were $10, belts $2, and so on—even covered buttons and clutch purses were available very reasonably. Not to mention the antique shops which were overflowing with wonders, and Chinatown, a browser's paradise, just sitting there waiting for you to discover some wonderful and exotic item you couldn't possibly do without.

Trips to the beauty shop were special. A good haircut, shampoo, manicure and pedicure cost altogether the astronomical sum of $3.50. The shampoo was wonderful. You stretched out on a big comfortable contoured couch, your head gently cradled in the basin. The attendant not only washed your hair but also massaged your scalp and neck for what seemed like hours. The pedicure was equally wonderful. Because of open shoes and going barefoot in the house, your feet took a beating. The massaging, oiling and pumicing did great things for your psyche. Noi, the pedicurist I regularly went to, became quite put out with me one time when I had shaved my own legs. You always felt like the proverbial million dollars when you left the salon.

Perhaps the most useful items we bought in Bangkok were a buffet and a china closet. For some utterly stupid reason I had all of my sterling flatware sent to Thailand. I guess it was some unfounded idea that we would be doing a great deal of entertaining. At any rate, I had it with me, and had no place to store it properly. We had become friends with Montlee and Princess Chumphot and often visited their home, a magnificent collection of old Thai houses called Suan Pakkad Palace. Ancient ceramics, Buddhas, and numerous other art objects were on display. It was truly lovely and always a pleasure to see. There were many examples of Thai bookcases, which are tall pieces of furniture with graceful sloping sides and very sturdy shelves as the Thai books are heavy "accordion pleated" objects of paper that is made from the bark of the *koi* tree. The bookcases at the Palace were of wood covered in black lacquer with charming scenes of the Buddha's life painted in gold. Jim measured one of these bookcases and had it reproduced in teak for us to use as a china closet. Then he took the design, squashed it to buffet height and extended it to a two-drawer width. He added several more drawers and we had our buffet design. We also had this made of teak. The two top drawers were modified by inserting wooden holders covered with tarnish proof cloth to hold all the sterling flatware I had so foolishly brought with me. Those two pieces of furniture are my treasures.

The best shopping of all was at Jim Thompson's silk shop. Jim was a former OSS (Office of Strategic Services, a forerunner of the CIA) officer who served in Southeast Asia and who had personal connections with Thailand. After World War II, he settled in Bangkok and was instrumental in reviving the Thai silk industry. This objective was primarily achieved by going to Switzerland and consulting with dye manufacturers to develop dyes compatible with the silk. Before that the silk was colored but the dye did not adhere to the fibers properly and there was a great deal of running and streaking. They also added some Japanese silk fibers to the mixture which helped to even out the fabric and make it a bit more durable. However, the silk was still woven on hand looms as a cottage industry.

By the time we arrived these problems had been solved. The shelves of his shop were groaning with bolt after bolt of shimmering elegant silk of every color of the rainbow and then some. He had also had the imagination to send artists to the National Museum to copy ancient Thai designs that would show up well on the silk. The designs were then silkscreened on the fabric thus generating a whole new and beautiful product.

Above I referred to "bolts" of silk. They were not bolts of cloth as we know them, but were lengths of fabric based on the size of the loom used and then folded and refolded to make compact packages to put on the shelves of the shop. They were usually arranged by color and by weight. The silk came in four or five weights, from light for clothing to heavy for upholstered items.

The Thompson showroom had an antique Thai bed in the center of the floor. The bed was made of teak and about ten feet by ten feet and stood about a foot off the ground. It was hand carved and had been polished to a gleaming sheen by the passage of time and the touch of many hands. When you wanted to see a certain color, one of the salespeople would gather up the package of fabric you had selected and literally throw it across the bed. The explosion of color and shimmer as it unfolded was wonderful to behold.

Princess Chumphot, Montlee and another female relative with the unfortunate name of Soon Torn Tit helped us purchase some good pieces of Thai art. The paintings were done on *koi* paper and were painted in brilliant colors that dried to a finish that had a somewhat chalky surface. I always took these pictures to Jim Thompson and he willingly helped me select just the proper shade of silk to use as matting for them. Sometimes many, many different colors were thrown on the bed before he and I were satisfied with the results. I'm sure his salespeople hated to see me come into the store as we made such a mess.

Back of Jim Thompson's store was a concrete area where Mr. Uthai, a Vietnamese man, had his framing shop. The pictures were matted with the silk and then framed with either a simple gold edge or plain teak. Either way, Mr. Uthai did a beautiful job. The pictures still look lovely, although in a few cases the silk has changed color slightly with the passage of time and exposure to light.

In that same area back of the store, Jim Thompson had his semi-annual silk sales. Portable tables were set up with the silk bolts thrown helter skelter. I always loved going. It was great fun and something of an endurance feat combined with a tug of war. First, you spied a piece of fabric in a color you liked, grabbed onto it and started pulling. The idea was to pull until you got the entire piece of fabric in your arms and could carry it triumphantly to the cashier and pay for it. I never succeeded in buying too much as there was always a French woman at the other end of my piece who pulled harder than I did, all the while giving me filthy looks.

Jim Thompson's house was utterly exquisite. He had six ancient houses made of teak brought from upcountry and set up around a deck with the open side facing one of the tidal *klongs*. The houses were, of course, on stilts and had the graceful curved Thai roof lines with the peaked corners. Inside the floors were of huge teak planks, again polished and worn with age. There were statues, paintings, porcelains, celadon objects and innumerable Buddha heads and hands, plus other works of art. It was a living, breathing inhabited museum. The grounds were planted with tropical flowers and greenery and were meticulously maintained. It was great to walk in the gardens in the evening when it began to cool off.

In the hot season the area under the house was used as a dining room. We had the pleasure of being invited to dinner one night. There were drinks and hors d'oeuvres upstairs in the living room. Then we went downstairs for dinner itself. The area was cooled by a light breeze and the fragrance of the garden flowers added just the right touch. There were a number of other guests, including Mr. Stouffer of Stouffer Foods and Dr. Elizabeth Lyons, a woman from the Metropolitan Museum of Art, whose field was Chinese art, particularly porcelains.

We had been able to acquire some antique Chinese porcelain bowls. Both Jim Thompson and Elizabeth Lyons came to our house to look at them and pronounced them genuine, which pleased us. We still enjoy them.

Easter weekend of 1967, after we had left Thailand, Jim Thompson and some of his friends went to the Cameron Highlands in Malaya for a vacation. That area is mountainous and cool, an ideal place for relaxing. One afternoon when everyone was napping, Jim went for a walk and just disappeared. Naturally a great hue and cry was raised, but no trace of him was ever found.

Many, many theories were offered—he had a heart attack, died and animals consumed his remains; his Thai business partners had him killed; people wanted the exquisite antiques in his house; someone from his OSS days wanted revenge; and many more. His nephew was his heir.

When we returned to Thailand on one of our visits, we went to the shop and were quite shocked and disappointed. Gone were many of the brilliant colors and designs. In their places were muted browns, beiges and greens that could have come from anywhere. It looked like any other commonplace shop. His nephew had inherited the business. His house had been turned into a museum but many of the antiques were missing, the gardens were not well maintained and the whole place had an air of neglect and sadness about it. If you wish to see the house as it was in its prime, there is a book called *The House on the Klong*, by William Warren and Brian Brake published by Walker/Weatherhill. It is a beautiful book and shows the house and grounds perfectly.

*   *   *

The city of Bangkok is an incredible place. The temples are colorful, peaceful and so exotic you think you are in another world. Traffic is nasty so you have to steel yourself to be in a hot car while getting to them, but they are worth it. We eventually saw most of them and were impressed with each succeeding site. Another place we loved visiting was the Sunday Market. At that time it was held on the Pramane Ground, which is a huge open oval of land in the center of the city. It was actually the royal cremation ground so there were no buildings on it, which enabled the weekend vendors to set up their booths with little difficulty. The National Museum was across the street as were other government buildings.

Almost everything in the world was sold at that market. Food of every description—from raw fruits and vegetables (most of which we didn't recognize) to cooked meals and irresistible grilled *satays* or skewered meat. All sorts of seafood, meat, poultry—I could go on and on for hours. In addition to food products, clothing was offered for sale, hand woven fabrics, shoes, toys, books, and anything else you might want including antiques, both fake and real. I bought Mark's clothing there, too.

One afternoon I was there by myself and spied a soft bluish green bowl I just had to have. I didn't quite know what it was, but I knew the dealer so he allowed me to take it across the street to the museum. The people there knew that it wasn't Thai, but they weren't sure what it actually was. I bought it anyway and paid the equivalent of twenty dollars for it which was a lot of money for something from a market. When I got home Sangob was visiting with Jim. I showed off my bowl and the two of them ridiculed me unmercifully about it saying that if I paid more than fifty cents for it I had been taken. I just listened to them, smiling quietly to myself. Later when we lived in Walnut Creek, we had it appraised and were told it was Sung Dynasty Chinese and worth about two thousand dollars.

Sangob and Krishna, his wife, became our very good friends. Perhaps this would be a good time to mention that never in my life have I ever met a person with such an innate appreciation of and knowledge of food as Sangob. He was simply amazing in his ability to cook a totally delicious dish out of virtually nothing. He could also cook a delicious dish out of expensive and exotic ingredients. In all the time we knew him during our stay in Thailand and on our several trips back to visit did we have a meal he cooked that was not stupendous.

Sangob and Krishna in their kitchen in Bangkok in about August of 1961

Sangob spoke very good English, although every once in a while he would say something wonderfully outlandish. One time Jim was giving him a hard time about something and Sangob replied in a hurry, "Are not to make worry on me." I thought it an excellent response. He also called cilantro or coriander "Chinese parsley." However, he would pronounce the word parsley as though it were spelled "pearsley." I loved it.

Nearly every weekend we would plan a trip. He knew that we were interested in Thai art, so often our destinations were abandoned *wats* with beautiful frescoes still on the walls. Even though abandoned, the buildings were still considered holy, so we had to take off our shoes before entering. Many times I have walked barefoot through a two-foot accumulation of bat dung. It looks somewhat similar to and crunches like a certain dry rice cereal and put me off that breakfast for years.

Other *wats* were not abandoned but nevertheless were not kept in the best condition because of a small "congregation" and lack of funds. Often only one or two monks were in residence. It was always fun to go into the "inner sanctum" of the *wat* (I really don't know the proper terminology for that room) where things the monks considered valuable were kept. We sat on the floor in contorted positions because we could not show the bottoms of our feet to the monks. Actually, it was disrespectful to show the bottoms of your feet to anyone. You were not to touch people in any way, especially the head. It was also bad to have your head higher than anyone else's, so people were constantly stooping over, ducking and scooting quickly past murmuring apologies.

In the "inner sanctum" there would be serene and beautiful Buddha statues and heads, lovely old ceramics, handsome religious carvings and also items like old television tubes and Christmas ornaments all jumbled together. It was hard to tell which things they considered good and which things were just there because they were different and had never been seen before.

*   *   *

We could talk to Sangob and Krishna about virtually anything. One time we had a strange conversation about how people smell to other people. We claimed that Thai people had a very strong garlic odor. They laughed and said that Americans smelled of sour cheese and rancid milk. It was all understandable—we don't eat that much garlic and, as there are no dairy herds in Thailand and dairy products are imported and expensive, they don't eat much milk and cheese. They really don't like them, especially cheese. Thais are very clean and Sangob once confided to me with much horror that he knew some Americans who took only one shower a day.

*   *   *

Krishna's family lived in a compound that was in the center of a square city block in downtown Bangkok. There were businesses on all four sides, but once you entered the middle of the block it was as though you were in the country—tall trees, vegetable gardens, flowers, shrubs, several houses, soothing shade and even a wooden *wat*. Every young Thai man becomes a monk for a period during his lifetime if he can possibly manage it. It might be a day, a month or a year. We were extremely flattered when Krishna asked us to come and witness her brother's induction into the priesthood.

About five o'clock in the morning of the scheduled day, we arrived at the compound and found several monks in their saffron robes chanting and praying near the *wat*. Her brother approached and sat on a stool. He then had the hair on his head and his eyebrows shaved off by one of the monks. He donned a white robe after which he was carried, so that his feet would not touch the ground, to the *wat*. The procession circled the *wat* three times carrying gifts of new robes and candles for the monks. More chanting followed with the monks performing certain rites and asking him questions. When that was successfully concluded, his white robe was changed for a saffron colored one and he became a monk. During this time there was much food in evidence. After the monks had their meal, everyone else joined in and ate their fill. It was a joyous and exceedingly colorful occasion. We were very happy to have been included.

*   *   *

One long holiday weekend the four of us flew to Chiang Mai in the northern part of Thailand. In 1961 it was a sleepy little village with a thriving craft industry but had no hotels except the railroad hotel, a wooden structure with overhead fans and a single light bulb in each room hanging from the ceiling on a long wire. It was clean, inexpensive and comfortable, so we stayed there quite happily.

Sangob and Krishna boarding the plane to Chiang Mai, Thailand, sometime in 1962.

We made a trip into the jungle to visit one of the Akha tribes, which was an incredible experience. The women's coin jewelry was magnificent and was draped all over their black and red clothing. Quite spectacular. I desperately wanted a piece or two but was unsuccessful in obtaining any.

The highlight was Jim's invitation from the chief of the village for a return visit *without* me when he could have his choice of any of the women of the tribe, including his wife or daughter. What a deal. There was one small drawback (other than me). The Akha seldom, if ever, bathe. Jim graciously declined.

We saw an indescribably beautiful silver bowl in the window of a shop. It had been hand made by hammering a lump of silver from the inside out. Then it was further refined with scenes from Thai mythology, delicately chased and marching around the outside. We both liked it but wanted one quite a bit bigger to use as a punch bowl. We asked about having one made to order. They had never made a large one before but were willing to try. We agreed. A month or so later, Jim flew to Chiang Mai and triumphantly brought a real beauty home. After they discovered that they could make big ones and people would buy them, we later saw several in silver shops in Bangkok. I still admire ours every time I look at it.

Our beautiful new Thai punch bowl, sometime in 1963.

An exterior detail of the punch bowl, sometime in 1963.

As usual, the meals Sangob ordered while we were in Chiang Mai were good. On one occasion there was a plate of squares of what looked like milk chocolate fudge on the table. Jim thought they were delicious, not sweet but very tasty, and after he had eaten two or three, he asked Sangob what they were. Sangob replied with a chuckle, "congealed blood." Somehow that took a bit of the attraction away. That was the last taste I saw Jim have of the "delicious" dish.

At least we were spared the most famous of the Chiang Mai dishes—warm monkey brains. Let me describe how it would be if you were to order that. A cart loaded with cages with a live monkey in each cage would be wheeled into the dining room. The diner would then inspect the monkeys and pick one—much like choosing a lobster at a seafood restaurant. The attendant would then extract the monkey from the cage and wrap a towel around the body. Then using a machete, he would cut the top of the skull off, rather like opening a coconut, revealing the brain. The monkey would then be reinserted into the cage to hold him upright. The diner would be given a spoon and immediately indulge in the delicacy of warm, recently alive, monkey brains.

Sangob and Krishna had been badly frightened by the flight to Chiang Mai, which to us was just an everyday sort of flight. They had never flown before and the whole thing was extremely upsetting to them. To make them feel better, we decided to take the train back to Bangkok. It was one of the most uncomfortable trips of my life. Chiang Mai is in the mountains so, as it was a night train, the temperature was chilly and a blanket was needed. The train company supplied blankets to be used on the bunks which were merely thin pads on wooden boards. However, the real problem was that the pads and the blankets had been used time and time again without laundering and were not only utterly nasty, they were stiff with dirt. (I have smelled that horrible body stench only once before when an Arab sheik and his entourage boarded our plane in Tehran and one of his oldest and fattest wives sat beside me and put her feet up on the pull down tray in front of her.) If you hunkered down and put the blanket over your head for warmth, you nearly died of the odor, and if you kept your head out, you froze to death. In the meantime, your hip bones throbbed and there was little or no space to turn over in and try to get comfortable.

At least we had *lam yai*, which are a small somewhat gelatinous fruit, slightly sweet with a nice protective covering which we peeled off before eating. We bought them at one of the stations, since there was no food service on the train. Considering the state of their bed linen, I don't think I would have eaten their food anyway. The trip to Bangkok was one of the longest of my life and one I hope never to repeat.

In spite of that sort of problem, we kept on making the weekend trips and always had a good time. We didn't take Mark and Alix with us on these short trips for several reasons. Number one, it was extremely hot and humid, the car was not air conditioned and their delicate baby skin would have suffered badly. Number two, Alix's red hair was a magnet for every *betel-nut* (an astringent nut of a palm tree, that when chewed with lime, produces a red spittle) chewing old woman in Thailand to make a grab for her, touch her all over and croon at her, meanwhile drooling red spit on her. Number three, safe food and drink were a problem on these outings. Jim and I could cope but the children couldn't. Number four, we had bought a number of tricycles, scooters, and wagons for use on the big driveway at our house. There were always four or five Chinese or Thai neighborhood children who came to play with Mark and Alix, with Soh and Daeng to supervise. Our children did not want to come with us anyway. They much preferred staying home and playing happily with the other children.

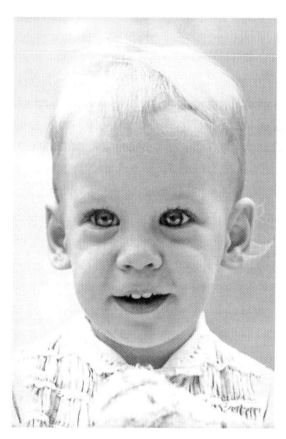

Alix in early 1962, taken in Bangkok.

Mark in early 1962, taken in Bangkok.

Mark and Alix in early 1962, taken in Bangkok.

Jim not only took these three pictures, he also developed and printed them. Frankly, I'm not sure how he could stand to work in the hot, steamy little closet he used as a darkroom. Somehow he did and I'm so glad because the pictures are my very favorites of the children.

During one of our trips to Sunday Market, we bought little Thai drums for the children. The drums were essentially fairly deep pottery containers with leather stretched over the open end and secured with leather thongs. They were small enough for the children to manage them easily while sitting on the floor with the drums between their legs. Jim and I were startled when the rhythms coming from these children of ours became more and more Thai and Oriental in nature. Fortunately for our nerves, the playing of the drums was something of a fad and didn't last too long.

The Chinese family to one side of our house had two of the children who came over to play with Mark and Alix. Piak was their little boy. Cheop was a little girl whom the mother had actually bought on a trip to Chiang Mai, as she had no daughters of her own. Piak and Mark played well together making up all sorts of games—one of them being "King's Boat" based upon imaginary doings of people and the golden boats and barges the king used once or twice a year for ceremonies on the river. Both boys had a good time. They also played other games relating to things they both knew about.

The real King's Boat that inspired the boys, taken in Bangkok sometime in 1962.

We bought some Tonka toy trucks for them. Strangely enough, they were never touched. We took the toys back to the States with us when we returned. When Mark saw trucks like the Tonka on the American highways, he immediately began playing with them once he realized what they were. They had had no relevance to him in Bangkok.

The Thai holidays entranced Mark and Alix, especially *Loy Kratong* which occurs on the night of the twelfth full moon which is sometime in November. Small boat-shaped containers are made of banana leaves. These are the *kratongs*. They are decorated with lighted candles, flowers and incense and are perfectly charming. You can make your own or buy one. When we lived in Bangkok, the *kratongs* were launched on the tidal *klongs*. They glided silently toward the river, bobbing up and down. You made a wish. If your *kratong* faded into the distance and did not capsize, your wish would come true. The *klongs* were crowded with *kratongs* and you had to watch yours carefully. Mark and Alix, as well as Jim and I, always enjoyed it.

Mark holding his *kratong*, Bangkok, November 1962.

One weekend we went to Hua Hin, a sleepy little ocean front town on the west coast of the Gulf of Siam. It was not developed at that time and I have no idea *how* Sangob found the rental. It was a typical tropical wooden bungalow all on one floor facing the ocean. I do know *why* he found the rental—it was squid season and he wanted his fill of the delicacy fresh from the sea.

Squid season was certainly the operative phrase. We had toasted dried squid as a snack with our cocktails, stir fried squid, stuffed squid, tentacles-only-in-a-dish squid, squid with eggs, squid with vegetables, and so on. The only thing Sangob couldn't make with squid was a dessert. However, I'll bet given time he could have come up with one. Finally we revolted (including Krishna) and he went back to his wonderful straight Thai food.

We also went to another sleepy little town on the coast with a lovely beach. It was called Pataya and is now one of the prime destinations in Thailand for people seeking relaxation in a tropical beach setting. There were only wooden buildings when we were there. Now I understand that it is filled with luxury hotels, fine restaurants, and so on. One thing I hope they do not have is the violent storm we experienced when we hired a boat to take us to one of the outlying islands. The boat nearly capsized several times. Our picnic paraphernalia was sliding from one side of the boat to the other crashing into everything. The waves were breaking over the gunwales and washing over the deck. A fierce gale was blowing. It was a miracle that we got back safely. That was one of the few experiences in Thailand I really did not like.

En route to one of our destinations, we passed some women planting rice seedlings in an already flooded paddy. They were barefoot with their skirts hiked up about their knees. I couldn't stand it another minute, so I hiked up my skirt, too, threw off my shoes and waded into the paddy to see what it felt like.

The author trying to pull her foot out of the rice paddy mud, upcountry Thailand, sometime in 1962.

Well, it feels like walking in quite oozy diluted clay. Your feet go way into the slimy bottom. When you want to take a step you have to pull your first foot out with a great obscene sucking sound, place it in front of you, and then repeat the action with the other foot and another obscene sound. Strange feeling. Another problem is that you wonder what little beings you're sharing the mud with. Also, the mud is so fine that it gets under your toenails and takes lots of hard scrubbing to remove. However, it was worth it. Now I know what it feels like.

The author walking back to the car with Sangob, still muddy, upcountry Thailand, sometime in 1962.

On a brilliant sunny day, we drove around a corner and were nearly blinded by line after line of drying cellophane noodles. They are made by grinding *mung* beans and adding other ingredients I'm not familiar with, then stretching the resulting dough out into the traditional noodle shape. They are then put over the lines to dry. As they dry they become clear and when fully dry are crystalline. When the sun hits them they are magical and look like thin icicles glistening in the sun.

One of the staples of Thai cuisine is *nam pla* or fish sauce. *Nam* means water, and *pla* means fish. It is made very simply by layering small anchovy-like fish with salt in huge wooden vats with a spigot to draw off the liquid at the outside bottom of the vat. As the fermentation process takes time and the vats are out in the sun, a very penetrating stench develops. It is so bad it almost makes you not want to eat Thai food any more. However, if they didn't use it, the food would lack something. The thing to do, of course, is to avoid getting anywhere near the vats and just take the food as it comes. Incidentally the *nam pla* is something like wine—there are certain areas that make better sauce than others and some that are "vintage."

During the cool season, the trips would be punctuated by whiffs of the most seductive aroma—sweetish, coconutty and infinitely tantalizing. (If you weren't near a *nam pla* factory.) A woman would have picked tiny cooking bananas, peeled them, sliced them in half lengthwise, dipped the pieces in a batter made with palm sugar, rice flour and fresh coconut bits, and then deep fried them. The resulting delicacy is called *kui keck* and is incredibly delicious—hot and crispy on the outside, creamy and sweet on the inside—never to be properly duplicated outside of Thailand because of the banana variety and the fact that you are buying them hot just out of the pan unexpectedly by the side of the road. They are served to you in containers made of folded old newspapers. Jim declared that I could smell *kui keck* cooking three miles away. And I do believe I could.

Another time we had lunch under the largest *banyan* tree in Thailand. The roots of a *banyan* tree spread in all directions. Then they send up shoots that develop into trees, eventually making the original tree absolutely enormous. It covered at least an acre or two. We were extremely hot and extremely thirsty when we arrived. Walking into the shade was indescribably cool and refreshing, only surpassed by the ice cold *Singha* beer that was immediately set before us. The Thais had put the bottles of beer into a proper freezer to cool. Somehow they manage to run electric cords anywhere they want and under the *banyan* tree was no exception. They also seem to have a sixth sense about when to remove the bottles so that the beer pours into the glass, but is only a degree or two removed from ice. *Singha* is a wonderful beer at any time, but icy cold on a hot day in Thailand, it is absolute heaven. Incidentally, *Singha* means lion in Thai, just as *Lowen* in Lowenbrau means lion in German. The link is that German Lowenbrau brewmasters went to Thailand and set up the *Singha* brewery with German equipment. Small wonder it was so delicious.

In a very remote village (don't forget that this was sometime between 1961 and early 1963 before the Vietnam War and before the vast influx of tourists) crowds of children followed us as we walked down the street laughing and pointing at me. Finally Jim asked Sangob what all the fun was about. By this time Sangob was laughing too and it seems that the children had never seen a foreign woman before and because of my light skin called me "The Fairy God Princess from Heaven". What an honor.

Pale skin is a mark of beauty to the Thais. I was always amused by the fact that most of the road construction gangs at that time were comprised of large numbers of tiny Thai women. They were dressed in cotton skirts down to their ankles, jackets with sleeves to the wrist, gloves and hats with huge, wide brims. Most of them also wore scarves across the lower part of the face. If you happened to be driving by when the work day was over, you would see them take off this paraphernalia and turn into the most delicate, charming looking women you could imagine with their pale complexions intact.

In addition to the road construction workers, women of every class were deeply concerned with preserving their complexions at their lightest. Many women carried parasols when walking in the sun. Another strategy used by Thai women to keep the sun off their complexions was to stand in the shadow of anything they could find. At bus stops you would see the women lined up in the shadow of the nearest telephone pole clutching newspapers to shade their faces. I didn't blame them one whit, that sun was strong.

The trips throughout Thailand continued. Each one was a unique experience—to Ayutthaya to look at a virtual sea of temples and *stupas* (a building, large or small, with a pagoda-like spire) all the way to the horizon;

to Sukhothai to see more ancient ruins; to Kanchanaburi to see the bridge on the River Kwai, which was heartbreaking. The cemetery was especially hard to look at as the headstones noted the ages of the men killed, most of them pitifully young. Sangob told us that as a boy he had helped to smuggle food and medicine to the men working on the railway. We visited many more places than I can count or remember—each one more interesting than the last.

Near the end of our stay in Thailand, we joined the Siam Society, which is the Thai equivalent of our National Geographic Society and under the auspices of the King. We deeply regretted not joining it earlier as the trips and excursions were to out-of-the-way ruins and historic places which were truly interesting and unusual. However, the best part was that we drove to the sites aboard big comfortable buses and servants went on ahead to clear away the jungle, erect temporary latrines, set out tables and chairs, offer us ice cold towels when we alighted from the bus and then serve us a delightful lunch.

*   *   *

We also had a life within the American community that included many parties, dinners, and social events with military friends as well people from the Embassy. It was not as "exciting" to us because it was similar to life in the States, just in another setting. But we enjoyed it. Many of the American women had not found jobs, had servants to do their housework and cooking, and did very little but moan and groan about the heat, no television, no telephones and the fact that they did not like Thailand and couldn't wait to go back to the States. Of course I am exaggerating to a certain extent but not much. They had made up their minds they wouldn't like Thailand, and sure enough, they didn't. What a waste.

An incident that highlighted the negative attitudes toward the Thais that were exhibited by many Americans who did not, or would not, learn to appreciate Thailand and its customs was clearly demonstrated one evening. Jim and another officer decided to host a joint party for all their Thai employees. A local restaurant was rented, an elegant dinner planned to be accompanied by Thai music and dancing. At that time Thai dancing was not like Western dancing. You did not touch or hold one another. It was called the *Ramwong* and was very easy to learn as it is more of just a walk, bending and swaying to the music. Both Jim and I had learned it when we were with our Thai friends, so we danced happily and often during the party. The other officer either did not know how to dance the *Ramwong* or did not care to try. At any rate, he did not participate in the dancing. Also he had not learned much of the Thai language, so he conversed only with those few employees who spoke English.

Both Jim and the other officer were known in Thai as *Nai*, which means boss but with a connotation of a higher status than our use of the word boss. The employees came by the table where we were sitting to pay their respects to the two *Nais* throughout the evening with an embarrassing but decided difference. Jim's employees prostrated themselves flat on the floor in a classic Thai demonstration of respect. The other officer's employees came by and shook hands but without prostrating themselves. This evoked some rather emphatic words of amazement and criticism from Jim's compatriot. However, we had no sympathy as he had made no effort to get to know the Thai people, their language or their country.

I recount the next anecdote, not to demean the woman I am talking about, but to further illustrate the insular attitude of so many Americans to overseas experiences that could have enriched their lives. She was the wife of an enlisted man who had been stationed at one of the U.S. Army compounds outside Paris. When Jim realized that, he asked her how she liked the city of Paris and her time there. Her answer startled him—she had left the compound only once because outside of it there were too many foreigners who didn't speak English.

*   *   *

Not only was Jim the Exchange Officer, he also ran several restaurants, the enlisted men's club and catered a huge number of diplomatic and military parties. Anyone who was entitled to use the Exchange could use his catering facilities. Liquor was imported without tax so it was relatively cheap as was the food served. It always amused me that the most expensive item at these parties was the ice. It had to be made in special equipment with pure water. The charge was five cents for three ice cubes. Since there was no refrigeration at the sites of these parties and the only containers were clean metal garbage cans lined with clean plastic, the ice bill could be huge. Sometimes more than the food and drink added together.

Word got back to the people in Brooklyn, who were Jim's Stateside bosses so to speak, that he was catering for Embassy parties and JUSMAG functions that they did not think were in his mandate. So they sent an "inspection" team to Bangkok to see what was going on. (And incidentally see Bangkok, too. Also known in military parlance as a "boondoggle.) When they found that there were a number of so-called acceptable restaurants on a list put out by the Embassy, they questioned Jim as to why he was doing the catering since it was obvious to them that there were acceptable restaurants as witnessed by the "Embassy List." However the all-knowing inspectors were totally ignorant of the local sanitation standards. Jim said that he would be glad to take them to any or all of the restaurants on the list and show them the kitchens.

The restaurant ultimately selected by the inspectors to visit was The Golden Dragon, which specialized in Chinese food rather than Thai. Jim and I had gone there a number of times and always found the food good and had never been sick after eating it. The men were courteously received when they walked into the restaurant. The owner recognized Jim, so when he explained that they wanted to look at the kitchen, they were immediately escorted there.

Just inside the door to the kitchen were three dead suckling pigs soaking head down in buckets of filthy water. The cook, a Chinese with an enormously fat belly, was standing at the charcoal stove naked from the waist up while the stove spewed ashes and bits of charcoal over everything. He had a dirty rag over his shoulder and was perspiring freely as he stirred the contents of the wok. Eventually he turned the food out onto a serving dish, sprayed the wok with a stream of water to clean it and wiped it out with the dirty rag from his shoulder.

Then he relaxed for a moment wiping his streaming face and chest with the same dirty rag before replacing it on his shoulder. He then turned his back on the inspectors and urinated into an oriental toilet installed in the floor nearby, which was open to the kitchen area and had no door. Without benefit of washing his hands, he turned to the stove and began preparing the next order. After that incredible performance, the Admiral in charge was so appalled that there was no further criticism from the inspectors and Jim was no longer criticized for his catering operations. Jim invited the inspectors to pick a few other restaurants from the list, but there were no takers.

After Jim told me what had happened, I wondered why we were not violently ill each time we had eaten there. My theory was that we had built up enough immunity to the bacteria so that they didn't affect us. On the other hand, we had become ill in Bangkok, but each time it was after eating at an American home as I said earlier.

There was a bar on Patpong Road where Jim would stop for a drink sometimes on his way home from work. The "assistant manager" was a chubby Asian woman people called Mama-san. One evening Jim asked her why she wore a Christian cross around her neck. She quickly answered that she liked the Christian way of looking at death, because Oriental religions called for mourning for a long time, whereas Christians "die one day, forget next."

We made friends with several American couples and went out for "dinner and dancing" frequently with Walt and Polly Grahlert. In those days there were restaurants where you could go for dinner and then when you felt like it, you could get up and dance to a small band playing slow danceable Western music.

It was always pleasant. One particular evening, Polly and I excused ourselves and went to the ladies room. Polly was very tall and slender and she loved clothes. That evening she was wearing a Chinese *chongsam*, the tight dress with short sleeves and closures across the chest that Chinese ladies wear. It had been molded to her body by the dressmaker, especially over the hips, rear and thighs. Suddenly all sorts of laughter came from Polly's stall. The dress was so tight that she couldn't pull it up over her hips and therefore had to completely undress to go to the bathroom. Vanity, vanity.

Polly also had another experience. She had not been given an engagement ring when she and Walt were married. There are hundreds of jewelry shops in Bangkok, so Walt bought her a princess ring set with diamonds from one of them. Princess rings are shaped like the headdresses worn by the Thai dancers and are extremely attractive. Unfortunately, Polly's mother was taken ill and she had to go back to the States. While she was there, she went to the family jeweler to show him her ring. The news was bad—the diamonds were fakes. When Polly returned to Bangkok, they went to the store where they had bought the ring and complained. The proprietor was most apologetic, and said that if he had known they lived in the city and were not just tourists going through, it would never have happened. He replaced the stones with genuine diamonds and everyone was happy.

Another Polly (Polly Raven) and I decided that since her husband was tied up with business at the Embassy where he was posted and Jim was also tied up with a team of inspectors from the States, she and I would go to the Burmese Embassy and see if we could get visas to Burma. At that time Burma was basically closed to the outside world and visas were not being issued. However, we had high hopes and went anyway. After smiling our most engaging smiles, we were delighted when they gave us the necessary papers. However, we were not allowed to go outside the city of Rangoon. That really didn't matter as we had only a week and there was much to be seen in Rangoon itself. Polly had a number of friends from the Foreign Service who were stationed there. They showed us around and couldn't have been nicer once they got over the surprise of our being issued visas in the first place. Of course, the Shwedagon Pagoda was the most impressive place we saw and kept us occupied for hours—a huge temple complex crowned by a huge *stupa* covered in gold leaf. It was completely out of a dream.

*　*　*

Jim's parents came to visit us. We were a stop on their trip around the world. I'm not sure exactly where they went except for stopping in Cairo and Hong

Kong before Bangkok. When we met them Irene was on crutches as she had fallen and done something terrible to her foot. She had to go to the hospital immediately. Since she had not lived in Bangkok, she was unfamiliar with *chinchooks* and caused a terrible rumpus by screaming vigorously when one of them crawled down the wall in her room. Everyone reassured her, so by the time she was ready to leave the hospital and come to our house, she knew all about them and was quite an "Old Hand."

Ralph had written articles for his local paper at each stop and, of course, tried to bring something about the appliances he sold into the story. He had a fine time at our house because Soh and Daeng were using a Maytag clothes washer of the wringer variety that we had brought with us, which we had bought from him. His stories, which were printed in each weekly edition of the *Barber County Index*, the local newspaper, made quite a hit and substantially increased the circulation to its highest level in years. I hope they also increased his Maytag sales.

Ralph surprised us all by becoming interested in the rubbings at Wat Po. The *wat* had a series of carvings showing different aspects of Thai life and religion around the base of the main building. They were beautifully executed and at that time people were allowed to make rubbings from these carvings. The rubbings were made by securing sheets of thin rice paper over the carvings by means of flexible bamboo sticks which caught in the stone frame around them. At that point you gently rubbed blocks of charcoal over the paper and the carving appeared as if by magic on the paper. Ralph did some very good ones and seemed to take a good deal of pleasure in creating them.

While Ralph and Irene were with us, we made a number of excursions to the Bangkok zoo. Surprisingly enough, it is quite large with many types of animals. The children loved going and the animals were interesting, varied and well cared for. "Charlie the Elephant" was one of their favorites with one of the giraffes coming in a close second.

Mark touching Charlie the Elephant's trunk at the Bangkok Zoo
sometime in late 1962.

All of us were invited by our landlady's husband (but no landlady as he brought his No. 2 wife with him.) to go to one of the provinces for the day so that Ralph and Irene could see a bit of the countryside and taste some of the local food. The visit was highly successful. We were royally entertained by the Governor of the province who went out of his way to make sure each person enjoyed himself. The food was especially good. There was music and we all danced the *Ramwong*—Ralph and Irene happily joining in, too. Everyone had a perfect day. Jim and I were especially pleased that his parents were able to experience something like that.

In addition to the food and the dancing, at one of the *wats* Ralph was given a special blessing by the head monk to keep away evil spirits. As Ralph knelt before the monk, he placed his hands on either side of Ralph's head. Bending Ralph's head carefully toward him so that eventually Ralph's chin nearly touched his chest, the monk blew his breath softly out of his mouth onto Ralph's head as he gently moved it back to its normal position. This ensured that the evil spirits were promptly sent away. Just the fact that he had touched Ralph's head was unusual in that, to the Thais, the head is the most important part of the body and you do not touch a person there if you can possibly avoid it. Even married couples do not touch one another on the head.

*　　*　　*

For some strange reason the Navy considered Bangkok a hardship post. Perhaps it was the heat and humidity or perhaps the prevalence of tropical diseases. Whatever the reason, we were able to go on Rest and Recreation (R&R) leave during our stay using military aircraft. We had to sit on heaps of equipment in the cargo hold, or if we were lucky, there were some canvas seats along both sides of the aircraft. However, neither of us minded. I should point out that only the transportation was free. We paid for our own hotel rooms, meals, souvenirs, and so forth, which we were pleased to do.

Twice we were able to go to New Delhi. The first time we stayed in the Delhi area visiting Jaipur and Agra with its magnificent Taj Mahal. An Army couple, Pat and Bebe Rose, who had been on the same plane from Bangkok, went with us to Agra and caused a sensation with the locals. Bebe sang beautifully and inside the Taj Mahal she was persuaded to sing a particular high note. (Poor old LBJ was criticized for doing the same thing when he went there as President. However, it is one of the things that visitors are asked to do if they are at all musical. The acoustics are phenomenal and are beautifully displayed when that certain note is "hit.") Being totally unmusical I'm not sure what it was, but whatever it was, it echoed and re-echoed throughout the interior of the building as it was supposed to do. The locals were enchanted and Bebe could do no wrong. This was further reinforced by her accepting a huge snake with both arms and putting it around her neck like a necklace. One of the snake charmers had playfully offered it to her expecting, of course, that she would squeal and pull away. She could very definitely do no wrong after that.

At one of the railroad crossings on the way down to Agra, the barrier was down across the road as a train was expected. The barrier was put down much too early, as usual, so we got out of the hot car. There were also all sorts of snake charmers at the barrier. One of them had a really big, fat formidable looking cobra in his basket. The cobra took a dislike to Jim and slithered toward him. Jim took one look at the cobra and jumped up on the roof of the car. He regained his composure, took a few pictures and convinced the snake charmer to lure the cobra back to his basket. All's well that ends well—I think. At any rate we provided a great deal of amusement for the local people loitering at the barrier.

Jim's "friendly" cobra at the train barrier in upcountry India, sometime in 1963.

In retrospect it was an ideal visit as there was no smog and few people. We virtually had the sites to ourselves. Delhi itself was extremely interesting and Old Delhi, overflowing with strange things we had never seen before, was even more entrancing. One of the restaurants was Muslim and featured a deep, hot *tandoori* oven. It was called the Moti Mahal and served chicken, *naan* or bread, and other items cooked in the oven. Since they were Muslim, they theoretically did not serve any beer, which goes beautifully with that kind of food. However, the owner quietly went next door and brought back a conventional tea pot filled to the brim with cold beer and two tea cups to drink it from. Very accommodating and not at all conspicuous. We have returned to the Moti Mahal on numerous other occasions and the owner presented me with a beautiful rose each time. He also went next door to fetch us some more "tea." Good man.

The rest of our time in India was one long curry orgy. At every meal, including breakfast, it was possible to eat curry. The vegetarian dishes were infinitely better than the meat dishes except for chicken and sometimes not then because there was no meat, just bones. Some of the dishes arrived with a microscopically thin piece of real silver foil atop them, which you were supposed to eat. The foil had no flavor but was impressive and must have been left over from the days when people showed off their wealth that way.

At breakfast a number of Indian dishes were served—*dosas*, a kind of huge thin pancake with a texture somewhat like a thin unsweetened Chinese fortune cookie, were made on a convex griddle. A little batter was put on the griddle and smoothed out into a circle. Then a bit of spiced potato mixture was put in the center and the whole thing rolled into a log and placed on your plate. At that point, you then put a spoonful or two of a spicy *dal* or lentil dish on top and enjoyed a different, but tasty, breakfast.

Another breakfast treat was *uttapam*. Again a circle of batter was put on a griddle—this time flat and small. Then finely chopped tomato, pepper and onion were sprinkled on top. After turning once or twice, it was placed on your plate and you had a spicy tidbit to go along with your omelet.

There were several stores run by various Indian states. The Rajastani store was a woman's paradise. They had all sorts of already cut semi-precious stones stored in soft flannel bags. If you wanted to see topazes, for example, they would empty a bag of 75 to 100 of them onto a black velvet cloth spread out on a counter under strong light. The light would pick up the brilliance of one or two of the stones that were better cut than the others. If the price was right (and it generally was) you bought the stone, took it with you and had it set in either Thailand or Hong Kong.

There was also an emporium called The Cottage Industries, which sold articles made by hand primarily by the village women. I bought all sorts of lengths of hand woven fabric, napkins, placemats, tablecloths, and so on, which I have used for years. The colors are vibrant, the cotton fabric soft and pliable, and they wash and iron like a dream.

During our second Delhi visit, Jim went to the Nepalese Embassy on a lark to see if it were possible to visit that country. We were lucky and they issued the visas to us—numbers 883 and 884. Nepal had just recently been opened to outsiders so we were especially gratified that we were going to be able to get in.

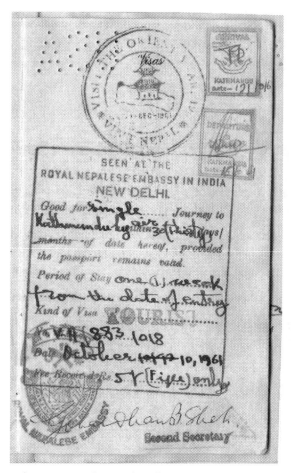

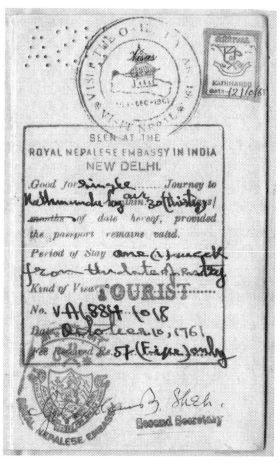

Jim's Nepalese visa #883, as shown in his passport, October 1961.

The author's Nepalese visa #884, as shown in her passport, October 1961.

The flight to Nepal was aboard an Air India DC-3 which could not fly *over* the Himalayas but had to fly *between* them. The weather began to get nasty and soon there was an announcement from the Indian pilot, issued in a clipped precise British accent, telling us that we could not get through the mountains and would spend the night in the city of Patna in north India and try again tomorrow. The pilot had already made three passes trying to get through. As the plane made its turn to go back, the pilot made a steep bank. If you looked out the window along the wing, the view was only of mountain—sheer rock and snow *above* the plane.

Our night in Patna was eerie. The lights had gone out all over town, so to while away the time we took a horse drawn carriage ride. There were old fashioned carbide lanterns on the side of the carriage so we could see a little bit. It seemed to me that we bumped into wandering sacred cows every ten feet or so. The dry drainage ditches at the sides of the road were dangerously close, not to mention the heavy bullock carts being drawn by huge oxen that tried to pass us. I was relieved when we finally returned to the hotel. Only a few lights had come back on by that time. It was probably good that I didn't get a good look at the room in its entirety until the next morning. We made it to Kathmandu the following day and checked into the Rana Hotel, the only one in town. It was the former palace of the Rana family, the hereditary prime ministers.

The hotel was square in shape with an open courtyard in the center. All the rooms opened onto the covered walkway that bordered the courtyard. It was there that a fifty gallon oil drum had been inserted into the outside wall of each room to emerge on the inside over the bathtub. Outside on the walkway, the servants had built a small fire under the drum hoping to heat the water inside the oil drum. There was a "cork" on the bathroom side of the drum that was to be pulled when filling the tub. Everything was fine in theory, but the fire was too small, there was too much water in the drum and when the cork was pulled the water fell too far in icy air and hit a cold tub. So much for a warm bath.

Kathmandu was beyond anything I had ever seen before. The buildings were constructed of wood with much delicate hand carving around windows and doors. The floors on all levels were of dirt and therefore always somewhat damp. (We were told that Nepal had a high incidence of tuberculosis and respiratory problems.) The moneychangers sat in rows on carpets on a huge dais in the middle of the square. Barbers shaved men and cut their hair nearby, talking loudly and gesticulating wildly. Vendors were trying to sell their wares advertising them with loud cries and shouts. Ordinary people were milling about. All of them were wearing colorful, exotic tribal costumes. It made the senses reel.

To add to the confusion and the color, the holiday of Holi was approaching and the villagers were bringing in goats, sheep and other animals to be sacrificed by having the head cut off with what they hoped would be one great stroke of a sword. The noise and the stench were incredible. We were told that when the animals were actually sacrificed that the streets would literally run with blood. I must say the thought of seeing it made me a little ill, but when would you ever see it again? Unfortunately, it would occur after our leave was up, so we had to go back to Thailand before the actual event took place. I've always been sorry I missed it.

Jim bought a huge handful of coins from one of the moneychangers to take back to Bangkok to Chief Church, one of the men who worked for him and was an avid coin collector. We never knew how much they were worth altogether, but he told us that even the least valuable were in the neighborhood of $35 to $40 each. The coins Jim bought were a real bargain as he got them all for about $20. I had also bought a handful of coins because I thought they were absolutely beautiful, but I had mine turned into earrings before I found out the value.

The Rana Hotel had a bar called the *Yak and Yeti*, named for the animal and the mythical "Big Foot" of the Himalayas. It was an interesting place to be. On one particular evening clustered around the huge circular fireplace were the Italian ambassador to God knows what country and his companion, a beautiful blonde woman; a Czechoslovakian doctor with an Auschwitz concentration camp identification tattoo on his arm, who had just come from Tehran where he had collected a suitcase full of priceless antiques; Boris, the Russian hotel manager, famous throughout the Far East plus a host of other characters who made me feel as though I had found a real live setting for a murder mystery *a la Agatha Christie*. The only problem was that I couldn't decide who to kill or why, or who the murderer should be. Does make a difference.

One night just was we were getting ready to go to bed there was a knock on the door that we barely heard because of the thunder and wild rain outside. Jim answered the door. It was Dr. Staub, the Czechoslovakian, who came into the room with his satchel of antiques. He opened the satchel and out came Iranian glassware, an exquisite ancient mirror with a silver handle embellished with much chased work and many other items I can't recall now. However, each was beautiful. The climax came when he thrust a coin into my hand and said that it was for me. It was an ancient Persian coin with a portrait of Darius on one side. I still have it. Every time I look at it I think of Dr. Staub and how strange and out of this world everything was in Nepal—especially that evening.

Even though the source was not as exciting as Dr. Staub, I also acquired a man's ring at a shop. It is very large, roughly triangular in shape, and made of bits and pieces of glass. It is very impressive and makes me feel like a *Maharani* or queen when I wear it.

We hired a 1923 Ford open touring car and a driver. It was great fun to ride in and when it had a problem or got stuck, you just got out and let someone else solve the problem.

The 1923 Ford stuck in the mud just outside Kathmandu, October 1961.

Just being out in the countryside with the temples flying colorful flags, the people in exotic dress and the prayer wheels turning was a treat. Some of the temples had huge eyes painted on the outside near the top. You felt as though the eye was following you and knew all your thoughts—good and bad.

One of the temples with eyes that followed you, Nepal, October 1961.

Another feature was the truly beautiful wood carving around windows, on door jambs and any other place where wood was used. Some of the buildings were so beautiful that you wanted desperately to dismantle one and take it home.

At one area where we stopped to look around, a huge goat fell in love with Jim. The goat was so big that he could rest his chin on Jim's shoulder, which he did—often. His fur was long and matted and he smelled just like what a huge goat in the Himalayas should smell like—perfectly awful. It took several washings to eliminate the odor from Jim's raincoat. However, I must say the goat was sweet and very gentle and *really* liked Jim.

We also visited a museum that displayed relics and mementos of the Gurka regiments that had served in the British army. The ceilings and walls were very high and painted white, which set off circle upon circle of antique guns and weapons. They were not all British made weapons, but came from all over the world. Jim was astounded to see several hundred Derringers in beautiful condition. There were all sorts of other guns, cannons, swords, and fantastic displays of armor and weapons.

Dr. Staub, the Czechoslovakian, had been raised in the Carpathian Mountains and took his mountain climbing seriously. With the assistance of Boris, the hotel manager, he hired a Sherpa guide and they started out. Boris rather disparagingly commented that few Westerners were able to match the Sherpas in climbing ability and that Dr. Staub would have his legs run off. When they returned, the guide was completely exhausted by the pace the doctor set, and the doctor had just gotten his second wind. Boris was dumbfounded. A day or two later, Jim and the doctor hired a jeep and drove toward Mt. Everest. They got as far as what was then the base camp. Jim took the strangest picture with banana trees in the foreground and Mt. Everest itself covered in snow looming up over the foliage in the background. Alas, that one is gone, too.

Looking back on that trip to Nepal, I still can't believe that I did all of that sightseeing, walking and climbing in a dress and wearing four inch red high heels. I must have been out of my mind. However, at that time people dressed up when they traveled. As a matter of fact, I don't think running shoes had been developed then.

The author sightseeing in Kathmandu in red high heels, October 1961.

*   *   *

On another occasion, we had a military flight to Singapore and stayed at the old Raffles Hotel. (Incidentally, the *Singa* in Singapore also means lion. Very popular animal in the Far East.) The hotel was in deplorable condition, but the famous Long Bar was in its original place on the ground floor even though it was in a bad state of repair. The gardens were lovely and well-tended. We knew we were there with the ghost of Somerset Maugham.

At that time there was still a cultural connection with Indonesia so *riijstafel* restaurants abounded. As I mentioned earlier, the word *riijstafel* means rice table in Dutch. "It was given its name by the early Dutch colonizers in Java who, being fond of their food, experimented with the many varieties of spices available and gradually introduced these together with the basic dish of Curry and Rice." (I quote from an old menu from Singapore.) It consists of rice with many, many different things with which to garnish the rice—curries, dried fish, shrimp, pickled vegetables, chutneys, peanuts, coconut, on and on. One of the garnishes, a dried meat very finely shredded so that it resembles steel wool, is called "monkey fur." However, it is tasty and is a good addition to the dish in spite of its name. The Cockpit Hotel on Orchard Road catered to Australians and New Zealanders and served a *riijstafel* to die for. We loved the raucous crowd and went there always anticipating a good time. We were never disappointed. We have counted as many as sixty-four different garnishes for the dish. Eating *riijstafel* was always an "occasion." Amsterdam was just a prelude.

In the evening incredible street food appeared in certain car parking lots especially on Orchard Road. There were electrical outlets available at the rear of each parking space. Vendors would plug in lamps, set up their tables and chairs, light their charcoal and begin cooking. One evening a parked car was left blocking the way by overstaying the departure hour for automobiles. The lot had two functions: one, a car park in the day time and, two, cooking and selling food at night. The outcry from the vendors was loud and vehement. The problem was finally straightened out and the car removed to everyone's satisfaction.

The eating routine was simple and efficient. A man would ask you if you wished to eat. If the answer was yes, he would select a tiny table for you and then walk you around the parking lot. You inspected the food that was being cooked, pointing at this and that, eventually coming up with a selection and number of dishes that suited you, choosing from Hokkien noodles, *dim sum*, curries, chili crab, soup, prawns, Indian pancakes, sugar cane juice, beer, regular Chinese food and all sorts of other tantalizing things. The aromas were enticing and by the time you got back to your table, the dishes were there. All you had to do was to begin eating some of the greatest food in the world.

Perhaps the very finest of dishes from Singapore is chili crab. The best restaurants are now down the coast at Changi beach, a little bit out of town. Changi beach is the site of the infamous World War II prison where the Japanese were excessively brutal to their prisoners. There are a few remnants of the prison but most of the area is now covered with apartment buildings and great restaurants. I don't know what species of crab is used for the dish, but it is large and has an extremely hard thick shell. They are kept in a tank and are sold by weight. After you have selected your crab, it is killed, then dismembered with the claws cracked and the body separated for easy eating. The cook then heats oil in a wok, adding spices, including mild chilies and certain other things I'm not quite sure of. The crab is added with a great deal of tossing, turning and showmanship. It is cooked until done which doesn't take too long. Then a beaten egg or two are mixed in forming threads like egg drop soup, and the dish is put before you. You dive in with your hands. I defy you to eat that dish without completely dirtying the bib they give you and having chili sauce up to your elbows. It is to my crab-loving heart one of the best feasts in the world.

The city of Singapore was full of incredible places to walk. The streets were lined with shop houses. This simply meant that there were businesses of all sorts on the ground floor with the people living above. There was a Chinatown, an India town, a place where transvestites congregated, a red light area and anything else of a depraved nature including opium dens. All in all Singapore was an exhilarating place to visit and one that you never tired of even if you *did* avoid the brothels and opium dens.

*   *   *

There were also several military flights to Hong Kong which were fun—intriguing food, great street markets, upscale conventional shopping, tailor made clothing, and anything else you might want. There were all sorts of exciting restaurants and cocktail lounges on the top floors of a number of hotels—all overlooking that classic neon jungle—Hong Kong harbor at night.

(I am jumping way ahead in time, but I must relate an experience Jim had on one of our later trips to Hong Kong regarding the harbor. We had dined in a restaurant on the top floor of the Peninsula Hotel, the premier hotel in Hong Kong. Jim excused himself to visit the men's room. It had just been renovated and was really quite beautiful. It had glass walls with the urinals placed against the glass so that the man using the urinal could do what he needed to do and at the same time have a superb view of the harbor. As Jim put it, "You are seeing all of Hong Kong and Hong Kong is seeing all of you.")

On one of the military flights, which probably occurred in 1961, we were aboard the JUSMAG plane which needed to refuel in Danang, Vietnam. For safety reasons, we had to exit our plane and stand on the tarmac a distance away. While we were waiting there were numerous A-26 two engine bombers taking off. They were unmarked and had exterior bombs under the wing. We, of course, did not know the destination, but did know that the plane could not land with the bombs still in place on the plane. This was well before the Vietnam War started in earnest and it seemed obvious that Air America was involved.

In Hong Kong we stayed in a Chinese hotel called the Luk Kwok where Jim had been staying since 1958. It was a long, low building with only a few floors. Each floor was presided over by a concierge who directed the other servants and was actually the person in charge. Jim had to make frequent trips to Hong Kong on Navy Exchange business so he stayed at the Luk Kwok often. One time when he was there by himself, he dumped all his money, including bills and coins, on the dresser and left the room. When he returned the coins had been stacked in order and the bills ironed and arranged by denomination.

In 1958 and for some years after that, Hong Kong had a water shortage and the hotels had water available for showers at only certain hours of the day. Since Jim and the concierge on his floor had become friends over the years, his room always had water. On numerous occasions he would come to his room hot and sweaty, remove his clothes and get into the shower. When he came out, his clothes would be gone. They were being washed and ironed. All this attention was amazing since Jim does not speak Chinese and the concierge did not speak English. It might possibly have been that the concierge always received a handsome tip to be disbursed at his discretion to the people working under him. Ah, what "filthy lucre" will do.

Jim was not the only one who had his laundry attended to. On one occasion I also sent out some things to be washed including two brassieres. They were white and had smooth cups. One bra came back with a bright yellow flower imprinted on each cup. Acquired, it seemed, by being washed with someone else's Hawaiian aloha shirt. The second bra was rigidly starched and made me stick out and resemble a short Wonderwoman. Not to mention that it was exceedingly uncomfortable. At least they were clean—I think.

The entire second floor of the hotel was a restaurant which specialized in *dim sum*, the small pop-in-the-mouth treats the Chinese so love. The most popular time for *dim sum* is Sunday noon when huge families gather to enjoy the food. There are grandparents, parents, children, tiny children, brothers, sisters and more family. The food is generally wheeled past your table on carts. You look at the selection, point to what you want, the cart girl places it on your table on a little plate or in the basket it was steamed in and off she goes. Some of the selections include pigeon eggs, small slightly hot green peppers stuffed with ground shrimp, rolled fish, shrimp in a clear pastry, ground pork surrounded by a noodle wrapping, chicken feet, buns filled with barbecued pork, and many, many more. You, then, proceed to eat with a big smile on your face, dipping the bits in chili oil, soy, mustard or whatever your palate dictates. When you have finished someone comes to your table, counts the empty plates and baskets, each of which represents a certain price, and then charges you accordingly.

Once we were seated at a table for three when a Chinese man asked if he could share the table. We gladly assented. Carts rolled by and we all chose what we wanted to eat. One cart held cubes of pale yellow with strange striations which did not look familiar. I asked the Chinese man what they were and he told me with a completely straight face that the cake was made of chicken guts. I passed on that dish and the rest of the meal went well. Years later in San Francisco we were again indulging our passion for dim sum, and a cart with a similar item came by. I asked what it was and was told it was noodles in egg. I burst out laughing and thought of the man in Hong Kong who probably chuckled to himself for years over the gullible foreigners who believed him and did not eat a perfectly acceptable dish.

Another sharing of the table took place during that visit. This time with a Chinese man who was manager of the "Happy Garage." We had the usual varieties of *dim sum* while he consumed a very large dish of sweetened chicken entrails.

After the Sunday diners had left, the tables were cleared and portable partitions brought in separating the tables. Then the real fun began. Innumerable *mah jongg* games were played simultaneously with great sound effects—the clicking and banging of the tiles, shouts of victory and defeat and heaven knows what else. *Mah jongg* is an addictive game and we were amused to see advertisements for withdrawal counseling in the newspaper. No wonder they had the partitions—the players didn't want other people to see them or what they won or lost.

* * *

In spite of all the trips and traveling, we did lead a somewhat normal life when we were in Bangkok. The children were well cared for and had many playmates. Jim enjoyed his work and I certainly enjoyed mine. We had lots of friends and went to many parties, dinners and social functions—some private and some official and all enjoyable.

Jim did not have Thai language lessons in the States before going to Thailand. The reasoning was that he had no Thai officer counterpart, therefore did not need the language. However, he *did* have about one hundred Thai employees, most of whom spoke no English so he began Thai language lessons on his own.

At one of the official functions, Jim, who had a good ear for the tones of the language and a good accent but had not acquired a large vocabulary, was talking to an older Thai woman. She suddenly drew herself up and left him in a huff. We later learned that instead of asking her how many children she had, he had asked her how many lovers she had. His tone was good, his vocabulary not so good. Needless to say apologies were offered many times over.

* * *

The man who was king of Thailand during our Civil War was Mongkut (Rama IV) of *Anna and the King of Siam* fame. He is a very special king to the Thais. He had been a monk for many, many years as he did not expect to ascend the throne. That fact alone made him very special. After he was crowned he did indeed have Anna Leonowens hired as a teacher for some of his children, but probably never met her himself. The play offended the Thais and it was banned, for which I really don't blame them.

King Mongkut must have felt deep sympathy for Abraham Lincoln as he offered him some war elephants to help the Northern, and in his eyes, legitimate, side of the conflict. I have always rather enjoyed that piece of information. After all, rulers must stick together.

*　　*　　*

In June of 1963 when the time came to leave Thailand, we were all heartbroken. Jim extended his tour of duty once by six months, but was not allowed a second extension. It was a very tearful departure at the airport. There were many people to see us off and our necks were hung with Thai-style flower leis, most of them of fragrant jasmine flowers. Thai leis are not circles of flowers, but long straight pieces of ribbon that go over the neck, and then have about ten inches of fresh flowers fastened to each end with many tassels and ornaments which go down the front on either side of the neck. I was absolutely enraged when the stewardess took them from us and enclosed them tightly in plastic bags saying that the scent from the jasmine would make some of the passengers airsick. Looking back on my perfume shop experience, I couldn't much blame her. However, when they emerged from the plastic, they were as sad looking as we felt.

5

STATESIDE DUTY STATIONS—JIM TO VIETNAM

O UR ROUTE HOME TOOK US through Munich where I showed Jim and the children my apartment building, the opera house and some of the other sights. In the square where the famous automated cuckoo clock is located, we had to wait a few minutes for the hour to strike. Alix and Mark became tired of standing. To solve the problem, they both squatted on their haunches exactly as the Thais do. (I understand that if your muscles are used to it, it is very relaxing.)

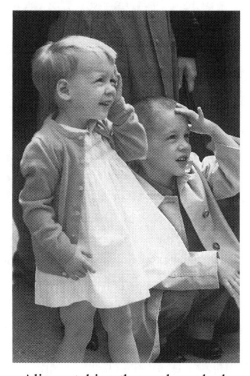

Alix watching the cuckoo clock with Mark squatting Thai style in in the square in Munich, June 1963.

We ordered a Volkswagen Beetle, paid for it and asked that it be shipped to the port of Baltimore from Hamburg since we would be staying in Annapolis with my parents for a week or two. The car failed to arrive on schedule. We had to go on to Medicine Lodge in order to see Jim's parents and then, of course, on to California where Jim would be stationed. While we were in Kansas, Jim got word that the car had finally arrived. He went back to the East Coast, got the car and proceeded to burn the telephone lines with his profanity. The car was filthy. It had been used to sleep in, eat in and who knows what else. The crowning touch was that he found a ski lift ticket in the back seat. Apparently whoever drove the car to Hamburg stopped along the way for a little skiing before taking the car to be shipped and didn't bother to clean up the mess.

After visiting our parents, we drove to California where Jim's next duty was at the Naval Air Station at Alameda just the other side of the Bay from San Francisco. We rented a house in Hayward, south of Alameda, which was a disaster. We lived there nearly a year, but everything seemed to be wrong. The landlady was nasty and it was in a fairly low class neighborhood. Even so, we never met any neighbors. Mark and Alix were still speaking Thai to one another, but that died out by Christmas. Mark had been enrolled at the local public kindergarten. He would go happily to and from school never saying very much about it. His teacher never consulted me with any problems, so in ignorance, I assumed that everything was fine. Eventually we couldn't stand Hayward any longer and bought a small house in Walnut Creek, which is a small town directly across the Bay from San Francisco, well away from Hayward. The house was on a *cul de sac* with enough room in the back yard for a small garden and some fruit trees. It suited us very well. The neighbors were exceedingly pleasant and there were other children for Mark and Alix to play with.

Alix painting a picture at nursery school in Walnut Creek, in early 1966.

Mark was enrolled in the first grade and struggled. I don't know if it was language or just simply that he was used to playing most of the day. The second grade was worse. Alix was attending a private nursery school. Although she was terribly shy, she seemed to thrive.

In order to be as frugal as possible (since Lieutenants do not make *that* much money), I did my grocery shopping at the commissary at the air station. It was a thirty mile drive away. However, once a month or so I would keep Alix out of nursery school and we would make the trip while Mark was attending school.

Those drives were delightful. Alix sat in the front with me very primly buckled into her seat with her little legs sticking straight out in front of her. Each time we made our grocery "run," she told me enchanting stories that she would make up as she went along. They were always filled with imaginative plot twists and excitement. She loved doing it, and I loved listening. How I wish that I had had a tape recorder.

*   *   *

During our time in Walnut Creek, I met one of the people I most admire. Her name was Norma Collier. She was British and lived on our *cul de sac* with her husband, John, also British, and their son, Adam. John was an architect and worked in San Francisco. Adam was younger than both Mark and Alix and did not go to school. Both Norma and I were full time *hausfraus* and therefore had some time to get together. She was an avid reader and interested in anything and everything. I would often see her returning from the library with a huge pile of books nearly falling out of Adam's push cart. She often invited me for tea, but not in the morning. Usually I went down to her house as Adam couldn't be left alone, but I could safely let Mark and Alix know where I would be. When she and I drank our tea together, her coffee table would be overflowing with books, the tea service set out and we would talk. Never, I might add, about babies or other domestic things, but about what she had been reading, my time in Thailand, current events and any other topic we both found of interest. She seemed to be able to discuss almost any subject anyone brought up. I found her fascinating and completely easy to be with. Jim and I were both astounded by her breadth of knowledge.

When Adam was ready to go to school, Norma and John freaked out, as the saying goes, and would not send him to a California school. Instead they went back to London to put him in what they called a "proper" school. Fortunately, we kept in touch and over the years I visited her many times as I passed through London, each visit more fun than the last. Several years later Norma and John were divorced. Jim also looked her up when he was in London and invariably took her out to dinner. On one occasion she recommended they meet in a small pub in Covent Garden. She got their first and when Jim arrived Norma was visibly upset. She insisted that they leave immediately as it was a "gay bar".

*   *   *

Our time in Walnut Creek passed quickly and very pleasantly. Both sets of parents paid us visits, which we all liked. I helped at Alix's nursery school which she and I both enjoyed. We went out to dinner occasionally and had people over. There were trips into San Francisco to the opera and to some of the great Chinese restaurants. Just walking the streets of the city was pleasure enough.

Petie and Jim Evans were living south of San Francisco in Monterey where Jim was attending post graduate school. We couldn't get together too often, but were able to see each other several times during our stay in Walnut Creek. Both Monterey and Carmel, a nearby town, were charming. Quaint shops, unusual restaurants and pleasant areas just to meander through. We were always amused by their daughter, Leslie's, name for a certain delicatessen. She called it the "cheese stink" store, which was an apt description.

Petie and Jim had their last child while in Monterey. They had had three girls: Anne, Laura (Laurie) and Leslie. Their fourth child was a boy they named James A. Evans, Jr., (Jimmy). With their four and our two, the family picture taken during one of our get togethers was impressive—at least in our eyes. Incidentally, Petie's girls are wearing dresses she made from fabric I bought on my trip to Burma. Each is a different color.

Family photo taken in Monterey, California, in the fall of 1963. Top Row from left to right: Jim Dickey, the author, Petie Evans holding Jimmy Evans, Jim Evans; Bottom Row from left to right: Alix Dickey, Mark Dickey, Laurie Evans, Anne Evans and Leslie Evans.

*   *   *

Through Elizabeth Lyons, the woman who had stayed with Jim Thompson in Bangkok, we met the curator of the Avery Brundage collection at the San

Francisco museum. Dr. DeArgensia was extremely gracious and took us for a tour into the storage areas to look at the items before individual selections were made to put on display in the part of the museum open to the public. It was a rare opportunity and we appreciated it. It was quite fascinating to see a bin of oxblood porcelain with twenty to thirty pieces of various sizes and shapes, each one perfect. We would then walk five feet and see another bin, this time with green porcelain, then another five feet for blue porcelain. Not only that, there were also Tang horses and camels by the dozen, incredibly early bronzes, weapons, incense burners, on and on ad infinitum. I don't know the full story of Avery Brundage, but it is my understanding that as a young and very wealthy man he went to China and bought everything he came across that was genuine and beautiful and perfect, then had it all crated and sent back to the States. The crates were put in storage and years later, he finally opened them and donated them to the museum in San Francisco. He is the same Avery Brundage who was head of the International Olympic Committee for thirty years and did much to promote amateur sports.

*   *   *

In June of 1966, Jim received orders to Vietnam where he was to be Senior Supply Advisor to the Vietnamese Navy Supply Center. Before he left for that country, he was to go to counter insurgency school in Coronado for a while. Since the Navy would ship our household goods anywhere in the country I wanted, I elected to go to Jim's hometown, Medicine Lodge, in the south central part of Kansas. His parents owned a house down the street from them that I could rent and they could get to know their grandchildren better. There was a chance Jim might be ordered to Annapolis one day, but no chance to Kansas, so it seemed like an excellent arrangement. Irene knew that I loved red, so she had the underneath side of the old fashioned claw footed bathtub painted bright red and installed red carpeting. The final touch was red and white checked curtains at the window.

Since Jim had to get to Coronado as soon as possible, he was to go ahead after packing up the household goods to be shipped to Kansas. We then put a few things in a small one-wheeled trailer to be pulled behind our Volkswagen beetle and off he went to Coronado. Our model VW had a storage area just behind the back seat and just in front of the rear window. The kids called it the "cuffy" hole and both of them enjoyed squeezing into it together.

The day came for Mark, Alix and me to climb into the VW and head for Coronado to be with Jim while he was still in the States. We got on the freeway and started out. The minimum speed limit was forty miles per hour, which is all well and good. However, the roadway was not quite as smooth as it might be today, and there were tar seams between sections of cement. Every time I speeded up above forty miles per hour, the car and the trailer set up some sort of harmonic with the road and its tar bumps causing us bounce so hard it was dangerous. Because of that I reduced speed and we were going around thirty-five miles per hour. Soon thereafter I heard shouts from the back seat that a big black car with a flashing cherry on top wanted me to pull over. I pulled over and was promptly given a ticket for driving too slowly. For some reason the policeman did not escort me off the highway, so I just kept going at thirty-five miles an hour. Before I reached Coronado, I had been pulled over a total of five times. I was given only one real ticket, and none of the men made me get off the highway. However, it was a peculiar trip—not one that *I* enjoyed particularly, but one the *children* thoroughly delighted in. They found all the police cars very exciting, especially when the lights were flashing and the sirens screaming. Anyway, we got to Coronado without further incident, but did have one of the best bacon, lettuce and tomato sandwiches that I have ever eaten in a tiny diner just off the highway when we stopped for lunch between tickets.

When Jim finished counter insurgency school, he had some leave, so we all got into the Beetle still pulling the trailer behind us, and headed for Medicine Lodge. The roads were a bit better so there were no "under the speed limit" tickets nor, lamentably, any good bacon, lettuce and tomato sandwiches.

Disneyland was our first stop. Mark and Alix were in heaven. I must admit that Jim and I thought it pretty spiffy, too. We all seemed to like the pirates the best. They were evil enough to be scary, but friendly enough not to seriously frighten children. In other words, perfect for the occasion.

We also stopped at Mesa Verde National Park and were quite impressed by the ruins. The Grand Canyon also impressed everyone, especially when we took a flight *into* the canyon in a six-seater Cessna. The pilot let Mark fly the plane. We had one thrilled boy on our hands. Mark and Alix did some trout fishing at a stocked pond near the side of the road and were pretty proud to have caught a number of fish.

*   *   *

During the time the children and I were in Medicine Lodge, which was from June of 1966 to June of 1967, we led a peculiar existence. Jim's Mother, Irene, and her best friend, Mary, were inseparable for they not only played bridge together, but Mary also worked at the appliance store that Jim's parents owned and where Irene also worked. Mary was funny, talkative, and kind. Mark and especially Alix really loved her.

Not only did Mary and Irene play social bridge, they also competed in tournaments. Each of them had a number of Master Points to their credit. They entered one to be played in Wichita. When they registered, they discovered that they were the "odd couple" and there was not another pair of ladies to play against. However, the men were in the same situation. Mary and Irene were invited to compete as a pair in the men's tournament, which they won. The following year the men were not so generous. As a matter of fact, they were downright chauvinistic and wouldn't let them defend their title. No, it didn't make the headlines then, but I'm sure it would today.

The people in Medicine Lodge didn't know how to treat us. I wasn't single, I wasn't divorced, I wasn't widowed and because Jim wasn't there, I really wasn't married in their eyes. Worst of all, I disliked bridge and refused to play and I still painted my fingernails bright red. However, with a number of pleasant things happening outside the confines of Medicine Lodge itself, we managed beautifully.

First of all, we got there in June and it was a long time until school started in September. Ralph, Jim's father, lent me a big car as he didn't like the idea of his grandchildren riding around in a small VW beetle. So off Mark, Alix and I drove to Annapolis to see my parents, and then to Virginia Beach to stay with my sister, Petie, and her children. The interstate highway system across our country had not been finished at that time, so the roads went through charming small towns with tall, arching shade trees and houses withhold fashioned colorful gardens. There were many antique shops and hotels with lounges where the children were allowed. Some of them even had people playing the piano. It was one of the loveliest long driving trips I have ever taken.

Jim Evans was flying jets off the coast of Vietnam from a carrier so Petie and I, with all the children, were on our own. We went to the beach, built sand castles, acquired tans and generally had a good time. The only untoward thing that happened was that one day the children were playing a game in the house that involved running. Alix came barreling out of the house proper into the sun room heading for the outdoors. Fortunately she had her head down as she hit the glass door of the sun room with her forehead and completely shattered the glass. The impact bounced her back into the sun room. I ran to her, picked her up, examined her and couldn't believe that she did not have blood streaming all over her. We were all amazed. After the mess was cleaned up and new glass installed, we put little pieces of duct tape here and there so that you could tell that the door was not wide open. I can't tell you how thankful I was that she had escaped with nothing more serious than a small bump over one eye. The angels were surely looking over her that day.

*   *   *

There was only one grocery store in Medicine Lodge. It was adequately stocked with basic supplies. However, the fresh vegetable offerings were limited to onions, potatoes, carrots, iceberg lettuce, cabbage, and the occasional tomato. If you wanted anything else, you simply had to drive the 110 miles into Wichita to visit a store that specialized in other types of food. There you could buy fresh broccoli, string beans, spinach, bread other than white and sundry other items that made life worth living. I usually made the trip every two weeks. In many ways living in Medicine Lodge was very much like living in an English-speaking foreign duty station in a third world country.

However, there was one place in Medicine Lodge where you could get hamburgers and French fried onion rings that would really make you sit up and take notice. That place was Charlie Bains' drive-in. Everyone loved going there. The hamburgers were juicy and flavorful and the onion rings hot, crisp and greaseless. The best of American fast food.

In all fairness, I should say that even though I do not like chicken fried steak, milk gravy and a large number of other Midwest favorites, the desserts that are produced in that part of the world are nothing short of miraculous. The women have access to extremely fresh eggs, milk and cream. When I say cream, I do not mean what is sold in cartons in the grocery store. I mean pale yellow cream that is so thick it has to be spooned out of the jar. All of this means, of course, that the ice cream, the cake frostings and the custards are something no one would believe until they saw and tasted them. Truly divine. Church ice cream socials are particularly well attended, I might add.

*   *   *

In September, I had sense enough to discuss Mark's school situation with the teachers at the local elementary school. We decided that since this was a new school for Mark and none of the students would know about it to possibly tease him, that he should simply repeat the second grade. He concurred. The difference was amazing. He turned into an active, bright child participating in class and taking an interest in everything. Wish I had had sense enough to do it sooner.

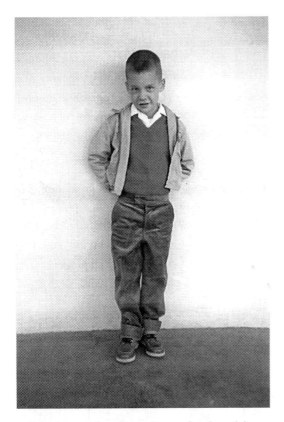

Mark on the first day of school in Medicine Lodge, Kansas, September 1966

* * *

In November, Jim, who was still in Vietnam, had to go to Honolulu for a conference. Irene kindly agreed to take the children, slipped me some money and off I went to meet him. We stayed at the Army's old wooden Ft. Derussy right on Waikiki Beach, ate spectacular meals and drank some pretty wonderful ChiChis. So wonderful were the ChiChis that I asked the bartender for the recipe. He pulled an already typed copy from behind the bar and gave it to me. (It seems a few people before us also thought the drinks good.)

We had a great week although I was surprised to see how thin Jim had become. Much later, when I learned the reason for this, I could understand it. It seems that one of his officer friends who worked in the Security Operations Group in the MACV Headquarters in Saigon told him that their counterintelligence group discovered that there was a price on his head of $5,000, which at the time and considering the poverty of the country, was a tremendous amount of money. This caused Jim to be extremely cautious wherever he went and it saved his life. He had rented a house only three meters wide (but quite deep

Jim at Ft. Derussy, Hawaii, on leave from Vietnam, November 1966.

157

with many small rooms and a partial second floor) with some other officers near the compound of the Commandant of the Vietnamese Marine Corps. There was parking space for his jeep nearby and the area was constantly patrolled by Vietnamese Marines.

One morning, just like any other morning, he rose, got ready for work and headed to his jeep. As usual, he checked the "tell tales," which were small pieces of scotch tape strategically placed so that if anyone tampered with the jeep it would be readily apparent. All of them were in place, so he proceeded to put the key in the ignition. For some reason, which to this day he does not understand, he had an uneasy sensation, did not turn the key and looked under the dashboard. There he discovered a ball of plastic explosive with the detonator hooked to the ignition switch. As he described it, had he turned the key there was enough explosive to have leveled the jeep and him along with it. Thank heaven he had that flash of intuition plus God watching over him.

After that incident, he was even more observant of his surroundings, and was constantly looking over his shoulder. Maybe he should have been looking in front of him rather than behind, because after he returned to the States and after the fall of Saigon, he discovered that his Vietnamese counterpart, Lieutenant Commander Du, with whom he worked on a daily basis, was secretly an officer in the *North* Vietnamese Navy.

*   *   *

While not as dangerous as Jim's experiences, I had a few problems of my own. I'm afraid that I inadvertently embarrassed one of the teachers from the high school dreadfully. She called on me to ask if I would speak to the students at the Christmas assembly about how that holiday is celebrated in Thailand. I had to tell her that they were Buddhists and not Christian, and therefore did not celebrate Christmas in any form. She blushed, thanked me and left in a hurry.

During Christmas I invited Irene, Mary and about eight or nine of their women friends over to try the ChiChis I had learned about in Hawaii. The drinks were so special and festive that I don't think that the ladies realized that there was so much alcohol in them. I must say that I refilled their glasses often and ended up with a bunch of little old grey haired drunks on my hands. Happy Holidays.

Christmas approached. I got a medium size tree, some new ornaments and a tree stand of the variety where you insert the tree into the stand, and then screw three screws into the tree trunk tightly to hold it upright. Mark, Alix and I were doing this together on Christmas Eve. All was going well. The tree was in place, the lights were on, the new ornaments gleaming—we sat back patting ourselves on the back that we had done well. Then, as we watched in horror, the tree slowly toppled over with a crash, breaking nearly everything. All three of us cried, and then started all over again. Eventually we got it right. Dads are sorely missed at times like that.

While we lived in Walnut Creek, we had played a great deal of the popular folk music of the day. The Kingston Trio and Peter, Paul and Mary were our favorites. When we moved to Kansas, I tried to play that music, too. However, even though the children didn't know how to verbalize it, they absolutely would not let me play any of the music. Apparently music has deep associations, even for young children, and it reminded them too much of their father.

When Christmas Day arrived, my spirits rose dramatically. Irene and Ralph had given me (I use the word "me" but it really was for both of us) an air ticket around the world so that I could meet Jim in Thailand if he could get leave. They offered to take the children and our two cats while I was gone. What an incredible gift.

*   *   *

The journey started out with a stop in Annapolis to see my parents. Then I was off to London. My friend, Eileen, had married a British man and was living in Cobham, a small village in Surrey. She invited me to come down to their home for a few days and I had a great time visiting with her and seeing all the renovations she and her husband were making to their "home," which turned out to be a twenty-eight room mansion oozing English country charm. Nothing, however, can help English plumbing. The bathroom I was assigned had a huge tub that absorbed all the heat from the tepid water and the ceiling was so high the air chilled you to the bone. In spite of that, they had made the rest of the house comfortable and attractive—many fireplaces, comfy furniture and beautiful paintings.

Eileen's sister-in-law invited us to lunch. It was extremely English and extremely entertaining. I don't remember what we ate but the conversation was good and the table was set with exquisite china and silver. I learned during the course of the afternoon that they had a booth at the Bermondsey Market (a glorified flea market sort of place) where they bought and sold silver. No wonder everything was lovely as they had definitely kept the best for themselves as they should have.

Eileen and her sister-in-law more than went out of their way to take me into London to Norma Collier's house. It was somewhat difficult to find, but we made it. They stayed for tea which was fun. Then Norma and I went to a revival of Sheridan's *The Rivals*. Margaret Rutherfood played Mrs. Malaprop,

Ralph Richardson was Sir Anthony Absolute and Daniel Massey as the young Absolute. Quite a cast.

The next day we did more sightseeing capped off with dinner at Rule's, an old theatrical restaurant with many caricatures, statues and other memorabilia around the walls. John Collier picked out a typically English meal—smoked trout followed by grouse pie which was served with soggy potatoes, it is true, but also the tiniest, most delicious Brussels sprouts possible. For dessert we had Drambuie and coffee. After talking for a long time we went home walking half way across London to locate John's Lotus which was parked in Soho where he worked. The drive home was wild with Norma perched on Adam's little seat over the battery.

The leg from London to New Delhi was aboard BOAC, a now defunct British airline. When the plane stopped in Beirut, I had to restrain myself from getting off as Baalbek beckoned, but went on, landing in Delhi in the wee small hours of the morning. Was kept waiting by the hotel clerk for an hour while he got himself ready to face the day. Delhi seemed dirtier and more run down than the last time, if possible. I wandered around visiting familiar shops, then crashed as I had to get up at two in the morning for the next leg of the journey which would take me to Bangkok.

Sangob, Krishna, Ken Dilks and Sangob's brother, Tawan, met me as Jim had not yet arrived. We parked the car, went into the hotel coffee shop and by some miracle ran into Soh, our former servant. By that time, it was about five o'clock. The others left and she and I settled down and talked until about seven. (I deeply regret not getting some kind of permanent address from her so that I could keep in touch. I found out years later from Ella Dilks that she married an American soldier and was living in the Philadelphia area.)

For the next day or two, I went shopping, to the beauty salon, dressmaker, Sunday market, jewelry stores, and on and on loving every minute of being there. Jim's plane finally arrived and my notes from the trip mention wonderful meal after wonderful meal, either cooked by Sangob or eaten at some of our favorite restaurants. It was all most enjoyable and very festive.

Roy Dickey, Jim's cousin, who had graduated from the Naval Academy ahead of him in 1952, but had gone into the Air Force instead of the Navy, was stationed at Khorat, a small town north of Bangkok. Roy was flying F-105 fighter bombers over Vietnam. We decided to drive up to see him. So off we went. Ubonsri (Tawan's wife), Tawan, Sangob, Krishna, Jim and me. After being refused entry to the base, we were all left as "hostages" while Jim, who had identification with him, bummed a ride to the Officer's Club and met Roy, who took him to his pad and showed him a picture from his gun camera of the Russian MIG that he had shot down just the day before, Roy was still very excited about it. F-105s are more bomber than fighter, so Roy had gotten the MIG when he came up through a cloud and it was directly in front of him. Since he had expended all of his other ordnance on his bombing run, Roy then opened up with his 20 mm cannon and blew the MIG out of the air.

We all had lunch and then drove to Phimai, an ancient city, and clambered over the ruins. It wasn't spectacular, but nonetheless interesting. Had dinner together and then Roy excused himself as he was flying the next day. We left in the morning returning to Bangkok via Ayutthaya, which is always spectacular no matter how many times you have been there. As I mentioned earlier, it is a plain of temples reaching to the horizon and you never fail to find something you didn't see the last time you were there.

Our last dinner in Bangkok was at Sangob's house—an Indian barbecue. Delicious, as always. Jim was amused to see the Frigidaire refrigerator and the Maytag wringer washer we had sold to Sangob when we left Thailand still in good working order. He took pictures of them to give to Ralph although I never heard if he did another article for the local paper about them.

Luckily Jim had enough leave so that we flew together to Hong Kong again staying at the Luk Kwok Hotel. We did a tremendous amount of shopping and a tremendous amount of wandering the streets savoring everything. We managed to have cocktails and dinner in a large number of restaurants on the top floors of various hotels overlooking Hong Kong harbor, that never ending kaleidoscope of color. In addition to eating all sorts of exotic Chinese food, we did have a memorable meal at the Parisian Grill—*vichyssoise*, snails for Jim (while I averted my eyes), *chateaubriand* for two, veggies and a bottle of 1964 *Chateau Neuf du Pape*. Not bad.

Eventually Jim had to return to Saigon, while I went on to Japan to stay a day or two with Fran and Wendy Powell, who met me at the airport. (Wendy was a classmate of Jim's at the Academy. We had become friends with them while all of us were living in Sanford.) We drove to their small Japanese house outside the air base at Atsugi. It was Washington's Birthday so Wendy was not at work. We went to Kamakura to see the Buddha and another shrine to see the Goddess of Mercy. Beautiful gardens and beautiful day.

That evening we went to a restaurant called the Water Wheel Court and had a beef *nabe*. (*Nabe* turned into one of our favorite dinners. I'm sure you'll see why shortly.) A special cast iron frying pan divided into five sections is put over an *hibachi* or small round cooker holding a charcoal fire. Each section is curved toward the outer edge and has a depression there for oil. Raw beef, onion, ginko nuts, mushrooms and green pepper are dipped in the oil and cooked on the curved part of the *nabe* or grill. After cooking they are dipped into a flavorful sauce that has sesame seeds, as well as a quail egg, in it and into which you put as much *wasabi* or horseradish and green onion as you wish or can stand. Then the pieces are put on top of the rice.

The center section of the grill is round and is filled with water. When the water comes to a boil, chrysanthemum leaves are added and then dipped in the sauce, placed in the rice bowl and eaten along with the other tidbits. Fran bought us one of the *nabe* grills, and went to the trouble of sending it to us in the States, which was wonderful of her. We have added chicken and shrimp to the selection of meat. I can't tell you how much we have enjoyed it over the years.

From the base at Atsugi, Wendy flew photo and electronic reconnaissance missions over Vietnam in an A3D. He was the pilot along with a flight engineer/recon officer. One of the evenings I was there, he was almost in tears as he described how he and his flight engineer would fly missions gathering information and taking pictures of what was happening on the ground risking their lives in the process. Then the information would be flown back to Washington and looked at by the powers that be. They picked out what could or could not be bombed. Then the instructions came back to bomb such and such. By that time, of course, several weeks had passed and everything had changed so that their initial risks and work had been useless.

I have never been able to understand why civilians don't let military people fight the wars. Every civilian interference seems to cause nothing but difficulties, additionally compounded by their lack of knowledge of strategy and tactics. But then, that is a "mere female" opinion.

Wendy briefed me thoroughly on how to get to Kyoto. Their servant's husband worked for the railroad system, so she had bought a ticket for me. Even without speaking any Japanese, thanks to Wendy's instructions, I managed to get myself aboard the bullet train to Kyoto. I crossed Tokyo in a taxi driven by man sitting tall and straight in his seat wearing a white jacket and cap, as well as white gloves. He was rather sedate and unsmiling—drove very carefully until for some reason it became necessary for him to go up and over a huge traffic island in the middle of the street. He accomplished this traffic violation without changing the expression on his face and proceeded just as sedately on to the train station.

My train seatmate was one of the Japanese public relations men for Canadian Pacific. We talked at length about Kyoto and Nara, Buddhism and Christianity. He was extremely courteous and spoke excellent English. In addition, he told me about the sights we were passing, Japanese customs, what to see while in Kyoto, and in general was very helpful.

The inn where I stayed was pure Japanese, no English at all, so there was a great deal of arm waving and pointing, not to mention hissing and bowing. I liked it all but I must say I had some trouble getting into the bath. There is hot water and hot water, and I swear this was beyond human endurance. It felt hot enough to blanch vegetables.

Kyoto itself was exotic, charming and everything it was said to be. I went to a *geisha* house and readily understood their popularity. Lack of a common language was no barrier. The *geisha* made me feel at home and comfortable immediately. She played games, did some pantomime and entertained all of us there in a universal way.

Had a Japanese breakfast the next morning, but didn't eat much as it was too early for raw fish. Took a tour of castles and palaces in the morning and in the afternoon went to temples and gardens. The gardens were not to be believed and the nightingale floors in Nijo Castle were unreal to walk on. It must have been a trial to construct. The floors were designed to emit the sounds of a nightingale so that no one could sneak up on the Emperor, either day or night.

After Japan, I went back to Kansas since I had promised to be home for Alix's birthday on March 2nd. I'm not sure who was happier to see me—the children or Irene. She had had the children and the cats for six weeks and that was a long, long time for someone at her time of life and health. She was thanked profusely for what she did, and as I write this, I thank her again.

During the time we were in Medicine Lodge, Alix was asked to be Mary's daughter, Helen's, flower girl when she and a young man named Mont were to be married. We gladly agreed and were caught up in the preparations for the wedding. It was a lovely ceremony and Alix did a fine job.

June of 1967 finally arrived and Jim returned from Vietnam. He came directly to Kansas. We all went to the airport in Wichita to meet him. In spite of being exhausted from the long flight and terribly thin, he was smiling and we were all delighted to see him. Within a few weeks, we had packed up that house and were on our way to Annapolis.

6

RETURN TO ANNAPOLIS

AFTER FINISHING HIS TOUR IN Vietnam, Jim was to be stationed in Washington, D.C., working in the Policy and Plans Division of the Naval Supply Systems Command (what a mouthful). We hoped to be able to live in Annapolis. He held that job for a number of months, loathed it and asked for a transfer. Fortunately there was a billet open in the Naval Material Command for which Jim was selected and which he thoroughly enjoyed.

One of his auxiliary duties was to manage the noon meal Mess for nineteen admirals. He tells a wonderful story of going to Georgetown, a posh section of Washington, to personally select some food items from one of the better stores there. That particular day was cool and rainy so he was dressed in a black raincoat wearing a black derby Mother had given him and carrying his favorite furled black British umbrella. One of the stewards, Dean, accompanied him in his steward's uniform of black trousers and white jacket with a bow tie. They pulled up to the curb in front of the store in a huge black limousine that normally carried admirals around town. The crowd parted as for royalty, and he entered the store. The other customers drew back as he pointed to various items and Dean carefully took them to the checkout counter and then to the car. Jim still laughs about all of the obviously upper class patrons who were wondering who on earth this strange person might be.

Of great significance to Jim was the fact that when he was promoted to Commander, Vice Admiral Jackson Arnold presented him with Commander collar devices which in turn had been presented to him by Admiral John Sidney McCain, the Commander of Fast Carrier Task Force during World War II and who was Senator John McCain's grandfather. It was especially appreciated since Admiral Arnold had just won the Navy Cross for his performance during the Battle of Midway when the collar devices were originally presented.

* * *

We stayed with my parents when we reached Annapolis unnerving them by arriving with two cats. We ultimately bought their house which was the house on Cherry Grove Avenue that I had grown up in. It was good for everyone. Mother and Father could move into an apartment and not have the responsibility of a house and a large yard. Jim and I would have a house we could afford and the children would be close to good schools. The house needed a tremendous amount of work, but the basic structure was sound. It was constructed of red brick with a slate roof and copper gutters. (One night we were awakened by thieves on the first floor roof right outside our bedroom window hammering and banging trying to detach the copper gutters and sell them for scrap.) The floors were of oak downstairs and pine upstairs. There was a full basement and a garage. The furnace and laundry facilities were also in the basement. The main floor had a large living room, small study, dining room, kitchen and half bath. The house was in the shape of a letter "C". Upstairs were three bedrooms and a full bath.

There is no need to go into all the details, but over the course of the next five or six years, the house was air conditioned, a new kitchen and laundry room added, a door between the garage and basement cut, a greenhouse constructed and the open part of the "C" closed by adding a sun room thereby improving the flow of traffic on the main floor and turning it into the perfect "party house." Jim's experience as a young man working for Ralph really "paid off" and under his tutelage, we were able to do a large percentage of the work ourselves with much help from Mark and Alix. Jim even made the kitchen cabinets and countertops.

Irene bought an upright piano so that Alix could continue her music lessons. (Mark was playing the guitar.) It was placed in the sun room which had a red and white color scheme—red carpeting with vintage wicker furniture painted white with red cushions. Jim also painted the piano white. Then he and Alix decided that the black keys would match the décor better if they were red. The piano was taken apart and the black keys given several coats of shiny red paint, much to Alix's delight. We used that room a great deal and I was always happy in it. The piano never failed to attract people of all musical persuasions—it was irresistible.

The neighborhood had many older houses. However, when we moved in, those homes were occupied by the next generation of younger owners. We had a lot in common with most of them—young children, not much money, houses that needed attention, love of getting together, and so on. After a severe snow storm one winter, the men cleared an area in the middle of the street, wheeled out portable barbecues, cooled beer in the snow, and constructed a life-like Dolly

Parton snow woman emphasizing her formidable attributes. We all partied. It was great.

The house to one side of us was occupied by Richard and Mary Megargee, their two daughters, Anne and Martha, and son, Michael. Mark and Michael were about the same age and became good friends. Mary and I became good friends, too, and still have our annual catching-up telephone conversations.

When the Megargees moved to Rhode Island, John and Peg Fenton bought the house. Jim and John became quite close. One thing that drew them together was their love of shooting British style darts. They eventually became proficient enough to get their team qualified for the "A" league. This category did not carry any great distinction since their league's venues were some of the raunchiest red-neck saloons in the county. The house across the street was owned by Peg and Bill Andahazy, who were always fun to be with.

We also had good times with one of Jim's classmates who also happened to be in the Annapolis area. Hoyle H. Miller, Jr., known by the fun name of Poppy, and his wife, Jane, had bought a beautiful long, low house just across the Old Severn River Bridge. It had the most spectacular view in town—the river, the Naval Academy and the lights of Annapolis. Poppy and Jim had been in the same Company at the Academy and not only knew one another well, but became lifelong friends. Hoyle resigned from the Navy after his obligated service was up and joined IBM where he did exceedingly well. Jane is a dear. All in all, we had a wonderful time living on Cherry Grove Avenue, especially with friends like Hoyle and Jane.

*   *   *

Mother and Father had experienced a truly hilarious event while we were in Thailand. The people who bought the Coe house next door were named Huff. The man's nickname was Ruffie, Father's nickname was Tubby and another neighbor was Rookie and, believe it or not, a fourth neighbor was Knockie. As if that weren't enough levity, Mother and Father had a cat. I don't know what the cat's name was, but it made a habit of using Mrs. Huff's flower garden as its litter box. Mrs. Huff took offense to this and told Father to make the cat stay at home. Father said he had no control over the cat, so Mrs. Huff sued him. In today's world, she probably would have won the suit, but at the time it caught the fancy of the town and everyone had an opinion one way or the other as to what to do about the cat.

The newspaper had published some facetious bits and pieces about the upcoming trial. On the day itself the courthouse was packed. By this time public opinion was in Father's ball park and Mrs. Huff hid in the basement in the ladies room to escape humiliation. Because she failed to appear, the case was dismissed and everyone went out to lunch to celebrate. The cat was declared "Not Guilty."

*　　*　　*

Every year the neighborhood had a "Whale of a Garage Sale." Everyone saved their junk during the entire year so there was a great deal of "stuff" offered for sale. Both the day and the sale were usually very successful. We straightened out our cupboards and made money, too. Everyone had a fine time and at the end of the day we had a barbecue, a keg of beer and partied. One year our family sold both a sail boat and the famous VW beetle of Hamburg fame.

Mother and Father introduced us to Mrs. James Doyle (Marie), the widow of one of Father's old Navy friends. She lived in a wing of the Bordley House in downtown Annapolis. We were much too young to call her anything but "Mrs. Doyle." No one in my parent's circle of friends really knew very much about her background. She claimed to have been raised in Hong Kong by two uncles, but little slips here and there made that seem improbable. We never did learn any further details, but she was a delightful person and was always fascinating and interesting to be around.

For some reason she took a fancy to Jim and me and invited us often to dinner at her home. The dinners were very formal with the women in evening dresses and the men in tuxedos. Mrs. Doyle had a servant who served at table, so the formality continued. I always liked going, not only because the conversation was good, but also because her wing of the house was where Francis Scott Key had had his law office and where *The Star Spangled Banner* had been written. It gave me goose bumps to think of the things that had been said and done in those chambers over the years.

After dinner was served, we always retired to the drawing room. She placed herself on a small stool with her back to the unlit fireplace with a low table in front of her. The table held what she always referred to as "the Baltimore silver." It was comprised of a coffee pot, creamer and sugar bowl. All the pieces matched and they were made by one of the famous Baltimore silversmiths during the Eighteenth Century. The workmanship was exquisite with delicate *repoussé* work over the entire surface of each piece. The coffee always tasted wonderful and I'm sure the silver had something to do with it.

*　　*　　*

Father belonged to The Annapolitan Club, a men's organization devoted exclusively to the pleasures of life. Luncheons, card games, billiards, and reading, along with good conversation and good liquor, were the mainstays. I'm sure that there were other things that the men paid attention to, but it was primarily a typical men's club. To this day it has not accepted female members although two or three times a year female guests are entertained at evening parties. Father thought that Jim should belong and put him up for membership when he was still a Midshipman sometime during 1955. He was duly accepted and is still a member. I always thought it rather amusing and rather nice that my grandfather, Dr. Washington Clement Claude, my father, Walton Runnells Read, and my husband, James Allen Dickey, all belonged to this somewhat biased, but nevertheless pleasurable, local club that they all enjoyed.

*　　*　　*

One spring we decided to have a family party. Since our house couldn't handle hordes of people, we elected to begin in the front yard under the shade of a huge maple tree with drinks (whiskey sours by the pitcherful) and appetizers. Jim secured the off-duty services of Dean, the steward, and one of his fellow workers, so that the serving of the drinks, the cleanup and so on would go smoothly. Inside, we set up bridge tables and chairs in every nook and cranny we could find with the main courses set out on the dining room table and the condiments on the buffet. The house was air conditioned by this time, so everyone could cool off inside.

The main menu was a bastardized version of beef curry that Mother and Father learned from British friends in China during their time there. It is easy to make, very filling and quite appetizing to look at. The curry is beef, onions, curry powder, and other seasonings that eventually become a thick, tasty stew. There is rice, of course, and the best part is a huge selection of Westernized condiments to sprinkle over the top. Rather like the *riijstafel* I have mentioned previously but without all the odd and peculiar things. Most Americans like this version as there are, among other items, chutney, sieved hardboiled egg, crumbled crisp bacon, plumped raisins, chopped red and green pepper, peanuts, fresh grated coconut and chopped scallions—everything familiar and safe.

One of my elderly aunts kept trying to figure out how Dean fit into the family. She never did get it straight. After the guests had departed Dean couldn't help but remark that he had never seen so many little old ladies and gentlemen put away so many drinks. The pitchers were filled time and time again. The party was a success.

*   *   *

In August of 1970 when Jim's tour in Washington was over, he was ordered to the Naval Academy as the Financial Advisor. He was offered quarters within the Academy grounds on Porter Road where most of the residents were Captains. However, as a Commander, he felt that it would not be prudent to live there. Also we had not finished the renovation of the house we were living in and it was not rentable in that condition.

*   *   *

Just one week later Father died of a massive heart attack. His funeral was held in the small chapel at the Naval Academy. Jim wrote and gave the eulogy and I quote it below:

"We are here this morning to pay our respects to Captain Walton Runnells Read, affectionately known to all as Tubby.

As each of you recall memories of Tubby, remember him in each of his roles:

As a naval officer he gave devotion and service to his country.

As a husband and father he gave love.

As a friend he gave sincerity.

And to all, he gave a sparkling sense of humor and gay happy music.

Remember then, if you will, that Tubby brought to each of you a little more joy and happiness."

*   *   *

I have always thought that to be a beautiful tribute to my Father.

Father in his Captain's uniform, probably taken sometime in 1947.

*   *   *

There followed a difficult few years. On one hand, Jim loved his job and we both loved the activities and social life at the Academy. On the other hand, Mother hated living alone and kept needing more and more care. Eventually she had to go into a nursing home and died eight years after Father in March of 1978. I am virtually sure that the cause of death was a broken heart, although the death certificate says something else, of course. Mother and Father had been extremely close and she just simply couldn't do without him.

*   *   *

During this time Mark and Alix graduated from St. Paul's Lutheran School, which was an elementary school, and went on to Severn School, a private institution, ten miles or so north on the road to Baltimore. This was thanks to Irene and Ralph who paid the tuition. Mark and Alix seemed to like it as they both did well academically, and Alix particularly liked the sports. She was the first female inducted into their Sports Hall of Fame. Only a year or two before Mark and Alix enrolled did the school begin taking girls. Before that it had been a preparatory school for young men wanting to go to the service Academies. Jim Evans prepped there before he entered the Naval Academy.

Since Annapolis is virtually surrounded by water, we sent Mark and Alix to Severn Sailing School where they not only learned how to sail, but honed their swimming skills as well. Swimming and sailing were just two of the things that were vitally necessary for them to know if they were to live safely in Annapolis. In addition, of course, they had a good time at the school. They enjoyed the other young people and as well as the parties and other activities.

Also, during this time Mark became a bicycle racer and a very good one, winning the Maryland-Delaware time trial championship two years in a row.

He and Jim would drive to the races weekend after weekend while Alix and I remained at home. Our noses were a little out of joint, so I found a very inexpensive tour with British Airways to London for a week and off we went. She was thirteen and duplicates of the trip became the "coming of age" trip for Alix's girls too when they became thirteen. Sort of a Christian Bat Mitzvah, if you will.

Our time in London was primarily spent looking at the new "mod" clothes on Carnaby Street, (of course, buying a few things for Alix), visiting Mme. Tussaud's Wax Museum, the Portobello Road antique market, Westminster Abbey, the British Museum and eating, eating, eating. The Tower of London is an incredible building with much too much history surrounding it for anybody to absorb. Alix enjoyed the Crown Jewels and the Beefeaters in their colorful medieval uniforms, but was hideously embarrassed when we arrived at the Armory where she saw Henry the Eighth's suit of armor with an enormous extension to allow plenty of room for his private parts. We also had tea at the Ritz which was unbelievably elegant, and which became part of the coming of age trips of the future. The tour also included tickets to five different plays, which we liked, although Alix, out of modesty, refused to attend *No Sex, Please, We're British* which I understand was just a light comedy. One of the plays starred Peter Ustinov's daughter, who was an excellent actress. However, I never heard of anything she did after that. Perhaps she confined her work to the UK.

Norma and John Collier, along with son, Adam, invited us to go to Bath for a day. (Norma and John were not yet divorced.) It is an interesting place to spend some time, but the city was far overshadowed, in Alix's eyes, by the fact that we were driven there in some sort of snappy sports car (I don't remember the make. It may have been John's old Lotus). She took one horrified look at the speedometer and gave me a hard poke in the side when she saw it register over one hundred miles per hour. They also took us to dinner at The Anchor Inn, a delightful old, old pub on the Thames embankment. Alix was secretly pleased that she could maneuver her fish knife better than Adam.

We located Gennaro's Restaurant, which Jim had discovered when he was in London as a Midshipman, and found it had the best food we had yet eaten. We went there several times. On one of the evenings Alix chose an outlandishly large slice of chocolate cake from the dessert trolley. The waiter asked her if she wanted thick wonderful English cream or thick wonderful English chocolate sauce poured over it. She sat there dazed, looking from one pitcher to the other and simply could not make up her mind. The waiter did it for her by pouring lots of each over her cake. Incidentally, our tea at the Ritz was no slouch when it came to desserts, all delicious.

At lunchtime one day we were wandering in the Fleet Street area looking for Dr. Johnson's house and stumbled onto an ancient pub called The Cheshire Cheese. It was too incredible to pass up, so we went in for lunch. So far our diet hadn't included much salad, so when I spied a listing for chicken salad on the menu, I ordered it thinking in terms of cut up chicken, a little mayonnaise and celery on top of glistening fresh greens with some sliced tomatoes. I was wrong again—it was a plate with half a small roasted chicken on one side and a few dismal lettuce leaves lying limply on the other side. Foiled again. However, the pub oozed antiquity and was a pleasure to be in.

At one of the antique markets we saw a Chinese export ware punch bowl dating from about 1850. It was in perfect condition and I drooled myself silly over it. Eventually my resistance evaporated and I bought it. The seller wrapped it carefully and placed it in a used cardboard box that had once held apples. For some reason, the airline allowed me to take it aboard the plane as carryon, but it did not fit in the overhead bin above the seats and it would go only halfway under the seat in front of me. Therefore my legs straddled it and I smelled rotten apples for the entire trip home. It was worth it. I have loved and cherished that bowl ever since.

*   *   *

While we were living at Cherry Grove, I belonged to a cooking group at the Naval Academy. It met nine times a year during the fall and spring. Seven of those times, the wives prepared the food, sharing recipes and sampling the dishes at noon with no husbands in attendance. (Some of the recipes I acquired are still favorites.) On the remaining dates, we met on a Saturday night and the men prepared the food. I will never forget one particular evening. The men decided to have an Hawaiian *luau*. However, no one lived in a house where the yard could be torn up to make room for the pit to cook the pig in, so they compromised and used a regular kitchen oven. The only problem was that the pig was too big to fit into one oven. Talk about ingenuity—they cut the pig in two through the middle and roasted the front half in one participant's oven and the rear half in another. When the two pieces were reassembled, the cut was much too visible for their taste, so they unearthed some Christmas tree lights, wrapped them around the pig over the scar. They lighted the string somehow and gleefully carried the glowing pig into the dining room with great ceremony accompanied by much applause.

*   *   *

For some childish reason, I thoroughly enjoyed dressing up as a witch with a pointy hat, black lipstick and all the trimmings at Halloween to greet and frighten the trick or treaters who came to the house. The door squeaked loudly and quite eerily. As I slowly opened it, I would screech something which terrified the little ones to their great delight. I would then, of course, hand out candy and everyone was happy. I did it for a number of years and eventually children who came as tiny tots were growing up and were bringing their little brothers and sisters. It was great fun. Jim's dad, Ralph, did not know of this tradition. As a great fixer-upper, he located Jim's oil can and put a quick and emphatic end to the squeak in the door. We were all somewhat upset, but by that time Mark and Alix were off at college and Halloween wasn't celebrated quite that faithfully any more.

*   *   *

Several months after the fall of Saigon in 1975, I was talking with a friend who mentioned that she in turn had a friend who was looking for housework for a Vietnamese evacuee who was living at her home. The Vietnamese woman's name was Nga Thi Cao. She had two children with her—a girl, Linh, of about eight years and a boy, Phong, of about six. She had worked in Saigon for an American colonel (the friend's son) who helped her get out when the city fell. However, three extra people in the house were just too much and she had to find Nga work so that she could be on her own financially and have her own place to live. I agreed to try her out.

She arrived a few days later with both children and promptly made them sit under our kitchen table and not move. Jim was on leave that week to work on renovating the house so he was home and needed lunch. I took one look at the three Vietnamese, scoured the refrigerator for vegetables and made a huge stir fry and a big batch of rice sending everyone out to the picnic table to have lunch under a tree. Fortunately, Jim still spoke some Vietnamese, so the children, Nga and Jim had an Oriental lunch with some conversation. Afterward Jim gave the two children a tour of his garden. The children were comfortable with him and his limited Vietnamese and chattered like magpies with him. Jim thinks he may have understood at least two percent of what they were saying.

I learned later that they hadn't had any Oriental food or rice in several months, so it had been a good idea—especially the rice. I'm not sure about the Vietnamese language, but in Thai you don't ask someone if they have already eaten, you ask them if they have had rice yet. That clearly indicates how important a part of their diet rice is, and I'm just glad that particular day turned out the way it did.

Another problem was that Vietnamese people are very clean and shower two or three times a day as the Thais do. The woman they were living with wouldn't allow this because of the water consumption, which made Nga and her children very uncomfortable.

That was the beginning of a very long and satisfactory relationship. Nga asked me to call her ChiBa, which I understand means second daughter or sister. However, she would never call me anything but "Madame." I'm sure that was because of being raised in a former French colony. She secured several other cleaning jobs and eventually moved into her own apartment. I helped her with innumerable forms and papers over the years both for herself and for the children. We paid her, of course, to clean our house and she also watched our rental properties when we were overseas or out of town. She also taught me to cook some Vietnamese dishes, and always made Mark and Alix their favorite pork barbecue stuffed buns, called *bao*, whenever they were home on visits from school.

ChiBa in our newly re-done kitchen at Cherry Grove Avenue holding a platter of newly made *baos*, sometime in the late 1970s.

As the years went on ChiBa bought herself a car and furniture for her apartment. Her children went on to college with a car each. Linh kept her name, but Phong changed his to Tom. He went through the Army ROTC program at his college and was eventually commissioned a Second Lieutenant in the Army and married a little blond American girl. Linh became an executive at State Farm and also married an American. ChiBa opened a mutual fund account with Jim's company and always added to it each month accumulating a sizeable nest egg. It never ceases to amaze me what people can do if they are willing to work hard.

*　　*　　*

At Severn School, Alix made friends with a girl named Estalena Corey. Her mother, Jane, opened a cooking school in West Annapolis. Estie had come to our house for sleepovers and knew that I cooked Chinese food. She told her mother about it. Jane and her business partner, Phoebe Bender, asked me to teach at their school. I eventually taught a course in simple Cantonese cooking. I received a small amount of money for the work, but in turn I could attend any of the other classes I wished. Some of the guest instructors were the wives of foreign officers stationed at the Academy. I remember taking classes in Italian and Viennese cooking which were great.

One afternoon while I was at the cooking school, the Australian Exchange Officer arrived to pick up some sort of catering order. He was very prim and proper, not smiling, and being very official. The weather was warm and he was wearing his white summer uniform. I helped by carrying a few things to the car, waiting while he stowed them. As he bent over the trunk his uniform became taut over his rear revealing the wildest most colorful under shorts I had ever seen. I guess even outwardly formal Australians are exuberant underneath. (Maybe he was related to one of the Aussies we met at the Cockpit Hotel in Singapore.)

Phoebe taught classic French cooking and was an excellent instructor. I truly believe that that was the time when my food experiences in Europe slid into place and a true appreciation of what I had eaten all those years ago came into focus.

During that time Wan Li, the Premier of the Chinese Province of Anhui, came to Maryland as a guest of the Governor. He was primarily interested in the Eastern Shore chicken raising methods and wished to inspect them. There was no place on the Eastern Shore to house him and his large entourage, so he was accommodated at the William Paca House, an Annapolis colonial building that had been restored and was used occasionally for guests of the state. (William Paca was one of the Maryland signers of the Declaration of Independence.) I was asked to cook for them. I prepared breakfast each day as well as several dinners. In spite of being a tremendous amount of work, it was also quite a bit of fun. Jim helped me and we did a good enough job that we were on television and had our "fifteen minutes of fame." Two Baltimore television stations each did a short "article." The kitchen was incredibly small so that with the camera crew, as well as Jim and me, there was no room left to fall down.

The look on the Premier's face when he found out that I was a woman was worth everything.

My cousin, Billie, who had also been born in China, told me that my mother was writhing in her grave at the idea of my being a "cook" for a Chinese, but I had a good time and am glad I did it.

Sometime that year we decided to have a cocktail party with Chinese egg rolls as the only food. I was surprised at how easy it was to organize. By that time the house had been finished to our liking and the kitchen was very bright, cheery and pleasant, even spiffy (if I'm allowed to use that word again), with lots of red (my favorite color) accents. I made several enormous batches of egg roll filling, setting them near the stove. Then I filled my deep fat fryer with oil, heating it to the proper temperature. I filled and assembled three egg rolls at a time, frying them together. As I finished each batch of three, Jim cut them into bite size pieces and put one roll and some dipping sauce on some antique Chinese plates that I had inherited from Mother and Auntie Lila, passing them to our guests. Most Chinese restaurants in today's world fry egg rolls ahead of time, so that when they are served they are not at their best. In fact they are downright nasty. I will never forget Henry Barton, an older friend of ours who had worked for Standard Oil and lived in China for a number of years. I truly do not know how many he ate. However, the number he consumed, as well as his enthusiasm, were very flattering to the cook.

*   *   *

As you have no doubt observed by this time, I am very fond of flowers and plants. I received a stupendous present sometime during 1974 when Jim and Mark built me a greenhouse. It was a twelve foot glass-to-ground building in a typical greenhouse shape with flat ends and curved sides. However, its capacity was increased by placing it on a three foot tall foundation of brick that matched the house. It was entered from a door just off the little study near the living room and also had its own door at the far end which led to the outside so that supplies and so on could be brought in without going through the house. It was heated in cold weather and had adjustable shadecloth to control the heat in summer.

Jim built all sorts of storage drawers under the benches; there was an easy mess proof watering system; and all in all, I really enjoyed it—especially on a cold winter day when you opened the door from the house, sat on the little steps, had a cup of coffee in your hand and inhaled the green and growing smells around you.

A kind and generous woman named Hildreth Morton owned and ran a small commercial greenhouse in Davidsonville, a small community south of Annapolis. She specialized in geraniums for the summer and poinsettias for the winter, but had many other plants for sale. She hired me to work several days a week during the school year. I could leave early to be home when the children came home from school. Although married to a judge and really quite ladylike most of the time, she totally broke me up one morning when she told me not to "fuck up the blossoms" when I was repotting a plant and inadvertently got water and dirt on the flowers.

Through this experience, I learned how to pot seedlings, propagate other plants and to see how a greenhouse is run. It certainly helped me run my own and I still thank her. There were several other women working there who became friends. Most of them were older than I and have since died, including Hildreth.

One afternoon Alix and I were standing at one end of the kitchen looking out over the backyard at the group of trees that Petie had expected the Japanese to come through to "get" her. We were discussing something innocuous while watching the build-up of some dark rainclouds. Suddenly, with no warning whatsoever, a huge jagged bolt of lightning hit a large branch about halfway up the tallest of the trees. There was a ball of fire, lots of steam, an immediate clap of thunder, then pelting rain. We were so startled that we couldn't move.

After the storm was over, we went outside to investigate and found that the lightning had superheated the sap of the tree which made the bark separate from the trunk for its entire length. In a few weeks it was obvious that the tallest and stateliest of the trees was dead. What a shame.

By that time Jim had finished his tour at the Academy and was back in Washington. He retired from the Navy in November of 1976. Because he had prepared himself for another career by attending Johns Hopkins University at night to become a Certified Financial Planner and to acquire the necessary licenses and so forth, he retired on a Friday and immediately opened his insurance business the following Monday. His broker/dealer was Western Reserve, which he found good to work for and with. His office was located in a building on Francis Street in downtown Annapolis, which we had bought. I also worked in his office as secretary. It seemed at that point that we were settled in Annapolis for the foreseeable future.

Jim at his office desk in our
building on Francis Street in
Annapolis, probably taken in
early 1977.

The author at her desk in our
building on Francis Street in
Annapolis, probably taken in
early 1977.

*   *   *

Irene's health became worse and worse. She eventually died in 1977 of heart failure after a lengthy illness. There were many trips back and forth to Kansas and consultations with many doctors, but in the long run nothing could be done for her. Alix, who was only sixteen at the time, had truly loved Irene and was extremely upset at her death. So much so that she ran off during the funeral service, and we had a hard time locating her.

*   *   *

By dint of great enthusiasm and hard work, Jim qualified for the January 1978 company convention after only six months in business instead of a full year. It was to be held on Maui, one of the Hawaiian Islands. Still bitten by the travel bug and not having been able to travel much in recent years, we decided to go to the convention via San Francisco, enjoy Maui with the other qualifiers and then continue on around the world.

The following is an account of our trip and reflects the experiences we had traveling eighteen years after our Bangkok days, but thirty years earlier than I write this memoir. Things do change over time.

On Friday, 6 January 1978, Mark drove us to Friendship (now Baltimore-Washington International) Airport and we caught the plane to San Francisco. We checked into the Beverly-Plaza Hotel, which we had enjoyed in prior years (now very modern and awful), on Grant Street just outside the Chinatown gates. At that time it was a Japanese hotel. Our room was on the top floor and very nice—at $25 a day. We then went out walking in Chinatown taking in the sights and smells. We had a drink at The Iron Horse (now closed, to our sorrow) on Maiden Lane and looked into shop windows. We then went back to Chinatown for dinner at the Hunan, a small hole in the wall on Kearny Street.

The next two days were spent going to familiar haunts, doing much walking and also much eating. On Sunday, we had *dim sum* and then boarded our plane for Hawaii. Bad headwinds made the flight excessively long and we missed the connection in Honolulu to Maui and had to take a later one. After arriving in Maui quite late and tired, there is nothing like having the Chairman of the Board meet you in person and chase down your luggage for you.

After attending the required meetings the next day, Jim and I headed for downtown Lahaina, the main city on Maui. We ate lunch in what looked to be a beautiful restaurant right on the water with a big tree growing in the middle and all kinds of sparrows pecking up crumbs. However, the food was really nasty. As a matter of fact, all of Lahaina was nasty. (I was reminded of a meal we had at a famous Thai restaurant in Honolulu one time. We ordered a dish that included pineapple. When it arrived, we discovered that the pineapple was actually out of a can. Imagine that in Hawaii.) We did tour the Reverend Baldwin's missionary house and found it interesting to see how people had lived in the tropics in the previous century. The Hawaiian woman who showed us around was knowledgeable and charming. She also recounted the severe dope problems in the islands and how their welfare program was bankrupting the state. (Sounds all too familiar.)

Back at the hotel, we changed clothes and went down to freeze at cocktails near the sea. We went to a "First Timers" meeting and reception where we were given white carnation leis. Then led by torch-carrying and conch shell-blowing Hawaiians in costume, we were all escorted to gather with the others. The buffet was extravagant and the show afterward quite good. The next few days were filled with meetings, dinners, sightseeing and, best of all, whale watching. We were lucky and saw quite a number of whales—two even swam under our boat.

January fourteenth we left Maui and flew to Hong Kong via Tokyo losing the fifteenth to the International Date Line. We stayed at the Luk Kwok Hotel, on the back side, which butts up against some tenements, so we were rudely awakened in the morning by a very early rooster doing his crowing in earnest. The waiter in the *dim sum* dining room made arrangements for us to go into the kitchen early the next morning to watch them cook. I was able to see the chefs rolling and working with the dough for three different kinds of *dim sum*. It was especially interesting to see how they folded and pleated the *shiu mai*. I had wanted to learn how to do that for a long time.

It is really quite easy to do. You simply gather up a small ball of the filling you have made, being careful not to squeeze it too hard or you will toughen it. Then you place it in the center of a round dough wrapper that you have either made or bought. At that point you pinch the wrapper carefully around the circumference, making small pleats. This leaves a ruffle around the top, which you fill with one green pea and a small cube of carrot for garnish. It is now ready to be steamed and enjoyed.

The next few days were spent walking around Hong Kong, shopping, eating and having cocktails in the rooftop lounges of some of the better hotels. The view, as always, was spectacular and not to be missed. We also browsed in wonderful antique shops. Both of us entranced by everything we saw.

Thursday we flew to Singapore. That city is always a treat. Barbara and Dale Hardy, friends from Annapolis, were living there. Dale was walking on air. He worked for Sikorski Helicopters and had just sold two of their luxury "choppers" to the Sultan of Brunei. They invited us to their apartment for drinks and then took us to dinner. Their lovely apartment was on the top floor of a building in a residential area and their rent was $1300 per month—in US dollars. (An absurdly high amount at that time.) They drove us out to dinner on the East Coast Highway to one of the special seafood restaurants. We had chili crabs, and vegetables prepared in the Nonya style with a little bit of ground meat sprinkled through it, and deep fried crisp squid. We enjoyed them—the dinner *and* the Hardys—very much.

We had to check out the Raffles Hotel. It was still in deplorable condition. The Long Bar was simply disreputable. On one of our excursions along Orchard Road, we stumbled onto the Salvation Army Headquarters, which were located in the former home of a wealthy Chinese merchant built in 1885. It was lovely, but in need of repairs to the tile work around the roof. There were a number of tile animals parading on the peak of the roof line which were almost like animated cartoon characters—simply charming. One of the officers, who was from Canada, spent an hour showing us various parts of the building and discussing the problem of repair and maintenance with us.

On Monday, 23 January, we flew to Bangkok on Singapore Airways, always a great treat and a great experience. As we rode into town from the airport we couldn't get over the changes in Bangkok. Much construction was already completed and much still under way.

After a great deal of difficulty, we finally located Sangob. Since a telephone number stays with the house, Jim called and reached a Thai woman who was living in Sangob's old house. Jim claims he got a charley horse of the brain talking with her since he had to recall his long unused Thai language skills. Talking on the phone without benefit of sign language and frantic hand gestures is hard. Fortunately the Thai woman had Sangob's new phone number and we eventually got in touch with him. He and Krishna drove down to the Oriental Hotel where we were staying and we all went out to dinner together. The Oriental was strikingly beautiful. I have never been in a hotel that opulent and that well maintained and appointed. Our room was just as lovely—huge bath, couch, chairs, table—but the best part was an unimpeded view of the river to the north without the sun shining in.

On Wednesday we rose very early and drove to Ken and Ella Dilks' home which was south of Bangkok. It took about three hours. Ken had been Jim's office manager at the Navy Exchange when we lived in Bangkok, and we were anxious to see him and Ella again. On the way we stopped in Pattaya, a beach resort on the east coast, and couldn't believe the changes. It was quite developed. (When we went there in 1962, there was nothing but sand and a few wooden shacks for rent. During that earlier visit, we had been caught in a violent storm in a small boat that very nearly capsized. I'm still not sure how we survived.) The Dilks' home was very attractive and it was obvious they had worked very hard on it. It is surprising how quickly trees grow. Their yard was just sand ten years ago and now it was lush. Ken laid 30,000 bricks around the house in different areas for patios and walkways. He used slender Thai bricks set on edge and the effect was quite handsome. I also checked out Alix's orchid. It was in bloom and doing very well.

We were offered cheese for lunch which definitely didn't thrill Sangob and Krishna. A far cry from the luscious Oriental food available and what Sangob prepares. On the way back to Bangkok, we went off the main road into BangSaen to a special place on the water where Sangob bought some weird looking shrimp-like creatures and some vintage *nam pla*, as well as some other types of fish. We also stopped at the market and got some sticky rice cooked inside large hollow pieces of bamboo, which I thought quite tasty. In addition, we bought all kinds of dried clams and fish, most of which were to be eaten as snacks, especially with beer.

On Friday we called Alix in the States via satellite and couldn't believe that the connection was so clear. It was as though we were calling across town. We ate Shanghai noodle soup at the Red Door Bar on Patpong Road, an old haunt of Jim's. We asked if I could go into the kitchen. The answer was "No." We found out why—no kitchen. The bartender had obviously gone next door to a stall and bought for five baht what she sold to us for twelve.

We then hired a taxi to take us to some places we wanted to visit. By some miracle Charoen was at JUSMAG. He looked wonderful, had married and had two daughters. I failed to get his address as I thought he would be coming to the restaurant the next day. However, he didn't and we again lost touch.

Our house on *Soi Klang* was occupied by a Burmese woman who let us come in and look at everything. The horses and buffalo were gone, and the duck farm also. The front of the house had been remodeled and my favorite *lantom* (frangipani or plumeria) tree removed. *Lantom* has the most tropical floral fragrance there is, and the configuration of the flower's stem makes it fit perfectly behind your ear so that you can pretend to be a Polynesian maiden, if so inclined.

Amara, one of the women who had worked for Jim, organized a luncheon at the Red Stone Restaurant for us the next day. It was excellent. We had *dim sum* with several other dishes. It was exceedingly kind of her to have arranged everything. However, it was somewhat sad to see how many of the people wished for the Americans to return and had jobs that obviously were not as good as before. Sangob in particular was really hurting financially.

After several additional days of visiting, chatting, eating and generally enjoying ourselves, we left Bangkok on January 31. A number of people accompanied us to the airport and again it was sad to leave Thailand. The relatively short flight to Columbo, Sri Lanka, (Ceylon) didn't leave until ten thirty at night so we arrived at our destination in the dark of very early morning. The drive into town was depressing as we saw many homeless people sleeping in bus stop shelters and wherever else they could find cover.

We woke up rather late the next morning and found that the Galle Face Hotel was indeed an old fashioned British colonial hotel right on the beach. High, high ceilings, overhead fans, palm trees and rattan furniture upholstered in white linen all added together to make it reminiscent of the days of Empire—not to mention the sparrows nesting in the lobby. They also serve the most delicious cold lobster possible. We had seen one being served the evening before. It looked so tempting that we had one sent up to the room for our late lunch. Unfortunately, half a lobster arrived for the price of a whole one, so there was a bit of an emphatic one sided discussion on Jim's part. We finally got the other half of the lobster, and thoroughly enjoyed it.

We went on a tour of the city with a driver who didn't speak very much English, visiting an antique jewelry shop, the zoo, a *batik* or tie-dye shop, and the Lanka Oberoi. Columbo was quite a provincial place. It reminded me very much of Merida, Mexico. Probably quite pleasant if you lived there and knew people. We also went to the Pettah district of the city, which was the bazaar area. It was unbelievably filthy. I got a cookbook in English at Cargill's department store. I had to ask the clerks for help regarding some of the definitions and terms because the translations were wonderfully bizarre. For example, a *chundu*, which holds about a cup, is an old Prince Albert tobacco can that has been squeezed into a roundish cup shape. A *hundu*, which is a fraction of that measure, is the same Prince Albert tobacco tin in its original flat shape.

I also bought a book written by an Englishman, a civil engineer sent to Ceylon to build roads in the eighteenth century. He stayed for fifty years and obviously loved the country and the people. At retirement time, of course, he had to go back "Home" to England, and the last chapter is pretty sad in that he missed everything, the cold climate was ruining his health and he had little in common with his new neighbors.

On Wednesday we rented a car (an Impala) and a driver (Mohammed) to drive about seventy-five miles into the interior and up (1600 feet elevation) to Kandy. Sri Lanka is very tropical and very lush. We passed terraced rice paddies, tall coconut palms, rubber trees, cashew nut trees, tea plants and many things we didn't recognize. Stopped at both a tea plantation and a rubber processing plant. Enjoyed seeing everything but was amazed at how you are "*rupeed*" (their currency) to death. Each time we saw someone doing something, from tea man to rubber tree cutter, it cost something. Hard to add it all up.

Had lunch at the Queen's Hotel (another relic from the days of Empire) after we convinced the waiter that we did *not* want the set lunch, which was pork with cabbage and sounded inedible. We asked for exactly what the staff was eating. He brought a good rice and curry which suited us well. It was rather an amusing lunch as many of the kitchen staff stood around and watched the mad foreigners eating their type of food with great relish. Everyone had a fine time.

Kandy must have been quite lovely at one time. If you use your imagination, you can erase all the dirt and neglect and make it seem the way it was. However, it was now a sorry sight. Mohammed wasn't waiting for us after lunch. Although we didn't worry about it then, we should have. We walked around by ourselves for about an hour, finally caught up with him and went to the Buddhist Temple of the Tooth and to its museum. The temple is a very holy place, quite ancient and is supposed to have a tooth of the Buddha as a relic. However, after the temples of Nepal, Thailand and India, it was somewhat bare and sterile. Even so, it was worth seeing.

We drove around the manmade lake that is the center of Kandy, and on up the mountain road, for a panoramic view and realized why it was a retreat for the British from the heat of the coast. It was lush, green and cool. I neglected to mention that we stopped at the botanical gardens on the way into Kandy and found them to be the most unusual we have ever visited. Trees of all sorts including camphor, sandalwood, nutmeg, clove, rubber, black pepper, tea, allspice, cocoa, coffee, enormous bamboo nine-inches in diameter, and heaven knows what else. The orchid house was unsurpassed. Elegant was the only word to describe it. One orchid plant actually had a fragrance similar to chocolate. The begonia house (my favorite plant) was amazing, too, and there were also double bougainvillea and poinsettias.

Later we climbed what seemed like nine million steps to see another Buddhist temple. We enjoyed the climb especially since some children came with us. They were great company until we realized that they, along with half the population of Sri Lanka, also wanted money for their escort up the steps.

When we were ready to go back to Columbo, we got into the car and mentally prepared for a harrowing journey down the mountain. On the trip up, there had been a large number of people on the highway—going to school, work and other errands, walking on both sides of the road. Little did I realize that that was the normal state. Not to mention the presence of livestock of all sorts, including big, black lumbering elephants.

We started off calmly enough but by the time we got very far, we realized that something was definitely wrong with Mohammed. He kept fidgeting and blinking, and his driving became more and more erratic. Finally he admitted that he was "sleepy." Jim told him to stop the car and he took the wheel while Mohammed collapsed in a heap on the back seat. That was when we discovered that the brakes on the left were gone and that the car pulled strongly to the right. The Sri Lankans drive on the left side of the road so the rest of our trip was one nightmare in living color and indeed as harrowing as I had imagined. The traffic was really bad and the pedestrians calmly proceeded to walk with their backs to the oncoming traffic moving not one inch even though the car horn was wailing like a banshee. As we approached the city, Mohammed finally came around enough to drive through the traffic. We went immediately to the bar and had a quadruple martini. That sounds like a lot, but they dispense the gin only in tiny portions of a gill, so it came out to about one good drink. Heaven knows we needed it. When Jim and I discussed the matter later, we came to the conclusion that during the hour Mohammed was missing in Kandy, he was probably taking drugs.

The rest of our trip home was tame by comparison. We did not have another stopover, but went through Tehran, Amsterdam and New York arriving back in Annapolis a few days later. What a great first convention trip it was.

7

SAUDI ARABIA—SAND AND CAMELS

I N 1980 HUGHES AIRCRAFT COMPANY somehow located Jim and hired him for one of his Navy specialties—inventory control. The contract they offered was too good to turn down, so he closed his financial services office temporarily and accepted the job in Jeddah, Saudi Arabia, to work with the Saudi navy on their SNEP (Saudi Navy Expanesion Program.). Not only was the salary excellent, but the leave policy was very liberal. We looked forward to many exotic trips, not only for ourselves, but also for Mark and Alix who were still in college and therefore considered dependents.

Jim went ahead to Saudi in November 1980, while I stayed in Annapolis to pack up our household goods for storage and find a tenant to rent the house. Mark was at the University of New Mexico in Albuquerque and Alix was attending Gettysburg College in Pennsylvania. It took me a while to pack and get ready but as the Saudis hadn't yet issued me a visa, it really didn't matter.

During that time I was invited to dinner by a couple we knew from the Little Campus Inn, our favorite restaurant and bar in Annapolis. He was British while his wife, an American, was a flight attendant. They both obviously enjoyed travel, but he was a fanatic about it. He schemed to get upgrades on British Air (he knew one of the executives), and every other perk he could possibly wrangle, including maximizing the use of his wife's free tickets on her airline. I accepted the invitation because I was curious about their apartment and frankly I quite liked them when he wasn't using the words "First Class" spoken with the broadest possible British "A". When I arrived, I was ushered in with much courtesy and immediately given the drink of my choice. We chatted for a while and then sat down to dinner even though it was still fairly early. He immediately broached the subject of the entire charade. "When could they come visit us in Saudi?" Today the occasional tourist can get into Saudi with special tours, but then no one who wasn't going there to work or was a dependent of a worker could possibly get in. I said as much to them and watched their faces assume a peculiar expression. Within minutes dinner was over and I was out the door.

I have often laughed about that experience. I think I was in and out of their apartment within an hour.

The packing was finally finished. I found a tenant (who turned out to be utterly horrible) and decided to wait for the issuance of my visa in London where Hughes also had an office. My British friend, Norma Collier, was living there and that, of course, was another inducement. Unfortunately by this time she and John had divorced, but I saw her often enough during that time in London to realize how unique she was and how much I truly admired and liked her. I found a room in a bed and breakfast near Victoria Station and proceeded to explore the neighborhood.

There was a pub called the Duke of Wellington around the corner which I had been told about. It turned out to be a great place—the neighborhood was safe, the people were pleasant and friendly, the food acceptable and I actually had one of Winston Churchill's daughters pointed out to me when she came in for a drink. Apparently she was a regular and went there often.

There was a young American woman living in a bed and breakfast across the street. She was in London to practice the piano in preparation for her concert debut at Wigmore Hall a month or two later. We couldn't do much daytime sightseeing because of her practicing, but we did have dinner together a number of times and I found her delightful. When she learned that I was going to Saudi Arabia, she told me the most unbelievable story about the landlord of her bed and breakfast. He had rented rooms to male Saudis who came to London on vacation until one group approached him and asked him to get them some women of easy virtue. He absolutely refused. At that point one of them then casually asked for the use of his wife. After that there were no more reservations accepted from Saudis.

To keep busy I volunteered to wait on tables at a little restaurant where society women cooked light gourmet lunches and other society women came in and paid to eat them. The proceeds went to a charity and everybody was pleased. Actually it was fun and I rather enjoyed it. Another time-filling occupation was the Victoria and Albert Museum. Their textile section is outstanding. The British never throw anything away so the textiles date back centuries. There was actually a small oil portrait of a man from the Elizabethan era wearing an elaborate lace ruff at his throat. I am not joking when I say that directly underneath the picture was the actual ruff in a display case, washed, starched and looking brand new. It seemed impossible that mere lace could be made to stick out quite that stiffly and that far, but there it was.

During this time I had not heard anything from Jim. I began to be concerned because he had always been a very good correspondent and had kept me informed about what was happening in his life. My visa finally came through and I made my way to Heathrow with great anticipation. When I arrived in Jeddah, I discovered that before Christmas he had had an upset stomach and passed out in the bathroom hitting his head on one of the fixtures. Since he was living alone, no one knew it had happened until he failed to show up for work the next day. When they entered his apartment, they found him a bloody mess lying across the bed. Off he went to the hospital where he was diagnosed with a concussion. For reasons of their own, the authorities decided it was best to keep me in the dark about his condition which accounted for the silence.

However, by the time I arrived Jim was out of the hospital and, although very thin, was much like his old self except for one very peculiar trait. Everything that I cooked for him tasted like "dirt," to quote him. Believe me, I tried my best to prepare things I knew he liked, but never succeeded in pleasing his palate for months. Years later we found out that altered taste sensations are a common symptom of concussion but the British doctors hadn't bothered to tell him. They also decided to let him "tough it out" when it came to his attacks of nausea and gave him nothing to alleviate those symptoms either. So much for British medicine.

Before I arrived in Saudi and before his accident, Jim had been taken out by various Saudi men to see some of the local sights. He and a Saudi named Boogamee Fahad got into a discussion about the relative merits of women. Jim asked Boogamee just where a woman fit into the scheme of things. The answer was incredible—just below a camel, and about the same level as a goat. Women's lib will be a long time coming to Saudi Arabia, if ever.

The naval base, where Jim worked and where we lived, was about ten miles outside the city of Jeddah on the Red Sea. Before you entered the base you had to drive through the port area. There were always delays getting through that area for one reason or another. My favorite was when they were off loading dozens and dozens of camels from Africa which would be slaughtered for meat. The animals were not the loveliest or most agile of that breed. They ran awkwardly across the road in front of the car nearly tripping over their own feet. They were amusing to watch, but you did have to erase from your mind the fact that they would soon be on somebody's dinner table.

The naval base was entered through a guarded gate and then the road proceeded around a very large shallow somewhat stagnant pond about a foot deep. The pond was the feeding ground for a huge flock of flamingos. As the car approached the pond, they rose in the air flapping their wings and screaming wildly as though the end of the world had come. They were always great fun to watch, especially the takeoff runs and the crash landings.

A camel sitting at the side of the road on the base between the gate and the housing
area in Jeddah, photo probably taken in early 1981.

The housing area sign stated quite simply 'FAMILY HOUSE". The compound
was a square around a central building which contained a library, mess hall for
the single men, space for the swimming pool, and tennis courts.

The Family House sign announcing that you had arrived at the housing area on the
base, photo probably taken in early 1981.

Jim had been assigned a three bedroom house as we expected Mark and Alix
to be able to enter the country. The house was fully equipped, down to linens,
kitchen utensils and furniture, because we were allowed to bring only seven
hundred pounds of personal belongings plus whatever we had in our suitcases
when we flew over. We were also assigned a car—a Chevy Impala. Of course

Jim was the only one to drive it as women were not permitted to do anything so macho or so much fun as drive a car. The Saudis obeyed very few traffic laws, so it was a brave person or someone with a death wish who drove into Jeddah.

The ground around the house was nothing but sand. A few people had planted *sansevieria*, and a coarse, strange-looking vine I had never seen before, plus several other peculiar plants, around their front doors. Jim knew that I loved plants, so he bought a departing couple's entire front yard and had it moved and replanted in front of our house. That was the definitive Yard Sale. Lovely present.

Just outside the chain link fence, which surrounded the housing area, were a few Bedouin living in their typical huge, low black tents and ramshackle huts with a pickup truck parked nearby. They kept donkeys among other animals. Occasionally the donkeys would wander into our compound seeking the plants in the front yards for food. They were no real problem and their owners came running after them fairly quickly herding them back home. Nevertheless, it was a bit disconcerting to find a donkey looking in your front window while chewing a mouthful of your garden.

Muslims believe that people should be buried the same day they die, if at all possible. One of the Bedouin died and was immediately buried in the sand between our housing area and the Bedouin tents. All well and good. Unfortunately, they did not bury him deep enough and some of the wild dogs found him and for a few days they dragged his arms and legs around the area eluding capture. Eventually he was gathered together and reburied to everyone's relief and we settled back into our routine.

The people working on the base were a mixed group. There were a number of Americans, including a few former naval officers, some British, and a couple of Egyptians all working in a management capacity. Since Saudis do not do menial labor, the lesser jobs were held by men from the Philippines, Thailand, Sri Lanka, Pakistan and other Asian countries. A large number of them were gay. There were also a large number of British men working at lower management levels. The mess hall catered meals for them as they were not accompanied by their wives. They usually shared housing and did not cook for themselves too often. We were allowed to go to the mess hall for meals by paying a small fee. We did that occasionally on Fridays for brunch. Friday was the day of rest so no one was working. The meal never failed to amuse me as it was so very English—eggs, broiled tomatoes, kidneys, mushrooms, non-pork sausages and some sort of undercooked meat streaked with fat that looked like bacon, but obviously was not due to the Muslim dietary laws.

The Saudis decided to re-organized the racial map of the compound putting all foreigners in one corner of the base so we had to move. We gladly left our front yard behind as we had discovered that the moisture left after we watered attracted hundreds and hundreds of the most bloodthirsty mosquitoes imaginable. It was better to have just plain sand than endure their nasty bites. We, too, had a Yard Sale.

```
"YARD" SALE!

Jim and Lila Dickey are selling every plant
in their front yard tomorrow, Friday, 9 Oct.
starting at 8:00 a.m.  They are in Quarters
B-164-1, across from the O&M Supply ware-
house, with the wooden fence.  Since they
will be moving next week, everything goes,
and the prices can't be beat!  C'mon over
and bring your own containers, please.

        *********       *********
```

Sign announcing our genuine Yard Sale,
photo taken the latter part of 1981.

Speaking of water, that indispensable commodity was supplied by a desalinization plant on the Red Sea run by people from Jim's company. I don't really know the actual process that they go through in its entirety, but it is my understanding that they take all of the salt and other impurities out of the water. What is left is bland and tasteless and you really wouldn't want to drink it unless you had to. At that point they start putting chemicals back into the water until it reaches a taste level that everyone likes. They certainly did an excellent job, because that water was some of the finest water I have ever drunk—truly excellent.

The daily schedule was somewhat odd, but pleasant. The men worked six days a week having Friday, the Muslim holy day, off as I mentioned. They left fairly early in the morning for work, but came home for lunch as there was no cafeteria or other place to get food at the office. In the mornings, if a wife wanted to go into town, she placed a cardboard plaque in the window and the ladies' bus, driven by an exceedingly pleasant and patient Sri Lankan man named Kassim, would stop and pick her up. Unless one of the women on board the bus had an urgent errand of some sort, the destination was always a matter of consensus. Sometimes we went to the gold *souk* where there were a huge number of dealers offering twenty and twenty-two carat gold jewelry made in Italy for sale. The jewelry was somewhat garish, not only because of the patterns and shapes, but because the carat weight was so high that the gold seemed almost artificial due to the color. I'm a silver person myself so I didn't worry about it. However, one Valentine's Day I happened to get on the bus. It was extremely crowded and no one would hear of going anywhere except to the gold *souk*. I soon discovered why. Almost every woman on the bus was clutching a huge handful of *rials*, the

Saudi currency, as a present from her husband and was hell bent for leather to get to the *souk* as quickly as possible to spend it all on gold jewelry.

Other destinations were the very fashionable and upscale malls where wealthy Saudi women covered from head to foot in black *abayas,* (long black robes that also cover the head), would buy other types of jewelry, clothes, and especially perfume and cosmetics. No women of any nationality were allowed to work in the stores, so it was always fun to watch the Saudi women as gay Lebanese men demonstrated the cosmetics on their own hands—the men's hands, that is—showing the Saudi women how to apply mascara, blusher and lipstick. It was somewhat reminiscent of the painted hand puppets on American children's television programs.

All of the famous designers were represented in these malls and sometimes quite odd things happened. One of the American women had some Louis Vuitton luggage she had bought in Europe. The handle of one suitcase had been accidently torn off on one of her flights into Saudi, so she took it to that shop to be repaired. She didn't hear from them for a long time, so she finally went into the store to check on it. She found out that the suitcase was still broken because it was made of pig skin, and they, of course, could not import any pig skin into the country to repair it.

Another destination, and I really think our favorite, was to have Kassim take us to the Afghani *souk.* It was basically a section of town where the Afghanis lived and worked. We liked them because they had a much less stringent attitude toward women, would let us take their pictures and they had inexpensive, but colorful, rugs for sale. One of the rug dealers had his shop on the second floor, which meant of course, that we had to open the street door, part the curtains and climb up. Opening the door was no problem and beginning the climb up the stairs was all right, but at about the sixth step, your eyes began to sting and your nose was assaulted by a penetrating, vicious case of body odor. It was particularly nasty and much different from the blanket on the Thai train. I didn't think anything could be worse than that, but this was. Perhaps it was because the Thai and Afghani diets are different. Who knows. I'm sure bathing and lack thereof also had a good bit to do with it. His prices and selection were good, so we put up with it. Heaven knows it was a test of our shopping endurance.

The odoriferous Afghani rug dealer, Jeddah, photo probably taken in early 1982.

Another enterprising Afghani had a shop with two or three *tandoori* ovens, which are large open deep vat-like containers that are actually ovens. He made crescent shaped pastries stuffed with a flavorful spicy meat filling. When he got ready to cook them he slammed them against the inside of the hot *tandoori* where they adhered and where the fire was located. He let them cook for several minutes. When he took them out of the oven they were browned, succulent and tasty. The oven was so hot and he leaned over so far to retrieve the pastries that he had virtually no eyebrows—they were almost singed off, as was the hair on his arms. We always bought enough for ourselves to eat on the bus back to the base, and enough for our husbands for lunch. They tasted even better when we found a shop next door that sold icy cold non-alcoholic beer to go with them.

Another meal we all enjoyed when out shopping was *kibbe* and *tabouli*. After shopping in the *souk*, we would agree to meet at one of the Lebanese hotels nearby at lunch time. Since women were not allowed to sit in rooms where men were present, (what a sin.) the Lebanese gladly set aside a small dining room for us. The *kibbe* arrived hot and delicious, the *tabouli* cold and delicious. *Kibbe* is made of ground lamb. It is shaped like a 2½ inch long football—thick in the middle tapering to nothing at each end. The outer shell is very finely ground lamb, the filling is also lamb, but ground more coarsely with spices and some bulgur wheat added giving a nice texture. Then it is deep fried and, when well prepared, is not at all greasy. *Tabouli* is a salad made from bulgur wheat, tomatoes, mild onions, huge amounts of chopped Italian parsley and dressed with olive oil and lots of lemon juice. Wonderfully refreshing on a hot day.

When Marty Mazzola, the wife of the US Director in Jeddah, asked me if I would like to learn to play *mah jongg*, I jumped at the chance. I had my grandmother's set but had no idea how the game was played. Marty arranged with the company for a special bus to take a number of us downtown to meet with other women who already knew how to play. We learned quickly, loved the game and played often. The game became a focal point of the women's activities in Jeddah and also in other cities I subsequently lived in. To this day I bless Marty.

One noon a fierce sandstorm developed. Somehow Kassim seemed to sense that we women should all be together, so he drove up to the front doors of all the *mah jongg* nuts, rounded us up and deposited us at Clara Davis's house and we played and laughed away the afternoon while the sand pinged at the windows and seeped under the doors covering everything with a pale brown coating of dust. After the storm, he carefully returned us to our homes.

At this point I should note that very solid and deep friendships were formed. Perhaps it was the fact that we were so confined; perhaps it was that those of us who chose to go to Saudi were adventurous; perhaps it was just serendipity. Whatever the reason, a number of us have remained very close over the years. Clara and Jim Davis, Cully and Sylvia Culpepper, and Jack and Nancy Holland were among our closest friends, as well as Judie Watson. Unfortunately several people have died, but those of us left are still firm friends.

Jeddah's airport at that time was very near the city as opposed to the present one outside of town. The old airport was the channel through which people making their pilgrimage or *hadj* to Mecca arrived. This pilgrimage is one of the Pillars of Islam and is something every Muslim hopes to do in his or her lifetime. The *hadjis* (people making the *hadj*) always had huge amounts of luggage wrapped up in tarps, old suitcases, canvas bags and anything else that would hold items. They also brought food, cooking utensils, bedding, tea pots, candlesticks and other things they thought might be of use.

Some of the *hadjis* with their luggage in downtown Jeddah, photo taken in 1982.

Frequently they ran out of money and had to sell something. Because of this, a small area of Saudi shops sprang up to buy from them and then resell the items. I was fortunate to buy a box made in the shape of a dog with its tongue sticking out. It is bronze, the back opens up to hold small items. The head of the dog is much like Assyrian art work. The dog is so charming he makes you wonder where he was made, who made him and who stored what inside. The shops in this area also sold bits and pieces of Bedouin jewelry, to which I became addicted. I managed to collect several quite handsome pieces.

As an aside, when we moved to Albuquerque, I was surprised to see that many of the American Indian silver jewelry designs were similar to some of my Bedouin pieces. I asked a professor at the University of New Mexico about it. In reply he gave me a short history of the rise and spread of Islam from the Arabian Peninsula. Apparently the silversmiths working during Mohammed's time (Sixth and Seventh Centuries AD) were Jewish. When Islam began its spread across North Africa and the Moors went into Spain, the silversmiths went along as part of the movement. The Moors were not expelled from Spain until 1492, so there was plenty of time for the Spaniards to absorb some of the Moorish culture as their own and in turn take it to the New World where it migrated from South America up through Mexico into what is now our southwest. The Spanish taught the Indians the art of silversmithing and so you come full circle. No wonder some of the designs were similar.

The women named another shopping area the "*Junk Souk*" because they sold everything under the sun. Most of the items were copper with some of the silver that had been used to line the interiors of cooking and eating utensils remaining on the vessels. This made them extremely handsome in my eyes. There were big milk and water pitchers, huge platters, plates, coffee pots, spice jars, and any number of other items. We bargained fiercely for them and I have found my *junk souk* purchases are among my favorites.

My favorite dealer at the *Junk Souk* in Jeddah, photo taken in 1982.

As foreigners and non-Muslims we women did not have to be veiled but we did have to wear skirts to the ground with long sleeved shirts that buttoned at the neck. If made of cotton, it was a cool outfit and frankly kept away unwelcome stares from the Saudi men. It was best to be covered anyway. Jim and I saw two French women beaten about the legs with rods by the religious police because the women stupidly wore tight jeans with sleeveless blouses. I did wear an *abaya*, the long black coverup, when I went with Jim to Riyadh, the capital. It is a much more conservative city and the protection of the veil was welcome.

It seems almost strange, under those circumstances, but we were allowed to wear typical American swim suits at the pool on the base. This is probably because the American and British women were the only ones who used the pool in the daytime and it had a big fence around it to keep prying eyes out. After lunch the pool became the center of our lives. We enjoyed going there, chatting with friends, playing *mah jongg* and generally socializing. Unfortunately, most of us did not use enough sunscreen and are now paying the price of millions of freckles and brown spots with a smattering of skin cancers.

Our walk from the housing area to the pool took us past a sandy spot where Korean men were building a small mosque for the use of the Muslims on the base. Near the sidewalk was a little "nest" of discarded construction material. Deep in the nest, out of the sun, a mother dog was raising her puppies. We all took a great interest in them and thought them playful and affectionate. One day they were gone. After a great deal of discussion and thought, we realized that they were being taken care of by *Korean* men and were probably on someone's dinner table. People over the world do eat strange things.

One afternoon three Saudi women arrived at the pool in their long heavy skirts and veils. One of them could not resist the lure of the sparkling water. She jumped in sinking immediately. The life guard, a Philippino man, rescued her, but had to give her mouth-to-mouth resuscitation. Her husband found her tainted because another man's lips had touched hers and divorced her. (How's that for a caring husband.) Jack Holland told me later that the life guard had been hustled out of the country within a very short period of time to keep him safe. Jack also said that one day a week the pool was opened for Saudi women after dark so that they could swim for a while. The only problem was that the women defecated in the pool and it always had to be drained and cleaned the next day.

Jack was one of the more adventurous of us. He and Nancy had worked in Iran before coming to Saudi. Jack liked to experience everything that he could of local life. This included voluntarily going to watch a beheading. The executions were held on Fridays after services in the mosque. Jack said that the prisoner was brought to an area in front of the mosque. He appeared to be lightly sedated. He was forced to kneel while someone walked around him chanting in Arabic. Jack thought it was a recitation of the man's crimes. Then the executioner jabbed the prisoner sharply in the back with his sword in order to have him jerk reflexively and throw his head up. Then the executioner lopped the head off and he fell to the ground in a bloody heap.

Nancy Holland did not like to be idle. In some fashion she secured a job with a Korean engineering firm that was under contract to construct buildings for the Saudis. The office was, of course, on the base in a somewhat secluded area so no one seemed to mind that she had the job. (Maybe no Saudis *knew* she had a job.) She and Jack wanted to take some leave, so she asked me if I would fill in for her while she was gone. I was delighted to do it. Fortunately, the Koreans conducted their business in English, were a pleasure to work for and I enjoyed my stint there very much.

One particular afternoon those of us at the pool became really bored. We finally talked Kassim into driving us to the beach just south of the base. It was on the Red Sea and we thought in terms of pristine white sand and clear water. We were mistaken. The sand was dotted with the remains of old fires and strewn with garbage. Conch shells, which had been roasted and the little creatures inside eaten, were discarded all around the fire sites. However, what really amazed us was that the sites were also littered with dozens of empty liquor bottles that had contained every brand and every sort of alcohol known—gin, vodka, bourbon, Scotch—you name it, the empty bottles were there. Since alcohol of any and every sort was banned from the country on religious grounds with dire consequences for disobeying, this really surprised us as these were Saudi picnic sites. Men only, of course.

The British nurse used to tell us incredible things about the Saudi women. Most of the stories derived from the fact that the women had so little education. For example, as a birth control measure they packed themselves with salt. The men butchered chickens, goats and other small animals in the kitchens as the floors were terrazzo with a drain in the center to catch the blood. A sheet of steel was brought into the kitchens, placed on top of the electric stove burners and used as a grill. The heat destroyed the burner units, popped the porcelain off the stove and probably created God knows what sort of fumes. It certainly created a fire hazard. When the Saudi men were transferred and the crews went in to clean the houses for the next tenant, they found the mattresses soaked with blood, urine and feces. Most of the appliances and all of the linens and mattresses were burned. As I said, most of it was lack of education, but it was nevertheless somewhat appalling.

One Saudi man was keeping chickens in his house. He had to go away for a few days, so he locked the chickens in the bathroom with the water in the tub slowly trickling. The chickens got into the tub, but couldn't get out. There were about eighteen dead birds floating in the tub with a few live ones out of the tub. The drain was plugged with rotting chicken feathers and chicken poop which caused all sorts of flooding and other problems. Very expensive cleanup.

*　　*　　*

Jim and I usually did our grocery shopping in the evenings when he could drive us into the city. There wasn't much to do, so it made a nice evening out and we could have dinner at one of the many restaurants. During our time in Jeddah, we went to Indonesian, Chinese, Korean, Indian, Lebanese, French and Thai restaurants, plus others I don't remember. Once when Jim was in Riyadh on business, he ran into the Thai *maître d'* from the old Oriental Hotel in Bangkok with whom he was well acquainted. Since they both recognized one another, there was an extra level of good food and service that evening.

When we first arrived in Jeddah, we went to a few open markets to buy fresh vegetables and items like eggs that were imported from Africa. The egg purchases were truly weird. You had to buy an entire flat of eighteen eggs. You brought them home and set them on your kitchen counter next to the sink. You then proceeded to wash off the chicken poop and feathers adhering to each egg. Then you filled the sink with clean water. After all eighteen eggs were washed and soaking in the sink, you removed and threw away any that were floating or had cracks in the shell. Then you drained the sink and washed the remaining eggs again. You were extremely lucky if you had ten eggs at the end of that process. As you can no doubt imagine, we did that only once or twice and after that always bought them at the grocery stores. Infinitely more expensive, but worth it.

The grocery stores were amazing. The Saudis wanted only the best. Therefore filet, prime rib and steaks of all sorts were readily available, but you couldn't find any bones for soup or stew meat because that was too plebian and lowly, so wasn't imported. A grocery store called Happy Family, owned by a French company, offered some of the most beautiful veal in the world. It was a pleasure just to look at it, let alone eat it. The cheeses and *patés* were also outstanding.

Jim unloading groceries at the front door of our house on the base in Jeddah, 1982.

If you wanted some brown sugar, you could certainly buy it, but the box it was packed in when it came from the States generally had a recipe for glazed ham on the side. The Saudis had actually used a black magic marker and inked out the word "ham" wherever it appeared in the recipe on every package in the grocery store. Although Muslims do not eat pork, what level of mentality dictates the obliteration of even the word "ham"?

The grocery stores sold an assortment of bottled and pasteurized Austrian grape juices (both white and red). Next to the juice were five kilo cans of yeast and ten kilo bags of sugar. Jim couldn't resist the hint, so he started making wine. He got a recipe, the proper equipment and started to work even though making wine was illegal. Each batch filled about eighteen of the juice bottles, which, with their heavy construction and bale tops, were perfect for aging the wine. We preferred his red and every once in a while he came up with a batch that was "vintage." He gave Ernest and Julio a real run for their money. On one occasion, the Philippino who was pushing his grocery cart to the car openly asked him how he made his wine and wanted the recipe. Jim mumbled wildly, told him he didn't know what he was talking about, hastily loaded the car and drove immediately home.

Jim bottling wine in our kitchen in Jeddah, photo taken in 1982. Vintage, of course.

The Saudi equivalent of our moonshine is called *sidiqui*. We never knew who distilled it, but if you spoke to one of the Koreans, he would secure a bottle for you. We also did not know what grain or other material was used as the basis of the liquor. Judging by the taste, camel dung is not too far off. However, it had high alcohol content and many people drank it mixing it with tomato, pineapple or orange juice, coke, lemonade or anything else that might kill the raw, almost brutal, taste of the *sidiqui* itself. We tried it once, but it was too nasty to drink a second time.

For some reason I can't remember, Jim decided to make homemade bean curd or *tofu*. He found the ingredients at the grocery store. They consisted of soy beans and vinegar. He also found a 9 x 11 x 2 inch open plastic container into which he drilled holes spaced about an inch apart. Then he cooked the soy beans with some water until they had disintegrated and the resulting liquid was thick and smooth. Then the magic began. He poured a certain amount of the vinegar into the pot and the mass began to coagulate. Quickly he poured it into the plastic container which was in the sink. The water drained out of the carefully drilled holes. As he smoothed the curds with a spoon, pushing them down slightly, they formed a beautiful block of *tofu*. It was quite truthfully the most flavorful *tofu* I have ever tasted, but I've never been able to get him to make it again.

On nights when we were at home, we often turned on the short wave radio and listened to the BBC (British Broadcasting Corporation) as the television was bad beyond belief. After we had listened to the news, we tuned to our favorite program, *The Brain of Britain.* It was a quiz program lasting half an hour. If we got one question right during the entire program we felt we had really accomplished something. The British educational system, as well as their frames of reference, is so different from ours that it was almost ridiculous, but great fun to listen to.

*   *   *

On 13 June 1982, King Khalid died and the country went ballistic. The Saudi hierarchy closed the country. Literally. If a commercial airliner was within Saudi air space, it could continue in and land. If not, it had to divert to an alternative airport. All non-official telephone and radio service was stopped. All businesses were closed, banks didn't function, grocery stores weren't open. The military bases around the country were closed. The television screen showed a red rose while a *mullah* or holy man shouted passages from the Koran.

Since the king had died in some undisclosed city outside the capital, they televised the return of the corpse to Riyadh as the Muslim faith dictates that people be buried as soon as possible after death. The king was wrapped in an Oriental rug. As it was removed from the plane, the body flopped about in an almost comic manner. The following day it was reported that the body was placed in a praying position in an unmarked grave pointing toward Mecca. After the brief viewing of the return of the body, the television programming concentrated on a marathon of minor princes and officials kissing the cheeks of King Fahd bin Abdul Aziz, the newly proclaimed king. After three days, the Kingdom returned to what the Saudis would proclaim as normal and Westerners would still describe as different.

Occasionally a notice would be circulated through official channels that a "C" service was going to be held at such and such a place. We understood that it was a religious service of some sort. However, none of us was particularly into that kind of thing, so basically we ignored it. Upon reflection, after we left Saudi, I began to ask questions. No one could tell me whether the "C" stood for Christian, Catholic or even Church. Jim did remember that the man who conducted the services was British and had six or seven passports under different names. None of us knew how he got around the country, how he was sponsored or how he got into the country in the first place. The only conclusion we came to was that he was an exceedingly brave man completely dedicated to his calling.

Our patio, which we never used as it was so hot, had a small storage room attached. The door did not fit snugly at the bottom. In fact it had a sizeable gap. I was looking out of the window that gave onto the patio one morning and couldn't believe my eyes. Something white and furry with bright beady eyes was looking out from under the door. I couldn't imagine what it was, so I immediately went outside to investigate.

The animal turned out to be a tiny Saudi kitten. His fur was very short and close to the body so that he looked almost bald. He seemed healthy and friendly, so I picked him up and took him into the house. Jim immediately named him "Fang" as he looked anything but fierce. He more than made up for any deficiencies in appearance by showing us how intelligent he was. Within hours he could open every type of door we had in the house. We, of course, fell in love with him.

Unfortunately the story does not have a happy ending. While we were on leave one of the Philippinos from Jim's office was to come to the house and take care of Fang. He completely ignored the cat and put him outside. A neighbor took him in for a few days, but discovered that Fang was eyeing their bird suspiciously. They put Fang back outside, and with no water or food, he wandered away. Unfortunately when we returned we could find no trace of him. I do think he was the most intelligent cat we have ever had.

Jim and one of the Saudi Lieutenants, Omar el Essa, had discussed food a number of times. Omar recommended a certain variety of spinach imported from Africa that was especially good. He offered to take us to the market one evening to buy some and we gladly accepted. He brought his wife along. I don't believe I have ever felt such pity for anyone before and been so frustrated because I was unable to do anything about it. Omar had married her when she was seventeen. He had been immediately ordered to Norfolk, Virginia, for training with our Navy. He took her with him as his tour there would be three years. He gave her a sports car which he allowed her to drive. He allowed her to wear American clothes, no veil, and astoundingly allowed her to wear a bikini at the pool. She learned English and had many American women friends. In other words, she led the life of a normal person in a normal town.

Then the blow fell. Omar's tour of duty in Norfolk was up and they had to return to Saudi where he was stationed at the Jeddah naval base. The evening we went out together Omar drove and Jim sat in the front seat. She and I were in the back seat. To make conversation Jim began asking her questions about their time in Norfolk. However, convoluted Saudi chauvinistic manners dictated that Omar translate the question into Arabic (even though she knew English), she would answer in Arabic and then Omar would translate it into English for us. Obviously no direct conversation between opposite sexes was permitted. It was a difficult and somewhat ridiculous evening, and got worse when we were invited back to their house.

Their living room had been furnished with many rugs and cushions and the two men went there immediately for refreshments. She and I were relegated to one of the bedrooms where she immediately sat on the floor and burst into tears. After she could talk coherently, she got out photo albums tracing everything they had done in the States which she showed me with more tears. Since their return to Saudi, she had had a baby, and I must say the little boy was beautiful. He was brought into the room by an exceedingly elderly Sri Lankan woman. The foreign workers are recruited, given passports, arrive in Saudi, have their passports taken away from them and, since an exit visa is necessary, can return home only at the discretion of the person who hired them. It was a form of slavery for both women of that household. The young wife's predicament was made even worse by having no household chores to keep her even slightly busy as the Sri Lankan woman did them all. She was further frustrated by the fact that although her family lived in Jeddah, she had no way to visit them unless Omar drove her and this he refused to do. I have never felt so helpless in my life. What's more I had the feeling Omar didn't want her to talk with me as I never saw her again.

*   *   *

The abominable exit visa affected all of the women on the base in the sense that many of the men had to go back to the States on Saudi navy business—to Washington or to one of the supply centers in Pennsylvania leaving their wives in Saudi. For example, we still had two children in college. If something had happened to either of them, I would not have been able to leave Saudi Arabia to aid them because my husband was not in Saudi to give me permission to go. I always felt, however, that the American Director would somehow have been able to get me a visa. Fortunately I never had to put it to the test.

It became necessary for me to make a trip back to Annapolis to check up on our properties. I broke the journey in London and was intrigued by the number of young women with scarlet, blue or green hair. I was still religiously wearing grey flannel suits looking quite straight and business-like. Petie was going to meet me and I thought I would give her a jolt by arriving in a prim grey flannel suit with green hair.

I went to a beauty salon and discussed the matter with one of the women. By that time, I was beginning to have quite a bit of grey in my hair. I was told that they had a wash-out green dye for the brown part of my hair, but that the green dye would stay in the grey until it grew out. This was because the grey hair was much more porous and would absorb and hold the green dye. The conservative side of my nature took over, and I didn't do it, much to my subsequent regret. I would love to have seen Petie's face as I got off the plane.

Coming back into Saudi after having been abroad was another test of one's patience. The customs formalities were lengthy and your luggage was opened and closely scrutinized. If, for example, you had been to one of the European capitals, including the Vatican, and bought an art book showing nude statues, you could expect the pictures in your book to be completely obliterated by heavy black magic marker over the offending body parts or confiscated entirely or the pages torn out. Censors would also sit and go through any magazines you may have brought with you page by page. They then proceeded to mark out unacceptable advertising or articles.

On one of Jim's trips back into Saudi he had something of a "double whammy." He was sitting in an aisle seat on the plane just watching what was going on and noticed a Saudi woman get out her tea making paraphernalia and squat in the middle of the aisle to light a fire to heat the water to make the tea. She was totally oblivious to the danger of a fire aboard an airplane. Jim called the stewardess and that was soon straightened out. A little while later an old man went toward the rear exit and pulled the door curtain around him and squatted down. Obviously he didn't know that airplanes had toilets as he was preparing to defecate in the aisle. Fortunately, this was also taken care of by another call, this time to the male cabin attendant. Again, a lack of education.

The duration of the flight from London to Jeddah was about six hours. If you were smart and had good bladder control, you used the toilet as soon after departure from Heathrow as you could because as time went on, the Saudis trashed the restrooms. It is quite upsetting to discover that wash basins have been used as toilets.

*   *   *

One restaurant we enjoyed was Lebanese. It served the many small dishes that make up a *mezze* or series of small plates of food. We loved the various choices. Perhaps the best part, for me anyway, was the fact that the owner would go into the men's room (there was no ladies room), chase all the men out and stand guard at the door while I used it. Along with the Afghanis, the Lebanese men were relatively understanding and courteous.

Occasionally we would go to a *swarma* shop. *Swarmas* are similar to Greek *gyros* or pita bread filled with meat and other food items. However they are much better. The meat is fresh lamb, seasoned and cut into strips about four or five inches long and one to two inches across. Not ground meat packed together as are American *gyros*. One end of each strip of meat is impaled on a two to three foot vertical skewer. The meat is pushed down and fanned out making a column. The skewer slowly revolves in front of a hot vertical charcoal fire roasting the meat perfectly. When you order a *swarma*, the attendant takes a warm Saudi version of pita bread, opens it and inserts slices of lamb cut from the roasting skewer, pickles, onions, a sauce made of yoghurt and dill pickle juice and hands it to you with a flourish for you to eat on the spot, which of course you do. In the process the juices stream down your hands and wrists. It is worth every paper napkin you use and every drip on your clothing.

Sometimes on Friday, the day of rest, we would get in the car and just drive around the city. There were all sorts of strange statues in the centers of the roundabouts—one was a huge iron bicycle two or three stories high. Another was a gigantic thumb sticking up in the air. I surreptitiously took photos of some of them as cameras were not allowed. Wish I had taken more.

The gigantic bicycle statue right in the middle of downtown Jeddah,
photo taken in mid-1981

On one particular Friday drive, we decided to find a *souk* we had heard about that was out in the middle of the desert on the outskirts of the city. After much searching, we finally found it. It was more like a flea market and was held on a street in what would, at some improbable date in the future, be a residential area. The streets were paved, and there were street lights, electricity and water—all waiting for something to happen. In the meantime, some enterprising Pakistanis imported items from their country and offered them for sale. We bought a hand carved end table and are still using it.

Building residential areas could be a tricky proposition. Someone erected six huge apartment buildings with at least sixty apartments in each building, probably more. Presumably the foreign builder had a Saudi partner as was mandatory, and presumably the partner looked over the plans at one point or another, as would be prudent. However, somebody made a serious error and the buildings were never occupied. They had failed to provide two sets of elevators—one for men and one for women, and of course, the two sexes could never get in the same elevator together.

We had heard about an area where clay pots were produced which could be used for plants. I was still missing greenery since I had had to give up my front yard with its mosquito attracting foliage. We decided to find the maker of clay pots. When we finally located him, he turned out to be a short, old, wizened Yemeni man hard at work. He placed a flat round piece of wet clay on the sand. He had no potter's wheel. In order to make the pot, he had to bend at the waist and *he* walked around the flat piece of clay pressing down the ropes of wet clay duplicating the movement of the wheel with his body. It was like going back to the Stone Age.

Taif is a small town about an hour and a half from Jeddah up the escarpment. It was something different, so we went there several times. The highway to Taif is also the route to Mecca, the holy city. Some distance out of Jeddah, there is a huge road block somewhat reminiscent of Berlin's Brandenburg Gate. It is *not* a temporary roadblock. All non-Muslims are diverted to a road to the right of this gate. The presence of armed guards insures that infidels cannot and do not go to Mecca. We would eventually arrive in Taif after a circuitous route and were always pleased we had avoided contaminating Mecca.

The Saudis seem to feel that since both Mecca and Medina, the two most holy cities of Islam, are in their country that they are special guardians and must keep infidels from defiling the cities. On one trip back into Saudi from London, the plane had to land at Medina for some reason before arriving in Jeddah. We were herded into the terminal like wayward camels and placed under armed guard. We were then subjected to all sorts of searches of our persons as well as our luggage. I very nearly had a fist fight with the woman assigned to me. She was just simply obnoxious in every way. Believe it or not, I ended up screaming at her not to touch me and to get away from me. Very loudly.

It was interesting just to walk around Taif, see the shops and watch what was going on. I saw a Saudi buy a striking looking piece of Bedouin jewelry from a hawker. The purchase was unusual to say the least. The man walked up to the vendor's table, picked up the jewelry, threw down some Saudi *rials* and walked away. No words were spoken. I nudged Jim. He chased the man down and eventually bought it from him after negotiating by writing the offers and counter offers in the sand with a stick. Arabic numbers are easy for a foreigner to learn because all the car license plates have our numbers written just below the Arabic numbers, so that when you are driving around town and get bored with the scenery, you just start memorizing. We bought a clock with the Arabic numerals on it and have it in our kitchen. While people very seldom ask about it, occasionally someone does a double take and wants to know what it is.

Earlier I mentioned that one of the perks of Jim's job was the liberal leave policy. We decided to visit Cyprus. I had failed to do research into the island and did not realize that it had many Greek and Roman ruins. It wouldn't have mattered anyway but I was irked with myself. Both Jim and I were aware that the island had been fought over repeatedly by the Turks and the Greeks and had ultimately been divided by the United Nations into two halves, one half for each nation. At the huge steel dividing wall, which was painted the blue and white of the UN colors, there was an area where you could look over and see the city of Famagusta, on the Turkish side. It was intact. The buildings had not been damaged, but it was totally deserted—no people, no cars, no animals—just buildings. It had been a very popular resort, and it seemed almost criminal to see it in that condition. On subsequent trips to Turkey, we have seen entire villages formerly inhabited by Greeks that are now standing empty and forlorn. No Turks will move into them.

The Cypriots drive on the left and as we walked, also on the left, along the waterfront our first evening there looking for a place on the beach to have a beer, Jim stepped off the curb into the street to get around a big tree. He did not look behind him because his reflexes and right hand driving experiences told him to look to the left for danger as we do in the States. He was hit by the left front fender of a big black Mercedes Benz. He flew into the air and landed on his back with the curbstone perpendicular to his spine. Everyone rushed to pick him up and I spent minutes pushing them away and shouting at them not to touch him. The driver of the car got out and added to the confusion with great grunts and arm waving. We later discovered that he was a deaf mute and probably shouldn't have been driving. Finally an ambulance came. I breathed a sigh of relief thinking that at last someone had arrived who knew what to do. I was mistaken. They picked Jim up like a sack of potatoes, threw him into a Volkswagen van converted into an ambulance and set off at a hideous pace over bumpy cobblestone streets, jarring every bone in his body.

The emergency room was ghastly. The walls were glistening with moisture. Peeling paint revealed mold and God knows what else underneath. There were two stone slabs in the room. Jim was put on one and the other slab already held a woman. Since there was no wall or curtain between the slabs, Jim heard her death rattle when she died unattended. The nurses finally arrived and removed the body. Soon a huge man appeared who announced in flawless English that he was a doctor. After hearing of the accident, he decided to visit the hospital.

Jim was then taken to the X-ray room which was like something in a World War I movie. No protective screen for the technician who probably glowed in the dark. It also wheezed and shook as it was taking the pictures. Fortunately, the X-ray showed that Jim had three vertebrae with vertical fractures which had not displaced. While he could have been crippled, he survived but to this day has a very temperamental back. He keeps his chiropractor in business.

The doctor was a very kindly man. He had been educated at Johns Hopkins University in Baltimore, so we trusted him when he said that there was nothing they could do for that kind of fracture. He continued by saying that there were only minimal services at the hospital and it would be better if we were to go back to the hotel as the hospital relied on the patients' families to bring in food, change linen and other chores. We went back to the hotel where at least the bed was clean and Jim could get some decent food. As the accident had happened the first evening of our leave, we spent most of the rest of our vacation at the hotel. Jim still complains that he was hit before he had even sampled a local beer.

The following day we were visited by the woman who owned the Mercedes and the deaf mute driver, who was her brother. We were asked if we would go to the police station to file an accident report, which we agreed to do. We made the trip to the station very slowly, carefully and painfully. When we arrived we discovered that the police chief was her cousin. With all the relatives involved, we quickly realized that it would be fruitless to file a claim against the driver. Talk about a stacked deck. The trip back to Jeddah was also made very carefully and painfully but Jim survived it.

*   *   *

During the summer of 1981 the Saudis gave Mark and Alix visas to come into the country. Their reactions to Saudi were somewhat mixed. All of us were glad to see one another and we spent a good deal of time catching up on all the news.

That first night Alix came roaring out of her bedroom claiming that something was living in her closet. Actually there *was* something alive in her closet. It was the yeast in the jerry can of grape juice that Jim was turning into wine. He had run tubing from the jerry can into a jar of water to keep out contamination. The bubbles popping and gurgling were what she had heard. Ernest and Julio were about to be outdone.

We showed Mark and Alix around the compound where we lived and then did a tour of Jeddah. Of course we had to visit the *souk*. It was summer and the weather was incredibly hot. (The temperature on our enclosed patio at the rear of the house registered 127 degrees Fahrenheit one afternoon.) The *souk* was almost as bad. The kids bought some bootlegged music tapes, visited the gold *souk* and generally wandered around. It was the first and, I hope, only time I have ever perspired so profusely that it ran into my eyes and stung them badly. While in the *souk*, I bought a small hand tied rug about two feet by one foot—it was just right to put on a table under a potted plant. It was made of camel hair and had a slight odor. I washed it and then set it out on the hot patio to dry. Several hours later I looked out of the window and couldn't quite believe what I was seeing—the rug was black and moving. After investigating the situation I discovered that the entire rug was covered with flies. I don't know if they were after the water I had washed the rug in or if the smell of the camel hair attracted them, but whatever it was, the rug went into the trash just as soon as I could get it there.

Shortly thereafter the four of us left for Bangkok to stay with Sangob and Krishna in Thailand for a while. They had three children quite close in age to Mark and Alix. The five of them got along very well and even though there was a language problem, we all had a good time. Of course we took the children to see our old house. We knocked on the door, introduced ourselves and were politely invited in. The Burmese family was still living there and still spoke very good English, so we were able to communicate. Alix remembered nothing as she was too young when we left, but Mark remembered the floor plan of the house and which room had been his bedroom.

As our vacation proceeded I was extremely interested in what they did and did not remember. Both of them remembered smells and certain foods. Their play language had been Thai for six months after we returned to the States, but now neither of them could remember any Thai other than hello and thank you. Mark had had a smattering of Chinese from the children next door and a little Laotian from Daeng. However, I think that knowing another language as a small child helps in the sense that both of them took French in high school and college and did extremely well. Later on I met Mark in Paris for a week. He had to do all the talking as I know no French. I was extremely proud of him as *no one* sneered at him in any way or asked him to repeat what he had said during the entire time we were there. Quite an accomplishment.

We showed them around Bangkok, going to all of the important temples and major sites, and of course the floating market as well as the Sunday market. Naturally there was a visit to Jim Thompson's shop, but as I mentioned earlier, it had changed drastically.

We were staying with Sangob, Krishna and their three children, making a total of nine people in the house, all beer drinkers. *Singha* beer was much in evidence and toward the end of our trip I went out into the yard to soak off some of the beer labels for my collection. The bottles had been saved because they are recycled and the bottle man had not been by since we arrived. *Singha* comes in cases of twelve *very* large bottles. As I looked around the yard, my chin dropped and I was completely astounded. There were sixteen empty cases, and twelve times sixteen comes out to one hundred and ninety-two large bottles of beer. Even better than the old drinking song about ninety-nine bottles of beer on the wall.

I tried to help Sangob with the cooking as there were so many people. He had already made delicious dish after delicious dish. One of the more curious ones was a fish curry. The white fillets of fish, plus a number of seasonings and other ingredients, were placed in a large bowl. I was given the bowl and a huge heavy spoon and told to stir it for a long time in one direction *only* while Sangob was working on other dishes. I did this until I thought my arm would drop off. It took nearly an hour. By this time the fish had disintegrated and the seasonings were well incorporated, believe me. When Sangob considered the job done properly, he made some small containers out of banana leaves just large enough for one serving each. The curry was placed in these and then steamed. After steaming, the curry had become somewhat solid like firm custard. At dinner time each person placed the curry on his plate after removing it from the banana leaf container and then poured a tangy sauce over it. It really was sumptuous. Like an exotic savory dessert.

The author filling banana leaf containers with Sangob's fish curry, photo taken during the summer of 1981 in Thailand.

After Thailand we went on to New Delhi, Agra with its Taj Mahal, Gandhi's burning *ghat* or funeral platform and other favorite tourist destinations in that part of India. By that time school was about to start and it was time for Mark and Alix to return to the States. So off they went and we went back to Jeddah.

*   *   *

Sometime during the winter we decided to go to Damascus and fell in love with Syria and its people. The *souk* is almost as good as the Grand Bazaar in Istanbul. You enter through a huge iron arch. After that the walls are of stone while the ceiling is of metal with skylights for illumination. This arrangement protects shoppers from the weather, but the building is obviously ancient, seemingly in a state of imminent collapse, with bullet holes showing here and there. The shoppers beneath, blithely intent on their errands, pay no attention. As we walked, or tried to walk, into the crowd it was obvious we were still in the Middle East. The body language was different. People edged up closely and the "crowd etiquette" was not the same as ours. A personal "zone of privacy" does not exist in the Middle East.

As we walked further into the *souk*, the passageways narrowed, the shops became less Western and to our eyes increasingly more interesting. A little old man tugged at my arm and we were on our way to a small shop built on several levels and crowded with merchandise. After browsing through all manner of handcrafted items, including beautiful Bedouin dresses encrusted with hand needle work and handmade Oriental rugs, we emerged on the top level. A flat terrace beckoned to us and we stepped out into a garden of potted plants nestled against the top of one of the Corinthian columns of the Roman temple situated just at the end of the *souk* and just before the walls of the mosque. We sat in the shade of the marble acanthus leaves of the column in Middle Eastern splendor looking at everything and sipping small cups of mint tea. The idea of living

211

every day rubbing shoulders with exquisitely carved Roman columns took my breath away.

Visiting the Ommayad Mosque is a sobering experience. It is old, enormous, serene and perfectly beautiful. It houses the tomb of John the Baptist and some magnificent Oriental rugs.

Interior of the Ommayad Mosque in Damascus, Syria, photo taken sometime in 1981.

We collected our shoes (one cannot enter a mosque wearing shoes) and went out the rear gate which leads immediately into the old living area of the city which is a warren of alleyways, shops, homes and crooked streets worthy of the Arabian nights. At that time the pedestrian lanes in the old part of Damascus were packed earth. It had rained and the lanes were not muddy, merely damp. Jim was walking ahead of me and with each step he kicked up a little bit of dirt. I was, as usual, watching to see that there was nothing to stumble over and saw something other than dirt fly off his shoe. I leaned over, picked it up and discovered that I had found a Roman copper coin. Incredible luck.

The doors of the houses were generally made of wood with a touch of ornamentation or carving. Many had door knockers in the form of a graceful human hand elegantly poised to tap. I am told that they are another version of the Hand of Fatima, which keeps away the Evil Eye. The part that actually knocks should be smooth as fruit, not knobby as a stone or it won't be as effective in keeping it away. (The Evil Eye is an old superstition going back centuries. Many cultures believe in it and have innumerable amulets to keep it from doing harm to animals and people, especially children. The Hand of Fatima and a blue glass "eye" are favorite items to ward it off.) We were content to wander aimlessly, enjoying just being there. We finally realized that we were hungry and stopped in a small shop tucked carefully between two houses. It sold primarily *fool mademes* which we ordered. They have that dish in Saudi, too, and we always referred to it as "foul madams." It consists of dried beans cooked in a special pot of bulbous shape over a slow fire. Then it is served with a sprinkling of lemon juice and olive oil, with romaine lettuce and bread. The bread is round, flat and thick and at the same time textured and full of bite and flavor—perfect for absorbing the liquid from the beans.

While we were in the *souk*, a tall hawker with a magnificent moustache sold us a set of six wine glasses that were among my favorite possessions. They were crude hand blown glass and sat on their bases cockeyed. They were full of bubbles and rings and undulations, so you knew they were handmade and wondered who had blown them. We took them back to Saudi with us and used them for our evening libations. Unfortunately they were somewhat fragile and now there is only one survivor.

We had dinner one evening in a large restaurant with many long tables. It reminded me somewhat of a college dining hall. The food was fine, but the main attraction was the vast number of cats allowed to roam freely about the room. The Syrian cats have shorter, squatter bodies and much shorter legs than our cats and are quite handsome. These cats knew enough not to get up on the tables, but they haunted the area near our chairs and under the table. Of course, we threw them scraps of food. What agile, quick animals. I don't think a single morsel ever hit the ground. They were always caught in mid-air. The cats were so hungry you didn't dare feed them by hand or you'd be minus a finger.

While we were walking in the city, we saw many other cats. One of them was a beautiful black and white male. His face was primarily white, but under his nose was a small rectangular splotch of black. He was immediately christened "Adolph" for Adolph Hitler. The resemblance was uncanny.

Aramaic, the language of Jesus, was still spoken in several small villages, among them Maaloula. The Lord's Prayer was first written in Aramaic, as well as the Book of Daniel. We searched for someone to drive us there and ended up with a nice man who was a college professor and owned a pickup truck. There was room in the cab for only two people, so in male dominated Middle East, Jim sat with him. In all fairness, I must say that it would have been unseemly for me to be in the front alone with him so I didn't really mind too much when I was very ceremoniously helped into the open back of the truck and discovered I would have several old tires as a seat. He drove carefully and I didn't bounce too much. To make up for this, he stopped at the side of the road and picked some fresh figs for me that were really delicious. Maalula was interesting and I'm glad we went.

We were staying at a Sheraton, believe it or not, and found it to be very soothing to our psyches after Jeddah. The rooms were lovely and the beds soft and comfortable. There was a bar, a good restaurant and we felt extremely civilized.

The daughter of the resident manager was a lovely child of approximately ten years of age. She had the poise of a grown woman and beautiful manners. She was charming to us and to all of the patrons and we enjoyed several lengthy conversations with her. Of course, we never saw her after that trip and I often wonder what happened to her. I hope she is well and happy.

*   *   *

The following summer, that of 1982, Mark and Alix along with Alix's roommate, Janet, and Janet's brother, Roe, wandered around Europe together visiting Spain, France and Italy.

They ended their trip in Vienna, where Janet's father was stationed at the Embassy. Jim and I flew to Vienna from Jeddah to meet them. This trip was less hectic since we boarded the plane at the new airport, which was almost surrealistic in appearance roughly resembling gigantic white Bedouin tents. We had to wait an hour to board and, as it was Ramadan, the month of fasting, there was not even a cup of coffee to be had. As soon as we were out of Saudi air space, alcohol was served on board the plane and we imbibed. The trip was longer than we had anticipated (seven hours). Even though Jim made wine, we hadn't had any strong liquor for months and I'm afraid that Jim and I arrived in Vienna in an alcoholic haze. We weren't helped by the fact that we had dinner with Janet's parents and drank more wine.

The next day, after lots of aspirin did its work, we took a cruise on the Danube to Melk, which was interesting. The day after that we walked around Vienna exploring the shops, visiting the cathedral, viewing the statue of Maria Teresa, and catching another glimpse of the Cellini salt cellar. Then Demel's, that fabulous restaurant I went to years ago, called loud and clear and we went for lunch. It was not quite as I remembered it, but close enough, and the food was even better. They had added a few savories to their menu. Mark had Beef Wellington, I had Galantine of Veal, Alix had *moussaka*, an eggplant dish, and Jim a beautiful ham and cheese quiche-like thing. We also ordered little open faced sandwiches. How in heaven's name we found room for dessert I do not know, but we did. They were as huge and as unbelievable as I remembered. Alix complained of a stomach ache later. I wonder why we didn't all have stomach aches.

Our next stop was Greece to introduce Mark and Alix to the Parthenon and the other wonderful sights of Athens. Our hotel was just off Constitution Square and at the edge of the Plaka or old city. At the Parthenon, the Greek guide pronounced marble and temple as mar-bla and tem-pla, both of which have become family jokes. She also told us with great solemnity that the rocks we were standing on were millions of years old. A voice from the back of the crowd said somewhat sarcastically that *all* rocks are millions of years old. Another family joke in the making. The rest of our time in Athens was spent wandering the streets, browsing in stores, visiting museums, taking horse drawn carriage rides and just soaking up the atmosphere. We all enjoyed it.

However, since our hotel was situated very near the Plaka, where numerous restaurants were located, the four of us went to one of the outdoor cafes there for dinner one evening. Things went very well at first, but after having only one beer, we were without a waiter. Good reason—all the waiters were watching a fight a few doors away.

Jim soon lost his patience about the lack of service, so he got up from the table, went to where the fight was taking place, and loudly shouted, "Stop. I need a beer." Those were the magic words. The fight stopped, Jim got his beer—and then the fight started up again.

An American in Jeddah had told us about a great place to take the kids on the island of Agistri that you reach by going first to the island of Agina via a huge Russian hovercraft. Then you proceed on to Agistri. There was no one to meet us, so Jim and Alix went off to hunt for the resort. Finally a motheaten jeep came and drove us to the club which hangs onto the side of a cliff with the rooms facing the sea. There was a disco at night and swimming in the daytime and that was about all there was to do. The meals were good and served in an area covered by a roof of grasscloth with lots of vines, oleander and other flowering plants nearby. Everything was whitewashed the stark clean white of the Greek islands and the view of the sea was superb. The meal hours were an indication of the success of the disco and the lazy days—breakfast, 9-10:30 am; lunch 1-2:30 pm; and dinner from 9-9:45 pm.

There were other young people of Mark and Alix's age at the club, which was a blessing. They swam together during the day and obviously had a good time at the disco at night after Jim and I had gone to bed. Because of the sailing lessons and experiences Mark and Alix had in Annapolis, Mark repaired a small sail boat owned by the hotel and entertained the young group by taking them out for short sailing trips around the island.

We enjoyed talking with the young people about their experiences bumming around the Aegean. Most of them were taking very cheap ferry boats from island to island. There were, at that time, three separate ferry routes. By using all three schedules, they were able to go to virtually all of the islands on a shoestring.

"On a shoestring" was the correct phrase because a number of the young people were leaving Agistri since it was so expensive. How expensive? The cost was approximately $10 per person per day which included room, breakfast, dinner and all the activities. Many of the group knew of islands which were far more reasonable. We could hardly believe it.

Then we went south to Cairo, toured the city for a few days and then we were to board one of the typical Nile cruise boats. Since it was summer and also Ramadan, there were few people on the boat and we had things pretty much to ourselves. I felt very sorry for our guide in Cairo, whose name was Moses. He was an elderly man, it was miserably hot, and the fasting and doing without water because of Ramadan was very hard on him. We found out later that he was a professor at the university—no wonder he was so good. We went to Giza to see the pyramids. Jim and I were shocked at the growth of the area nearby. Apparently the land around the pyramids had belonged to the king and was used as farmland. After Farouk was deposed, the land was sold very cheaply and people built houses on it. At any rate, the area is built up almost the entire way to the pyramids and the old Mena House Hotel was unrecognizable. There was even a sound and light show and souvenir shops. Father would not have known the area.

Perhaps I should say something about the Muslim holiday of Ramadan. It lasts a month and is determined, like our Easter, by the lunar calendar. As a devout Muslim you must fast from sun up to sun down. The fast starts very early in the morning as soon as it is light enough to see the color of a piece of thread held up to the light. The fasting includes abstaining from food, water, and sex. In the evening, the partying begins. The feasting and other festivities last far into the night. Of course, the next day people are tired, hungry and grumpy, so virtually the entire Muslim world comes to a halt for the complete month.

The Nile boat stopped at a number of temples which had many friezes covered in carved hieroglyphics. The guide from the boat, whose name was Raj, could read and write hieroglyphics. It was unbelievable to watch him write them on paper and tell us just what each character meant. He did it so quickly it was just like one of us writing English. The boat stopped at the usual places so Mark and Alix got a comprehensive look at most of the sites along the river, including Kom Ombu, Edfu, Philae and others.

Soon it was time for Mark and Alix to return to the States. I should mention that Alix had not particularly liked Gettysburg. Added to that fact, her brother was in New Mexico and we were in Saudi. So she did what every red-blooded American girl would do—she transferred to the University of New Mexico. We found out about the transfer after the fact, but it was fine with us.

Hughes Aircraft ultimately lost its contract with Saudi Arabia through sheer stupidity. The loss was due in large part from their practice of hiring people who were not qualified for the jobs they were hired to do. The Saudis quickly recognized that Hughes was clearing off all the bar stools on the East Coast of the States and Great Britain in order to fill middle management billets with warm bodies. That was unfortunate because the contract was one of the most lucrative in all of Saudi Arabia. We returned to the States at the beginning of 1983.

8

HERE AND THERE

THE NEXT FEW YEARS WERE rather odd in the sense that Jim was sent by Hughes to several different locations to work on various projects, but nothing permanent came of it. There was a year in Buena Park, California, which was pleasant and another year in Redondo Beach also in California and also pleasant. During the time in Redondo Beach, Jim organized a reunion of the people who had been involved in the SNEP (Saudi Naval Expansion Program), which was, of course, our reason for being in Jeddah. He did an excellent job of notifying people, finding housing, planning menus, and so on. However, the best part was the program he put together using bits and pieces from the Jeddah English language newspaper discussing the proper time to pray, who had left Jeddah without a proper exit visa, who first sighted the moon to announce Ramadan and all sorts of wonderful tidbits. Not to mention the severing of thieves' hands and the sinking of ships. It was a work of art.

Thief's hand severed for robbing 28 homes

RIYADH, Dec. 18 (SPA) — A man had his hand cut off here Friday after he was found guilty of several robberies. An Interior Ministry statement said that the criminal Khaled Ibrahim Al-Mis'ari, had been caught stealing in the bedroom of a citizen in Eleisha district.

The statement said that during the investigation, Mis'ari admitted to having robbed 28 homes and commercial shops. A Sharia court ordered his hand severed from the wrist. The ministry reiterated that it will strike with an iron fist to deter criminals and preserve the security of the country. The sentence was carried out at Justice Square after the noon Friday prayers here.

Clipping from a Saudi newspaper sometime in 1981 or 1982 regarding the severing of a thief's hand.

Clipping from a Saudi newspaper sometime in 1982 regarding the sinking of a ship.

It was always good to get back to the East Coast now and then, even if only on business. Fortunately or unfortunately, we spent some time in Annapolis, not so much because we wanted to, but to repair the extensive damage done to our house on Cherry Grove Avenue. It seems our tenant turned out to be a steroid crazed junkie. He was a physical fitness maniac and a karate instructor who not only terrified the neighbors, but trashed the house, including the greenhouse. He even bent the steel casement frame of the master bedroom window by hitting it with his fist. The damage amounted to a little over $8,000, which prompted us to sue him. However it was useless. He declared bankruptcy and left town owing us and others substantial amounts of money.

*   *   *

In 1984 while we were living in Buena Park, Jack and Nancy Holland, whom we had met in Jeddah, invited us to go on a tour of Russia with them in May of that year. Nancy was attending school in Arizona, while Jack was still working in Saudi. It was being sponsored and run by the Russian language department of the University of Arizona and sounded excellent. It was long before the breakup of the Soviet Union so we knew that we would be closely chaperoned by Intourist, not to mention the KGB and several other security organizations. We went in spite of potential problems and had an exceedingly fine time with the Hollands as well as having a firsthand chance to observe a Communist country.

Since we had to go to the East Coast anyway, we went to New York via Annapolis to further check up on things. A taxi (a clunker) with a young punk (another clunker) driver picked us up where we were staying to take us to the airport. We took a small plane to JFK where we were to meet Nancy. She was quite late and we were concerned. After she finally arrived, we boarded the Finnair flight to Helsinki where we were to meet Jack who was coming from Jeddah. However, we waited on board the plane for three hours before it could take off because there were a number of thunder storms in the area and over one hundred planes were backed up waiting to take off. We were seated in the last row in the middle of the center section with no way of reclining the seats. The three hours on the ground plus the thirteen hours air time to Helsinki plus the bad seats made it one of the trips from hell. Not to mention the time we had spent on the plane from Baltimore to New York. We also spent two and a half hours going through customs and passport control when we got to in Moscow. Never have I been stared at that hard by soldiers young enough to be my sons. However, we eventually arrived at the hotel and found the room comfortable and the bed divine.

Our first dinner was at the Aragvi Restaurant on Gorky Street, which served Georgian cuisine. As we were led into the room we could see the huge table for twenty-five all set with small dishes. Each place fairly bristled with cutlery and glassware (four glasses each) along with bottles of champagne, mineral water and fruit juice. Containers of Georgian wine and vodka were placed here and there. Much to our delight there were many little iced pots of caviar which we managed to polish off as no one else really liked it. The glasses were all cut crystal, the plates made of porcelain and the caviar containers silver plated. It was a lovely table.

The dinner was quite varied—cold meats and fish, pickled garlic, peppers, spiced beans, meat in sauces, cucumbers, onion, beet and cabbage salads, skewered meats and tasty coarse bread. After dinner we walked down to Red Square. The moon was full and luminous behind St. Basil's Cathedral. At the same time spotlights played on the Kremlin and two lighted red stars gleamed on top of two of the Kremlin's towers—it was *very* impressive.

Breakfast the next morning was odd. The liquid refreshment being offered was *kefir* or fermented mare's milk. I settled for cheese and bread and some delicious non-sweet eggy custard. Actually enjoyed it. Several times during the trip we would wander into a restaurant for lunch, be given a five or six page menu, choose something and be told it was unavailable. After a while we just asked what *was* available and were usually limited to two or three choices depending upon what they had in the pantry. So much for collective farming and government planning.

The Intourist guide assigned to us was former paratrooper named Boris. He was a somewhat pleasant man who reminds me now of Vladimir Putin in appearance. He, Jim and I got along well and though I am getting ahead of my story, I do want to say that toward the end of our trip Jim drew Boris aside and asked him if he knew of someone who could use several of the sports coats and other clothing that Jim had brought along with him and no longer needed. (These were still the days when one dressed fairly decently to travel.) The answer was an enthusiastic "Yes" since Jim and Boris were approximately the same size. Jim suggested that Boris come to the room to get them. Boris was emphatic that that was not the thing to do. Jim suggested that he bring them to Boris' room. That was even more of a no-no. So the two grown men, in broad daylight, behaving like actors from a James Bond film, actually set up a "drop" in the lobby of the hotel. Jim leaving the bag of clothes next to a chair he had sat in, and Boris sidling up to the chair later to pick up the bag.

One particular day Jim, Boris and I went out together while the others were doing something on their own. Jim asked Boris a number of questions about this and that. Boris finally stopped and asked Jim, "Are you CIA?" Jim answered,

"Yes, are you KGB?" He said "Yes." After that everything went smoothly, but there were no more questions.

Ella, our local guide (real name Eleanor—it seems Eleanor Roosevelt was visiting Moscow at the time of her birth) took us on a tour of five or six of the metro stations. They are remarkable in that each one is unique. They are constructed of marble, semi-precious stones, alabaster and so on with huge mosaics and statues sprinkled here and there. Amazingly enough there was absolutely no graffiti to be seen anywhere.

After a tour of the Pushkin Museum, the capitalist came out in everyone and we went off to one of the largest *Berioska* stores which were for tourists only—no Russians were allowed. These are state run shops which have a rather large selection of merchandise with the restriction that you must pay in hard currency. *Rubels,* the Russian currency, were not accepted. Jim bought me a beautiful long strand of amber with both opaque and clear natural beads, as well as a pendant with pieces of moss and insects visible. We were both somewhat startled by the variety and prices of the bottles of vodka offered for sale. They were priced from the very expensive to the very cheap with innumerable brand options at each price level. Astonishing.

Jim standing near the *Tzar Pushka Cannon* in the Kremlin, Moscow, May 1984.

I had not been feeling well the day that Ella took everyone around the Kremlin, so Jim and I took advantage of some free time the next day and he gave me his version of Ella's tour. One of the sights is a gigantic cannon called the *Tzar Pushka Cannon* as he was the person to have it cast in 1586. It is truly enormous and the cannonballs are not far behind. It must have taken a tremendous amount of gunpowder to fire it.

The Kremlin architecture is unique, and yet you can see much Byzantine influence. The interiors of the two churches we went into were indescribable. I never realized that such truly beautiful *ikons* or painted religious images existed. They were much larger than normal and painted in deep rich reds, maroons, and ochers with the recessed space for the face surrounded in chased silver. Really magnificent pieces of art and piety. The entire Red Square-Kremlin complex is enormous and very impressive. Jack and Nancy jointed us on a walk to the area of St. Basil's Cathedral with its bright and unlikely color scheme.

Nancy Holland, Jack Holland and Jim standing near St. Basil's Cathedral in Moscow, May 1984.

We then flew to Baku in Azerbaijan where we stayed for several days. The food on the flight was ghastly, but we knew it was chicken—there were still feathers on the meat. When we landed, the passengers stood up ready to off load. The stewardess, who resembled a football linebacker, shouted something in Russian and everyone meekly sat back down again. In a few minutes the door to the pilot's area opened and the pilot and copilot strode importantly down the aisle and out the door. After that we peasants were allowed to exit.

Baku is located in an industrial and oil producing area and is not particularly attractive. However, it was one of Russia's larger cities, and, as such, we were taken there to admire it. We did attend a circus, which was extremely entertaining. Their circuses have only one ring so that you can see everything. One of the performers was a woman who had taught very unexpected animals to do very unexpected things. She made cats jump through hoops and pull miniature wagons, plus other tricks I can't imagine a cat holding still for. It was quite amazing. The finale was a pair of porcupines parading around the edge of the ring with their quills fully extended, bristling menacingly while she smiled at them. The audience, myself included, applauded wildly.

Circus performer showing off
her trained porcupines in Baku,
Azerbaijan, May 1984.

The next stop was Odessa on the Black Sea. It is a gracious city with trees lining the wide streets and many views of the water. Odessa had been completely rebuilt after the war since bombing raids had virtually leveled it. Fortunately they kept the former architectural style. We went to see the famous Potemkin Steps, the museum, a kindergarten, and several other sites. The best thing about Odessa to me was a performance of the opera *Madame Butterfly.* The Cold War was still going on then and the Russians took full advantage of the American Pinkerton's infidelity to Cio-Cio-San by booing him loudly, vehemently and often. It was as though they were saying Cio-Cio-San *Da* or yes. Pinkerton *Nyet* or no. Jim was very much amused by the fact that Pinkerton's naval uniform included a dirk or dagger hanging below his uniform jacket—strictly non-regulation in the US Navy.

A few days later we were on our way to Kiev by train. It was a pleasant enough trip but for the crotchety old woman who was in charge of the tea *samovar*. She was downright rude and it took a good bit of doing to get any tea out of her in the morning. Kiev is one of Russia's oldest cities. However, there was not a great deal to see at that time as Kiev had been badly damaged during the war.

As sort of an afterthought, we went to Tallinn in Estonia and found it to be charming. The architecture was unusual, the people cordial and the open markets interesting to visit. I must admit I was a bit upset at our hotel room as it was on the twenty-fifth floor. I always make sure I know escape routes from planes and hotels, but this one really bothered me as the stairway entrance was just across the hall from our room, but the door was locked. Twenty-five floors is a long way to jump.

After Tallinn, we backtracked to Leningrad or St. Petersburg and had a rousing finale to the trip. The Hermitage Museum is unique, fantastic and wonderful. You could lose yourself in it for days. Not only are the things on display awesome, but the building itself is without parallel. Each room and staircase is different and feature rare and unusual construction materials such as amber and lapis lazuli. The collection of French Impressionist paintings is, of course, first class. Many of the paintings we had never seen even in picture books. When Jim mentioned to our guide that the Russians had "liberated" the paintings from the Germans who took them initially, she became quite angry. However, such is the power of propaganda. About two months after we returned to the States, TIME magazine ran an exposé on these same French paintings which had been "liberated" by the Russians from the Germans, particularly Herman Goering, but which the guide had denied were stolen. Everything at that time was so strictly censored and monitored, that she probably thought they had always belonged to Russia.

Since the Great Patriotic War, which the Russians call their hard battle to turn back the German invasion and we know as World War II, the Russian people had been almost completely cut off from knowledge of the West. Perhaps Voice of America or Radio Free Europe got through occasionally, but the Russian government blocked the stations as best they could. It was astonishing how little the average Russian knew of events that had taken place in the rest of the world.

Del Phillips, the head of the Russian language department and the person from the University of Arizona in Tucson who put the trip together, related an incredible tale about some Russian academics visiting Tucson a few years before our trip to Russia.

They were given a tour of the city which included a supermarket. If you have ever seen a Russian grocery store, you know that the contrast between our stores and theirs is dramatic. Jim and I visited a few stores in Russia and saw primarily empty shelves. Some of the canned goods were root vegetables put up in glass canning jars like we use in the States for home use. Most of the lids were bulging and ready to explode. The only fresh vegetables were sorry looking cabbages and a few sprouting onions. The butcher shops reeked and were full of flies. The full shelves were those holding bottles of vodka. At the end of the tour of Tucson, the Russian director was asked for comments. To Del's surprise and shock, the director berated Del angrily for taking them to propaganda grocery stores that were set up only to impress the group. The director said that they were all lies and could not possibly be legitimate.

At these comments, Del became quite angry and took the Russian group back to their tour bus. He told the Russian director to have the driver go wherever he, the director, wanted. It was a revelation. The group saw Albertson's, Safeway and many other grocery stores as well as several department stores, pharmacies and other retail operations. The Russians returned to the University in silence, completely awe struck by such plenty.

The city of St. Petersburg itself is well laid out with many onion-domed churches and buildings. There are also the more secular things like the Astoria Hotel, St. Petersburg's famous old standby, where we had a great cup of tea. We also saw the facade (the store is closed) of the Faberge shop where the famous eggs were made and sold. Peterhof, the *Tzars'* summer palace, is as ostentatious as the Hermitage, but wonderful, and somehow you have the feeling while in the gardens that it was made just for your own personal enjoyment.

As an aside, Jim's dentist in Buena Park was Slavic, however, I'm not sure which country she came from. Jim had an appointment with her when we returned. He opened his mouth and her first comment was—"You've been drinking Russian tea." She was right. We had drunk a great deal of tea during the trip and it had stained our teeth badly. However, it was worth it.

A good percentage of the rest of our time in Russia was spent visiting museums, schools, reconstructed ancient villages, boat trips on rivers, monumental sculpture memorials, watching folk dancing and so on. On the way home we had to land in Helsinki to change planes. As the wheels touched down, the pilot announced, "Ladies and Gentlemen, we are now in Helsinki, Finland." This generated a huge and spontaneous round of applause from the passengers—all of us had made it out of Russia in one piece and were now out from under the all-pervasive feeling of control and oppression.

We had to wait a while to board the plane back to New York, so we walked around poking and peering into the shops. Finland is noted for its furs and the airport is no exception. To my surprise and delight Jim gave me a thoroughly fun, fluffy white fur jacket. It was our twenty-eighth wedding anniversary. What a great present.

Jim and the author in the Helsinki airport just after he bought the author a fluffy fur coat for their wedding anniversary, May 1984.

*   *   *

One of Jim's temporary assignments with Hughes was in Norfolk, Virginia. Since we had business needing attention in Annapolis, I stayed there while Jim worked in Norfolk and came to Annapolis on alternate weekends. After Irene passed away in 1977, Ralph and Mary were married a year later. They then moved to Chowan Beach, North Carolina, which is about a two hour drive from Norfolk. This location proved to be most fortunate for both Ralph and Jim. Ralph became quite ill and had to have a major operation. Since he wanted to return to Medicine Lodge for his last days, he and Mary returned to Kansas while Jim was left to pack up their belongings for shipment to Kansas.

Although he did not know it at the time Ralph and Mary left for Kansas, Jim discovered some financial transactions while he was packing their things which told him not to send the original of Ralph's will and their marital agreement directly to Mary. This proved to be an extremely fortunate and important decision. When Ralph died in 1983, Mary immediately hired an attorney in Medicine Lodge and attempted to break the will as well as the marital agreement. Fortunately Jim had filed both original documents with the clerk of the court and was able to preserve them for the law suit which followed. Even though Mary was well provided for, the bulk of the estate was to go to Jim. Unfortunately, she wanted it all. This was a classic case of grief immediately turning to greed.

Court cases can often become quite lengthy. In this instance, it took exactly two years to the day to close it. Some eye-opening information emerged during the numerous trips to Medicine Lodge. It was common knowledge, expressed by many people, that Mary had been stealing from Ralph and Irene for years while employed at Ralph's appliance business. This seemed to be known to everyone but the Dickey family. To compound this, it was disclosed that both

Mary and her daughter, Helen, were telling everyone that they would soon be coming into a lot of money from Ralph's estate. This whole scenario was so unpleasant and shocking that it made us virtually ill. In retrospect, it was such a shame, since Mary had been Irene's best friend, and she ultimately married Ralph after Irene's death, becoming part of the family. Irene had discussed the possibility of the marriage with Ralph before her passing, and said she had no objection provided they wait a full year—which they did. Mary died shortly after the suit was settled. It seemed dreadful that after we had all loved and trusted her that this deception had been going on for so many years and finally came to a boiling point at Ralph's death.

*   *   *

The time had come to make a decision about the future. Jim decided to resign from Hughes and return permanently to Annapolis to reopen his financial services business. We would live in a house on Duke of Gloucester Street, which he had recently purchased. The story of this house is a classic example of what *not* to do when one wants to maintain marital bliss. Jim had seen the house when it first went on the market, and since I was not there at the time, he purchased the house without my seeing it or agreeing to the purchase. I did not like the house at all. Although I had never been inside it, I had walked past it many, many times while I was growing up, and it always gave me the proverbial creeps. He has since vowed never to buy another house without my concurrence. (Smart man.)

It had been built in approximately 1703, remodeled a number of times, turned into a duplex and thoroughly messed up. There was a small garden with dead soil and too much sun to the left and a two car garage which was shared with the person who owned the other half of the building to the right. The neighborhood had a sprinkling of old houses that had been converted to offices, so parking spots were nonexistent. However, if you were a resident, you could get a sticker that would prevent your car from being ticketed if you parked longer than the two-hour limit.

At that time we had two cars. Jim's was the better car so he got the garage. When I had to go to the grocery store or had to make other trips with many packages to carry into the house, I waited until I had secured a parking place near the house, perhaps in the previous day or two. Then I would go to my car, start it and wait for Jim who had gone to his car in the garage. He would pull up behind me, I would leave my parking place, he would take it and off I would go to the grocery store. After I finished my errands, I would head for the garage, park the car and we would unload the packages. Then I would back out, go where he had parked and the whole maneuver would be played all over again in reverse. What a mess.

After living there for a while, Jim decided that he did not like the house, either. (It was haunted, believe it or not, in addition to its other deficiencies. You could just feel that it was inhabited by the miserly spirit of an old harridan who lived there in the middle part of the twentieth century and badgered her husband to death. As you climbed the stairs to the second floor, you expected any moment to see her leering down at you shaking her fist.) So we sold it to a lawyer whose office was across the side street. He bought the house just to get the garage. Parking has always been a problem in Annapolis, and since he had received multiple parking tickets during past years, he desperately needed a parking space which was not on the street and susceptible to frequent ticketing. As a businessman and not a resident, he was not entitled to a parking permit. When he found out that the house and garage were for sale, the purchase was soon consummated. He was happy, we were happy. Then a truly hilarious thing happened. The first time he tried to park in the garage, he ran into the door frame and dented his Porsche.

To backtrack a bit, in January of 1985 (we were briefly in residence at our King George house at that time) Alix and Peter Benjamin, a young man she had met at the University of New Mexico, were married. In due time, Ana Irene arrived. For some reason I could never fathom, the pediatrician didn't believe in giving babies solid food until they were quite a number of months old. Alix brought Ana to visit us when she was eight or nine months of age—still no solid food. We were living in the Duke of Gloucester house and were sitting around the kitchen table eating grapes. Ana was frantically reaching for them and drooling. Throwing doctor's orders to the winds and relying on feminine instinct, we peeled a grape and gave it to Ana to eat. I had never seen a child act the way she did. At the first bite, she started to quiver and shake and actually began to cry. She had obviously never had anything that tasted as good and was crying from sheer pleasure and excitement. So were we. Needless to say that child did not go hungry again. Jim jokes that that might be the reason Ana loves good food today—she is making up for lost time.

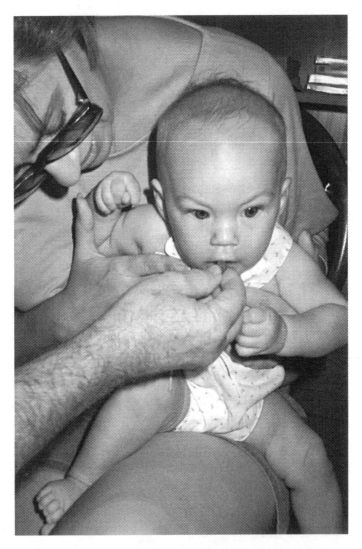

Jim giving Ana Benjamin, our granddaughter, her first solid
food—a peeled grape, in Annapolis, early 1988.

9

KING GEORGE STREET—HOME AGAIN

ONCE THE DECISION TO STAY in Annapolis had been made, we set about organizing our lives to make it simple and make it work. We moved back into the small house we owned on King George Street on the other side of town. Jim's office was set up in another building we owned on Francis Street, both of which were also in the Historic District. We could walk to and from work without moving the cars for days. Another plus was that that side of town had no offices so parking was a bit easier. At the halfway mark in either direction was The Little Campus Inn, a bar and restaurant that we had patronized for years.

It is something of a cliché to compare it to the TV comedy bar Cheers, but most of us who went there on a regular basis became drawn into the friendliness and warm atmosphere that reflected the owners, Angy and Mary Ellen Nichols. Angy, who is Greek, had also known Dr. George Basil, but in an entirely different way from my parents and me. There is a tight Greek community in Annapolis, and, of course, they all know one another. In the thirties, forties and fifties almost all the restaurants in town were run by members of that community. However, there was not a Greek doctor, so Dr. Basil filled that slot. As you no doubt gathered from his time in China that I wrote about earlier, he was always open to new experiences and a very likeable person. The Greek people, according to Angy, do not celebrate their birthdays. Instead they celebrate their name days on which they have an open house sort of affair with lots of food, drink and dancing. Dr. Basil went to these parties, and in turn held one of his own on St. George's Day. Angy told me that he will never forget Dr. Basil balancing a glass of wine on his forehead and performing the appropriate dance with great skill and even greater abandon. (Still wish I could have known him when I was an adult.)

The Little Campus patrons came from all sectors of Annapolitan life. There were lawyers, city officials, tutors from St. John's College, naval officers, business men and women, ordinary citizens and "ladies who lunch".

When patrons went to the hospital, other patrons visited them. When there was a wedding, everyone went. When someone died, we all went to the funeral. Several times a summer, a bus was chartered and we went to Baltimore for an Orioles baseball game. There were Fourth of July picnics in backyards around the city and other get togethers for no reason at all

Jim in front of the flag at a Little Campus 4th of July picnic, Annapolis, 1989.

In other words, The Little Campus was a smiling, friendly place. The bartenders, Gabe and Charlie; the waitresses, Peggy, Vernice and Sue; not to omit Patsy and Potsy, as well as other employees, including, Solomon, the cook, all helped to make it special. (Jim swears that he has never eaten a bread pudding as good as Solomon's, even though it has become almost a lifelong quest to find one.)

Many of the patrons were complete eccentrics, which just added spice to the general atmosphere. One particular lawyer in town would stop in for drinks in the evening. However, he also stopped in during the afternoon. At that time he would be attired in his running shorts and dripping perspiration. He would run into the bar for a quick Martini and a cigarette—then dash off to finish his "healthy" exercise.

Another eccentric was an older man who had diabetes and unfortunately lost the lower part of one leg. He was fitted with a prosthetic device. The wags at the Little Campus presented him with a certificate for a termite inspection to assure that his new "peg leg" would remain in good condition. He took the joke beautifully and retaliated by taking picture postcards of some of the Georgian mansions in Annapolis with him on a trip to London. The postcards slowly trickled back in the mail to the Campus with remarks like "My goodness, London looks just like Annapolis."

As I have mentioned before, St. John's College is located in Annapolis. It is very close to the Naval Academy and was only half a block from our house. It is a liberal arts college with a small enrollment and has only one "varsity" sport—croquet. There is a large grassy space at the front of the college facing College Avenue. The St. John's students challenged the Midshipmen to a croquet tournament one April. It was great fun. Everyone who could get there did so. We all sat on the lawn, sipping drinks, eating dainty sandwiches and cheering everyone on, being very impartial with our cheers. The event still takes place each April.

One year the navy coach, a naval officer and a Little Campus patron, secured an old "fore and aft" hat, a la John Paul Jones, as well as a set of ancient gold epaulets. He was splendid as he strutted up and down in his uniform exhorting his team to victory. Another year the St. Johnnies kidnapped the Navy mascot, a goat, and had him tethered to one of the trees near where the game was being played. Even if he was an American goat a continent away from Nepal, he smelled just as bad as Jim's friend from Kathmandu.

Another Little Campus patron was a tutor at St. John's. He was very gregarious, highly intelligent and amusing to be around. He always owed hundreds of dollars to various libraries in the area and really didn't care until they cut him off from any more borrowing. His house was almost sinking into the ground from the weight of the books piled here and there in every possible space. At the Campus there was a tradition of watching the TV show *Jeopardy* with the volume turned relatively low. Then when the final big question was about to appear on the screen, the volume was increased. People put their dollar bets near their drinks and wrote their answers on paper napkins. He almost invariably won.

Charlie, the bartender, was a student at St. John's. He was one of the most brilliant and versatile people I have ever known. At the wedding of one of the younger patrons, he barbecued a lamb (a bit rare), tended bar, and entertained everyone by singing Gregorian chants accompanying himself on a mediaeval musical instrument. As I mention above, St. John's is a liberal arts school with the students all taking the same curriculum to the best of my knowledge. It is based on one hundred great books. They may have a language choice. Anyway, Charlie, who was married, received a Watson Fellowship at graduation. The fellowships were endowed by Thomas Watson, who founded IBM. You do not have to pursue a particular subject and are not restricted in any way. You choose

233

what you want to study. Charlie chose Japanese papermaking, so off he went with his wife to Japan to study with a Japanese National Treasure. They were there a year apparently enjoying it all. If I am not much mistaken, they probably "shook up" the Japanese community where they were living to its benefit.

Another Little Campus patron was an ardent basketball fan. During the March Madness and Final Four business one year, he made a chart and was taking people's bets quite openly in the bar. He is a very sweet mild mannered man whom everybody likes. In some fashion word got out that there was a gambling ring operating at the Campus. An FBI agent appeared and promptly arrested him and took him off to jail. The situation was eventually resolved, but not until he was embarrassed and made to feel ridiculous. There was possibly not an office in the city of Annapolis (or the country) that was not doing the same thing that he was doing with full cooperation from bettors and onlookers.

Two of my cousins who were brothers also had their share of embarrassment. They were standing together at the far end of the bar when their discussion took a belligerent turn and they started hitting each other and fighting quite fiercely. Angy intervened, broke up the fight and barred them from the restaurant for a while. Bad news.

Another relative who patronized the Little Campus was my cousin, Billie. She had long black hair which she wore pulled straight back fastening it in a big bun at the nape of her neck. Her complexion was flawless and she intended to keep it that way. To do so, she always wore a hat with a large brim. You never saw her without a hat unless she was in her own home or at work. Unfortunately she died prematurely of cancer. When her apartment was cleaned out they found hat box after hat box, each filled to capacity with large brimmed hats of every description. I wish someone had counted them.

At Christmas time crazy, silly gifts were exchanged on a designated evening with everyone in festive dress. I don't remember the exact mechanics of it, but as I recall, person #1 picked a gift. Then person #2 picked a gift. Person #2 could keep his gift or exchange it for person #1's gift. Person #3 would have his choice of one the first two gifts as well as the one he drew. And so it went down the list of people. It was amazing to see what strange things were brought as gifts, and then to see what lengths people would go to in order to obtain the gift they *really* wanted.

When Bill Clinton was president, he and an entourage of around fifteen people or so came to Annapolis. They ended up having lunch at the Campus. Secret Service agents were all over the place, keeping regular luncheon goers from entering which was highly unacceptable to independent Annapolitans. After all, this was the city that declined Rockefeller's offer to renovate the colonial part of town and the poor man had to go to Williamsburg to mess *them* up. Angy's good temper prevailed and Clinton finished his lunch in peace. However, there was too much confusion for the person with the money. Believe it or not, the entire group of people left without paying a single luncheon tab.

The Little Campus was a congenial, happy place—one that you wanted to visit. The food was good, the people were pleasant and you always felt welcome. We met a number of people there whom we have remained friends with over the years. It is a nice feeling.

*   *   *

A favorite breakfast spot downtown is Chick and Ruth's Delly (not misspelled—as independent Annapolitans, that's the way they spell it) on Main Street. It is now run by their son, Ted, and his wife, Beth. (Long before, when I was young, it was called Bernstein's and they made the best chicken salad sandwiches on earth—Ted's are not far behind.) Ted and Beth have remodeled the upstairs, turning it into a very attractive inn named for their two children. We like to stay there. If you are in the restaurant part of the building at eight-thirty in the morning during the week, you will be asked to rise, face the flag and recite the Pledge of Allegiance with the words "under God" included. Since they are open seven days a week, this is done every day. However, you can sleep in a bit on Sundays, as they don't pledge until nine-thirty.

Chick and Ruth's is also a mecca for state officials (don't forget that Annapolis is the capital of Maryland and when the legislature is in session, it is overrun with all sorts of government people.) Various governors used to come to the delly also, so Chick, and then Ted, always roped off the first booth for the "reigning" governor. At one time the governor's name was Marvin Mandel. He was having marital problems caused primarily by the fact that he had a girlfriend living south of Annapolis off Solomon's Island Road. Once when he and his bodyguard were about to leave the restaurant to go south to a rendezvous, the bodyguard referred to their route as "The Road to Mandel's Lay" out of the side of his mouth. I always thought it was a great play on words. I wonder if Kipling would agree.

On the waterfront there was another of the old time "watering holes." I rarely went to it because it was Jim's lunchtime retreat and it was close enough to his office when he was stationed at the Academy so that he could walk. I always heard about all of the happenings, but I think it would be better to put them in Jim's words which follow:

"The bar was called Sam Lorea's and was located on the waterfront in an ancient building. It shared a stone wall with the old gaol or jail of colonial times. The bar had quite an interesting recent history. It was started by an ex-drunk.

The story is that Sam was a down and out alcoholic. I don't know the details, but somehow he acquired enough money to open a small bar, which was only about thirty feet wide. It has been said that after opening the bar, Sam never had another drink.

"Sam was a dyed in the wool patriot of the first order. He wrote patriotic poems on poster board and hung them across the back of the bar. He was also partial to the many Naval Officers who frequented his establishment. I used to go in for a beer at lunch time. The ceiling was so high I had to jump up to one of the exposed rafters to hang my uniform hat on a large nail. I often talked with Sam who sat behind the bar supervising Gabe and Ernie, his two black helpers. Actually they had been working there so long that they didn't need any guidance. Well, maybe they did need a little, because on a hot summer day your arm would stick to the table top if your glass sweated the slightest bit. A wet rag would have solved the problem.

"One noon when I was talking with Sam, who was facing the door, he jumped up from his stool and yelled, "Get your damned hands off that hat." A young man with long hair, obviously a "hippie" had taken my hat off the nail and started to put it on. Sam immediately ejected him since he had a fierce dislike for hippies and was particularly upset that one would try to put on an officer's hat.

"On another occasion, two young men came into the bar. This was a problem for Sam since their hair length was only bordering on long. Ernie had taken them each a beer and Sam sat glaring at them from his stool. Finally Sam could take it no longer. He went over to the table and asked the young men if they were old enough to drink and, if so, to show him their draft cards. Sam's words echoed up and down the street when they told Sam, the patriot, that they had burned their draft cards. When Sam told them to GET OUT, one of them replied that they had already paid for their beer. Sam immediately reached into his pocket, threw some money on the table and said, "I just bought the beer back. NOW get out."

"The only person, other than a hippie, who was not welcome, was the National Bohemian Beer distributor, of all people. Sam told me that the beer man had once told him that he could not survive unless he offered "National Boh" to his patrons. Sam got his hackles up and bought one case. However, he charged $1.50 per bottle while he was selling the other beers for 50 cents. He also sold a shot of whiskey for 50 cents. To make the Boh even less appealing, Sam never chilled it.

"While there were a few Naval Officers who were visitors to the bar, the regular cliental were usually local businessmen. Since Annapolis is the state capital, the lunch time crowds often consisted of legislators, the governor, mayor and often the entire city council.

"A crisis occurred when there were so many patrons that they spilled out of the front door onto the sidewalk. In summer, it often became quite warm since Sam's establishment was not air conditioned. Also, there was only so much room inside. Obviously some do-gooder complained to the powers-that-be and Sam was cited for allowing patrons to drink on the sidewalk. This dastardly situation was immediately sent to the City Council. The members who were regular patrons decided that if Sam painted a yellow rectangle on the sidewalk just outside the front door of the bar, leaving enough room for pedestrians to pass, they would consider the matter closed. Thereafter, drinking outside, but only if you were within the bounds of the yellow line, was legal. Oh the joys of a small town. Drinkers rejoice.

"Lunch time another of the regulars showed up, but only during crab season. This regular was an old, and I do mean old, black woman by the name of Florence. (Not to be confused with the woman who gave us the dandelion wine as a wedding present.) She was quite a sight. She wore an old, faded, but very clean dress, which came almost to her ankles, with her long handled underwear peeping out just above her tennis shoes. All of this was topped by a big apron. Often she had one of her grandchildren tagging along with her.

"Since Sam did not serve any food except chips and pretzels, Florence's appearance was a welcome sight. She was "The Crab Cake Lady." Her menu was simple and to the point. One crab cake the size of a saltine cracker, two crackers and a spoon to dip into the mustard jar which was in the upper fold down section of her grocery cart. Her price for this delicacy was a whole quarter.

"As many times as I had seen Florence and bought crab cakes from her, I had never seen her look up. One day when I was there for lunch, just to tease her, I walked up to her and said, "Florence, are these crab cakes a nickel?" Her response, still not looking up, was "Lordy me, they ain't been a nickel for years gone." One day she didn't show up for lunch. To my knowledge, no one knows what happened. It was the end of an era.

"Sam passed away a number of years later. His funeral mass was held on the Fourth of July. The church was packed."

*   *   *

An activity we looked forward to were the fall Redskins football games. There were about ten of us who were avid fans. The team was doing well—it was the era of John Riggins, Joe Theisman, Sonny Jurgensen, Larry Brown, Charlie Taylor, Billy Kilmer and Mark Moseley. We would have lunch or dinner at various houses depending on kickoff time. Then, watch the game, disturbing neighbors for miles around with our shouts and yells. It was much fun to be together and even more fun because at the time, although not always Super Bowl material, the team was doing well and won often.

We were always completely doubled up with laughter when the cameramen at the games homed in on the *Hogettes,* a group of about twelve adult, paunchy business men who dressed up in hideously out of style female clothing, including garden party hats, and cheered madly for the team. The best part of their costume was the wonderfully realistic pig snouts they always wore. They even followed the team to the out of town games and added a great deal to the festivities. They chose the name *Hogettes* and dressed like pigs in honor of the Redskin's offensive line, known as the "hogs" for their weight, endurance and success.

One of the couples who were Redskins fans lived on the Eastern Shore. They loved animals and had many exotic birds, which were truly fascinating to watch. However, Jim preferred their Yorkie, Vince, who virtually danced a jig whenever they told him that, "Jim is coming." Vince would jump onto Jim's lap, which they said was an unheard of occurrence, and snuggle down for the afternoon. He was disturbed only by touchdowns accompanied by loud shouts.

* * *

After settling in at King George Street, we really did not do too many "wild and crazy" things. Jim qualified for the annual company conventions, which were fun, but were usually held in typical resort areas—Acapulco, Cancun, Naples (Florida), Bermuda, Tucson, and so on. One rigid criterion set by the company was that there had to be a golf course, so that precluded most of the interesting destinations.

The first year Jim was back in business he qualified for the convention in Acapulco which was to be held in January of 1989. He had also qualified for the company Honor Society to which he had previously belonged. However, because of his break in "service" to Western Reserve, he had to go through the initiation process again. Each year that program is different. In 1989 the powers that be decided that it should entail having those being initiated become "Bunnies" along the Hugh Hefner line. The wives were allowed into the dressing room to help with dress, wigs and makeup, so I was able to take a large number of incriminating pictures not only of Jim, but of the other men, too. I will spare you the details of the backstage hilarity and simply show you a picture of Jim in all is glory. He was magnificent.

Jim as a bunny when he was re-initiated into his broker/dealer's honor society, Acapulco, Mexico, January 1989. Great legs.

To backtrack a little, in January of 1985, Alix and Peter Benjamin were married. We were living in the King George Street house for a few months at the time. Peter was from Lake Bluff, a suburb of Chicago. His father's name was Kenneth and his mother's Patricia. Peter also had two brothers, Eric and Tom. Alix and Peter had met at the University of New Mexico in Albuquerque. They chose not to be married in church, but rather at the Naval Academy Alumni House located directly across the street from our house. It is a former home of one of Annapolis's early wealthy residents, and is a graciously furnished and appointed colonial house. I have mentioned the house before as it is where Petie and Jim Evans had their wedding reception.

The ceremony was to be at 7:30 in the evening. Alix was dressed long before that as she couldn't wait for everything to begin. She tore out of the house with no coat on, lifting her long skirts and dashing into the traffic which came to a screeching halt to avoid hitting the white apparition in front of them. I was right behind her shouting motherly cautions.

The ladies room is upstairs. I was there with Alix and Mary Robillard, her bridesmaid, whom she had known since the eighth grade. They were touching up their makeup and hair getting ready for the procession. Finally the ceremony was about to begin. Something wasn't quite right with the fit of the bodice of Mary's gown, so Mary unzipped her dress and ripped off her bra in one swift motion, handed it to me, and proceeded down the stairs with the aplomb of a duchess. All went well.

The ceremony was simple and very short. It was held in front of the unlit fireplace in the main drawing room. The guests were close to the couple, so it seemed as though everyone was participating. Afterwards the reception spread out to include all of the ground floor rooms. The staff had done a beautiful job on the food. Jim and I were very pleased.

Peter's parents had hosted a rehearsal dinner the evening before at the large house my great grandfather had bought on State Circle which had been turned into a haven for the single ladies of the family. The dinner was lovely and most successful. The house had been bought by a man who made it the center of his five-building hotel chain in the city. By adding a new wing where the huge back yard had been, he managed to create fifty-five rooms, a banquet room, a welcoming entry area and a parking garage.

As an aside, a number of years before the sale of the house to the hotel man, it was sold to the Claude family heir who had the largest interest in it. That person was Frank Stockett. I am not a lawyer and do not know the legal ins and outs of the transaction but from what I have gathered one set of relatives had to sue another set of relatives in order to clear the title. It was all done very amicably as the ladies left in residence wanted Frank to have his share of the money. The sale, of course, meant that everyone would have to move. It worked out well to the best of my knowledge because most of them moved to an apartment complex in Eastport that was deemed acceptable and they were still near one another. (Eastport was considered a very "iffy" part of town for many years by those "in the know.") I do not mean to give the impression that all the money went to Frank. On the contrary, it was divided up in a strange way bordering on Black Magic—even Mother received a share of the proceeds. Believe it or not, she received $398.15 by check after a deduction of $194.44 had been made for legal fees.

There were a number of guests attending the wedding from Peter's side of the family, as well as friends of the bride and groom and our friends. People came for several days, so Jim and I arranged informal tours of the Naval Academy and the Historic District of the city hoping to make it more interesting for the attendees. I hope we succeeded.

After their marriage, Alix and Peter settled down in Lake Bluff. Both of them worked at *Nursery News*, a trade magazine to the floral industry that Kenneth published. Eventually they were able to buy a small house. However, they rented another house in the meantime. It was fortunate that they could buy later as the rental was certainly in need of insulation and other repairs. On one of our visits in winter we went to see the orchid greenhouses of one of their friends. I was generously given a blooming orchid plant which I gloated over and couldn't wait to get home. I set it near the back door inside the house to keep it out of the way. When I leaned over to pick it up and pack it the next day, I couldn't believe my eyes. It was completely frozen—killed by cold *inside* the house. We were delighted when they were able to buy their own place and live in more comfortable surroundings.

Ana Irene Benjamin, their first child, made her appearance 6 April 1987. Her middle name honored Jim's mother, whom Alix adored. I flew to Lake Bluff to help, while Jim followed a few days later. When he was first handed Ana, who was wrapped up in a blanket, he was taken aback when instead of cuddling up to him as Alix had done, she took a deep breath and pooped loudly into her diaper. She has been feisty ever since.

Jim holding Ana soon after her birth in Lake Bluff, Illinois, April 1987.

She was a real "cutie," however, and it was wonderful to be in on her arrival. I slept on their convertible couch in the living room, which was fine except when their enormous dog, Cammy, decided to join me. She was so big and so determined that I had to literally force her out of my bed with my feet, pushing with all my might. Eventually I succeeded. If you think Cammy took her defeat calmly, think again. You should have seen her pulling me along when we took our so-called walks. I was a mere scrap being dragged behind her.

* * *

In late November of 1987, just in time for Christmas, Alix and I went on a shopping trip to Asia. It was not a commercial tour, but had been put together by a friend who thoroughly loved to shop. She did an incredible job. We went first to Seoul, Korea, via Anchorage, Alaska. We landed in Anchorage to refuel in the midst of a truly horrendous snowstorm. The Maryland snowstorms I had been through were nothing like this. Snow was blowing almost horizontally. I'm so glad they had modern equipment or we could never have landed safely. Or taken off, for that matter.

The Itaewon area of Seoul was a large shopping section offering clothing, shoes, leather goods and any number of other items, both made to order and ready-to-wear. Our hotel was the Lotte, a big beautiful place in a good neighborhood. One wall of the lobby was glass. Behind the glass was a waterfall flowing down an artificial mountain. I knew it was cold, but I didn't realize how cold—the waterfall was frozen completely solid. I could then understand all the shivering of the cast of "MASH" in episodes that took place during the Korean winter. Incidentally, under the Lotte were literally miles of underground shops and small restaurants to keep the people out of the cold. Believe me, they were well patronized.

We did some touring of the city, ate street food, went to a dance performance and shopped. The highlight was a dinner of *bulgogi*, a type of barbecue. It was more than enough for Alix and me to share. We were served by an amusing young waitress who showed us how to cook the meat properly and what condiments to put with it. I must say it was delicious, but I couldn't quite get used to the *kimchee*, a formidable concoction of cabbage, garlic and hot peppers that made your eyes glow in the dark or, as Jim would say, curl the hair in your nose.

Our next stop was Hong Kong with more shopping, including visits to street stalls and flea markets as well as conventional stores. We broke the shopping by taking a train to Guangzhou in mainland China. One of the tour members had become fascinated by scarves and the various ways they can be tied. She entertained everyone on the train by demonstrating the various techniques and styles of tying to us and to a dozen or so Chinese women who were completely mesmerized watching her with their mouths open. I often wondered if they ever tied their scarves her way later on. We stayed overnight at the White Swan Hotel enjoying our stay in "real" China.

The last stop was Bangkok which, of course, has incredible shopping. We stayed at the Shangri-La Hotel, another lovely spot. Almost before we could catch our breath, Sangob and his brother, Tawan, arrived and began showing us new shops that had opened since we were last there, as well as new restaurants. Needless to say, we did a great deal of eating under Sangob's impeccable direction. Thai food is just simply glorious. Our trip home was uneventful. However, when Christmas arrived that year we had some marvelous presents for everyone.

*   *   *

While living in California, Mark met a young woman named Catherine (Cathy). They wanted to be married. Since they did not have a large number of friends there, we persuaded them to be married in Annapolis. They agreed.

They asked that the ceremony be held somewhere near the water. I located a restaurant overlooking South River that was under new ownership. It was being completely renovated and redecorated, so I thought it would be a nice fresh location. I made arrangements for the wedding to be held there about three months later on 28 May 1989. Then I simply forgot about it and went on with other things.

We had the rehearsal dinner in our backyard at King George Street. Our neighbors had offered the use of their backyard which joined ours, so there was plenty of room and it was quite attractive with lovely plantings and a huge, shady tree. We had it catered so there wasn't too much for me to do except choose the menu and get out the china, silverware, and so forth that I wanted to use. The weather was clear and cool, so everything went well.

The time came for me to discuss final arrangements with the restaurant where the wedding would be held and to select a menu. The minute I walked in I almost groaned in horror. The people were Italian and now, instead of being a calm lovely place to have a wedding, it was completely crowded with what Jim and I refer to as "grandmother Italian attic." There were cherubs, angels, and nude female statues on every flat surface with more hanging from the ceiling. Huge containers of artificial plants and flowers were everywhere with big swags of gold cloth swooping across archways. It was much too late to find another venue, so we made do.

The wedding was held in late afternoon. As it turned out, with the sun finally setting, a large number of guests milling about and the individual dining tables set with white cloths, crystal and china, it wasn't too bad. At least I told myself it wasn't too bad. The food was fine, the disc jockey was fine and everyone seemed to have a fine time. Cathy got her wish and was borne away to go on her honeymoon in a huge white limo.

Mark and Cathy started a unique business. It was called *Squeaky Floors and More.* There was much new housing being constructed in California at that time. Their business dealt with the aftermath of construction—repairing squeaky floors, re-hanging doors properly and any number of other items that the builder had overlooked. They were doing very well. However, Mark knew that he couldn't work that hard physically for the rest of his life. They eventually moved to Albuquerque where Mark began his career in the insurance and stock brokerage business with Jim.

Before their move, their first son, James Harrison made his appearance 22 September 1992 with Garrett Austin following on 30 January of 1996. Our daughter had two daughters and our son had two sons.

*   *   *

To be frank, I never knew exactly what Alix did at *Nursery News*, Kenneth's trade publication. I knew it entailed a great deal of the selling of advertising and the writing of articles about various nurseries and other horticultural enterprises. Beyond that, I really knew very little. Imagine my surprise when in late 1998 she invited me to go with her to France on a tour sponsored by the French government to promote horticultural endeavors in the region of Var, which is on the Cote d'Azur in the south of France. Of course, she was to write an article to be published by Kenneth, but that was expected. I was completely delighted and quickly made arrangements to accompany her. The trip was everything that I had imagined it might be, starting with a letter from the French Embassy in Washington personally inviting me. We flew into Nice, had a great time there wandering about in the open markets and peeking in the door of the famous Negresco Hotel. Then we went to Monaco for the day, seeing the casino and just soaking up the atmosphere before the tour began.

The tour visited all sorts of greenhouses and farms, including the famous Meilland rose establishment. We were taken to their breeding greenhouse where we were allowed to touch the half opened roses. I have never felt such substance and body in a rose. Totally unbelievable.

Alix inspecting a Meilland rose at their facility in France, late 1998.

Then on to the flower auction houses which were kept extremely cold in order to keep the flowers fresh. The bidding was incredible to watch—done very quickly to get the flowers on their way to the overseas markets. I enjoyed every minute of the time and every aspect of the floral industry that we visited.

Little did I realize, when I accepted Alix's invitation, that we would be spending our nights in absolutely perfect country inns, eating magnificent food and drinking wine the gods would willingly die for. All in all, it was a never-to-be-forgotten trip and I again bless Alix for the opportunity she gave me.

*   *   *

Callie Reed Benjamin arrived on 27 September 1990. (Her middle name was her Grandmother Benjamin's maiden name. I always laughed to think one grandmother was a Reed and the other a Read.) Of course, Jim and I went to

244

Chicago to see her and to help with Ana. We took her to the hospital to see her mother and Callie. She immediately jumped up on Alix's bed and wanted to hold her new sister. Alix put Callie into Ana's arms and a new and wonderful relationship was formed. They have been very close ever since.

Ana delightedly holding her new sister, Callie, Illinois, September 1990.

* * *

In October of 1990, we decided to go to Guatemala and Costa Rica. Our primary purpose was to see the activities and rites surrounding the Day of the Dead. We were also interested in the villages, the markets, Mayan ruins and the abundant wild life.

It turned out to be a completely fascinating and intriguing trip. We landed in Guatemala City where we spent the night. We left early the next morning driving to Chichicastenango (isn't that a truly unreal name?) which is in a mountainous area west and slightly north of Guatemala City. We checked into the Hotel Santo Tomas, a charming colonial type building. Our room had a *kiva* or round fireplace in one corner. I must say that the person who crept into our room while we were still in bed asleep to light the fire at about six in the morning performed a lifesaving service. The room was frigid but the fire took the edge off so that you could eventually steel yourself and climb out of bed to dress. It eventually warmed up later in the day, but the late nights and early mornings were COLD.

Our stay there was exceedingly pleasant. However, the drummer in a *marimba* band that played constantly in the late afternoon and evening was off a quarter of a beat. This drove Jim crazy, but he did manage to survive. One evening the buffet offered an enormous platter of bright green local broccoli swimming in butter. It was so fresh and so delicious that I had four servings.

The town was packed with people from the outlying villages coming to buy supplies to prepare for the Day of the Dead. Everything was available, from candles and food to incense and flowers—especially marigolds. To the Mexicans and Guatemalans the marigold is the flower associated with the dead. It is somewhat similar to our feeling about the lily. The people were all in native dress, which varied from village to village, so the entire town vibrated with color. It reminded me of Kathmandu many years ago.

That night the cemetery was full of candles casting a soft but eerie glow over the tombstones and the faces of the people intent on paying their respects to their dead family members. It was almost like a trip to the Underworld. We wandered around the cemetery looking at everything and were made to feel welcome. One small old woman told us a long rambling story about one of her relatives. We couldn't understand one word she said. But we nodded and smiled, listening attentively and it seemed to make her happy. We parted friends. The cemetery by daylight was almost as impressive, but in a different way.

The cemetery by day in Chichicastenango, Guatemala, October 1990.

The next day there was a great milling about of people in the square between two ancient churches. Men were dancing wearing masks with white faces, blond hair and beards representing the *conquistadores*. It was all very primitive and fascinating to watch. There was much brandishing of swords and sticks with mock fights here and there.

There was a taboo that we didn't fully understand. Apparently some of the Maya did not feel worthy to go into the churches, so they hired go-betweens to enter the church for them and place incense sticks upright in the big sand boxes that were placed in the church aisle near the entrance. This seemed to mean that their prayers and requests were there for the Deity to hear but that they were not contaminating the church. At least I *think* that is what was going on.

Later we went on to Panajachel on the shore of Lake Atitlan. It was filled with more markets and gaily dressed people with Maya profiles. Even the women washing clothes along the shoreline were colorful and cheerful. Then to Antigua, a lovely colonial city, after which we boarded an *Aeroquetzal* (named for the colorful national bird) flight to Flores in the north to see the Mayan ruins of Tikal.

We stayed at the Jungle Lodge, a short walk from the site. There were a number of small wild animals about, including turkeys with iridescent feathers. The ruins were overwhelming. In our subsequent travels to many other Mayan and Aztec sites, I don't believe I have ever seen a more magnificent ancient city. Go see it if at all possible.

Many years later, we returned to Tikal. I was entranced by a family, from grandma and grandpa to the youngest grandchild, enjoying a quiet picnic. Their modern Mayan profiles duplicated what had been carved in stone hundreds of years earlier. It was uncanny.

A few days later we flew to San Jose, Costa Rica. After some sightseeing in the city and a trip to Sarchi, the town of the hand painted carts, we boarded an old fashioned train of the type with open windows, no screens, and seats whose backs were manually moved back and forth when the train was going to reverse its direction. The tracks paralleled a river and stopped whenever anybody wanted to get off or get on board. All you had to do was pull the brake cord or hail the train—no stations—just where you happened to want to get off or on. It obviously served a large number of upcountry people. Very civilized.

Of course, if you are in Costa Rica you must go to a banana plantation. The one chosen for us was owned by Del Monte. The tour was interesting. I had not realized that when a banana shoot produces its bunch of bananas that that is the end of its life. The root mass has to put up another shoot in order to grow the next bunch. We watched the picking and the sorting and were duly impressed. However, the most amazing part was watching the last person in the process who put several little stickers with the Del Monte name on each hand of bananas. You know the ones I mean—the ones you have to take off before you can properly peel the fruit. Remember that they are applied manually and you can be thankful you do not have that job.

10

NEW MEXICO—RED OR GREEN?

W HEN ALIX AND PETER WENT back to Albuquerque to attend a wedding, they realized what they had been missing in the way of good weather and good friends. They convinced Kenneth that they could do the same work for him on telephones and computers from Albuquerque as they could from Chicago. So without further ado, they moved to New Mexico settling in a tiny town called Placitas, which is about nine miles north of Albuquerque on the way to Santa Fe. They were able to find a suitable house with the added luxury of a swimming pool and space for a garden. It stood on three acres of very high ground, giving it a magnificent view of the valley below. The best part, as far as I was concerned, was that there were a number of other young couples living in Placitas. I hoped that they would have the same happy experiences with their neighbors that we had on Cherry Grove Avenue. It turned out that they did.

Sometime during 1991, Alix called us in Annapolis and invited us to move to Albuquerque to "grow up with your grandchildren." We couldn't have been more pleased. Jim's business was "portable" in a way. So after discussing the matter briefly, we agreed and the upheaval of the moving process began.

We made several trips to Albuquerque during 1992 to house hunt, eventually finding a comfortable place on two acres in the North Valley on Rio Grande Boulevard. The North Valley is semi-rural and parallels the Rio Grande River. At that time you could drive around the area and see llamas, sheep, goats, horses and cattle grazing in fields. There were also many acres under cultivation planted with feed for the animals and other utilitarian crops. Now most of the animals are gone and the fields have been used as building lots.

When we were ready for the actual move to New Mexico, we were extremely touched and flattered by the reaction of some of the people in Annapolis. Linda Holmberg, one of our friends from The Little Campus, hosted a lovely farewell party at her home inviting other patrons we were close to, including Judy and Ray Neidhardt, Wil Shields, Jean Stephens, Charlie Stinchcomb, Bobby

Dunleavy and Angy and Mary Ellen Nichols. It was quite special. I was also pleased to have my *mah jongg* friends give me a marathon of games before we left Annapolis. I knew it would be a while before I could find another group

There was plenty of room on the property of the new house for a vegetable garden as well as a number of fruit trees. Jim planted several varieties of peaches, cherries, pluots, apricots and apples so that they would ripen at different times and there would be a succession of fruit. He also planted raspberries and asparagus. There was an area for thirty-four tomato plants as well as a huge area for sweet corn. Nine raised beds were in the center where lettuces, radishes, green beans and other annual vegetables were grown. It was a large and very productive garden. We wallowed in fresh organic produce all summer and into the fall.

The house was long and low, built in the southwest style. There were three bedrooms and three baths, the usual kitchen, laundry room and small dining room as well as an atrium with a skylight for houseplants. The living room and the master bedroom each had a *kiva* or round fireplace. The biggest asset was a long *portal* or covered area running along the back of the house facing east thereby avoiding the intense heat of the setting sun. The *portal* was supported by hand hewn wooden columns. It was also the site of a large hot tub which we both enjoyed and a gas grill which became one of my favorite ways to cook. The *portal* was used nearly all year long. It was pleasant to sit there in the evenings and watch the world go by.

The house on Rio Grande Boulevard in the snow, Albuquerque, 1992.

The author using the easy-to-use gas grill at the house on Rio Grande Boulevard, Albuquerque, 1992.

The huge expanse of lawn with its cluster of three large trees at one end near the *portal* created a place for volley ball, croquet and softball, as well as a shady spot for tables and chairs at party time. In the spring a long bed of bright yellow daffodils bloomed along the back fence. Peter gave us those bulbs as well as a number of short, yellow day lilies we planted along another fence. The changing colors of the foliage in the fall were lovely. In winter the snow was especially beautiful when you were up to your neck in warm water and looked at it from the hot tub. We were delighted with our new home.

In addition to the house itself, we had a shed for storing wood, flower pots, fertilizer and other farming items, including the riding mower. The crowning touch, however, was a chicken coop with thirteen very busy and lively chickens. I was pleased at the thought of having fresh eggs; however, I took one look at the inside of the coop and had it cleaned out. Little did I realize that it would remain clean for about a minute and a half. Callie was so small that she wanted to use the low chicken entrance on her hands and knees, which made her as dirty as the chickens. So, reluctantly, the chickens had to go.

Jim and Callie looking at the chickens on the far side of the yard at Rio Grande Boulevard, Albuquerque,1992.

One of the best things about the house was that Peter introduced us to a wonderful man named Manny Estrada who was able to work for us several times a week keeping the yard and garden immaculate. Manny was a great help in many ways. He took care of the house when we were away on trips, and looked after everything. If something needed to be purchased, he went ahead and bought the item, giving us the receipts for reimbursement when we returned. If something needed to be done, he did it. He was invaluable and became almost a member of the family.

When the fruit trees Jim and Manny planted (all twenty-five of them) began producing fruit, we had wonderful gatherings of Alix's young women friends with all of their children. Everyone helped in some way toward the production of as many pies as possible. Some picked the fruit, others washed and peeled, while others chopped and placed the fruit in the pie tins lined with pastry. It was a joint effort. We made pies of every fruit variety we had. One year when the time came to divide them up at the end of the day, we discovered that we had made fifty-two peach pies. Lots of work and lots of pies and lots of fun.

Ana's birthday is in early April. One year the day fell near Easter so we had her party at the house with an egg hunt, a *piñata* and all the birthday trimmings. The *piñata* (a paper container filled with candy) was hung from a lower limb of one of the trees near the *portal*. The children were blindfolded and one by one took turns trying to hit and break it with a stick thereby releasing the goodies inside. When someone finally succeeded, there was much cheering and laughter with everyone scurrying to pick up as much candy as possible. Children always enjoy *piñatas*.

Alix had bought some plastic eggs that opened, were hollow and could be filled with small objects—a coin, toy or candy. They were scattered about the yard, behind shrubs, in flower beds and so on. The children weren't quite as good at finding them as they were with the items from the *piñata* because we came across the plastic eggs for years. I didn't mind finding the ones with coins or toys inside, but the candy filled eggs were pretty disgusting by the time we got to them.

It was probably ridiculous of me, but I was quite thrilled when I introduced Ana and Callie to one of my favorite childhood treats. Alix had also enjoyed it as a child. It is the serving of Bunny Rabbit Tea. Petie and I had always liked it, too. It is a completely innocuous concoction of weak tea, a large amount of milk and a huge number of teaspoons of sugar. The fun for children is that they are drinking an "adult" beverage but enjoying the sweetness of the sugar along with it. When it is served in a grownup special teacup with a saucer, it is doubly wonderful. It even makes them pay attention to their table manners.

During one of our early Christmases at Rio Grande when Callie was quite young, I found some chocolate candy wrapped in colored foil. Each piece was provided with a short cord so that it could be hung like an ornament. We put a number of them on the tree thinking that it would be fun to see how long it took the girls to discover them. We didn't have to wait very long at all. Callie walked in the front door, wrinkled her nose taking a big sniff and yelled "cannie" as she made a dash across the room to the tree and the candy.

One day Manny ran up to me and said to come quickly as there was a kitten in the shed. When I got there the most adorable cat in the world was peering out of one of the shed windows. The kitten had long soft fur, perky ears and bright intelligent eyes. Her fur was a mixture of beige, tan and grey and she was totally beautiful. I picked her up, cuddled her and I was done for. She was obviously someone's pet, so I reluctantly put her out of doors that evening telling her to go home. There was a huge owl in the neighborhood and the occasional coyote, so she should have been kept indoors at night. She appeared the next evening while we were eating under the *portal* and that was it. If her family let her out at night with that owl in the vicinity, then they shouldn't have her. We had Sofie for sixteen years and enjoyed every minute. She was a complete delight.

Jim holding Sofie the cat at the house on Rio Grande Boulevard, Albuquerque, 1993.

Every time I string green beans for dinner I think of her. She loved them—not to eat, but to steal and play with. If I gave her one she would slap it around a little bit and then ignore it. However, if she stole it, then it was the perfect toy and she would play with it for hours. I can't tell you how many dried up old green beans I have found in odd corners of the house.

*   *   *

When we arrived in New Mexico an entire new world of food opened up before us. Even the names were evocative of something slightly foreign and wonderful: *tortillas, carne adovada, enchiladas, posole, sopapillas* and, of course, *burritos*. These food items are: flour or corn flat bread; marinated and cooked meat; various spicy fillings placed on the *tortillas* and covered with sauce; soup made of pork and dried corn; deep fried puffy bread served with honey; the *burritos* I describe below.

People do get set in their ways. One of our rituals was to go to Garcia's restaurant, one of a small local chain, for breakfast either on Saturday or Sunday morning. We always ordered a breakfast *burrito* with green chili. It is made by taking a large, fresh flour *tortilla* and placing it on a work surface. Then a nice fat ribbon of scrambled eggs is run down the middle of the *tortilla*. Next, seasoned pan fried potatoes are added, then chopped crisp bacon pieces (or cooked sausage or ham), cheese and green chili sauce. The *tortilla* is rolled up and placed on a large oval oven proof dish. More green chili is poured over the *burrito* with more cheese sprinkled on top. It is then run under the broiler for a few minutes and appears at the table hot, bubbling and fragrant. You can't wait to start eating.

Red chili can be substituted for the green, or you can order "Christmas," which is red at one end and green at the other. However, either of these alternatives is virtually a crime to real green chili fanatics. The difference between a breakfast *burrito* and a great breakfast *burrito* is, of course, the quality of the green. (You eliminate the word "sauce" when speaking with locals.) When the green is spicy enough to make your cheeks glow and your eyes water slightly, then it is just right.

Green chilis are prepared generally in two ways. They are either steamed to get the tough outer skin off or tumbled in a metal basket over a fire to achieve the same result. The steamed method gives a bland uniform mushy chili. The fire method allows the chili to keep its texture and also acquire more flavor from the charred bits and pieces. I don't know the complete secret of Garcia's green, but they not only utilize the charred green chili but also add garlic, spices, perhaps oregano and cumin, with a little bit of flour to thicken. At any rate it is delicious. On days when we have a *burrito* and the green is especially good, we usually buy a quart and put it in the freezer as it is good with many other foods.

During the chili harvest a number of flame roasters are brought into town and set up around the city. They go full time. You know you are approaching one when your eyes start to burn and you smell the unmistakable pungent aroma. People buy the amount of chili they want, as yet uncooked. Then the vendor puts them in the tumbler of the roaster and fires it up. After the chilis are roasted the prescribed amount of time, they are put in a big plastic bag and the buyer heads for home. During the drive home, the chilis sweat and the tough skin becomes easy to remove. The buyer separates the skin from the meat of the chili and prepares them for the freezer in his own way. The idea is to buy enough to last the year until the chilis are available the following season.

Our favorite Garcia restaurant chain roasts their own as I said. Most of the employees gather on a given day at their Fourth Street location and all participate in roasting enough chili for the year. Considering the amount they must use during that time, it is an absolutely mind-boggling affair. However, I'm so glad they do, as their green is absolutely *the* best.

Speaking of the best, we went to a pot luck party at Alix's one evening. A young man brought a big container of green chili stew. This is a soup-like concoction generally of pork, potatoes, seasonings and, of course, green chili. I complimented him on how good it tasted, and wondered if he would share the recipe. He smiled quietly and told me that the recipe had been mentioned in his divorce settlement, and that neither he nor his ex-wife could divulge the ingredients without dire consequences.

Jim and I have often been amused after returning from a trip and are standing at the luggage carousel to pick up our bags and head for home. We will talk about getting a "green chili fix" at Garcia's the following morning. Almost invariably someone near us will hear us and very fervently say "Amen to that" in agreement. Such is the New Mexican addiction to the green chili.

*   *   *

Life settled down nicely. Jim found an office and began working diligently to build a clientele in our new part of the world. He did very well, eventually utilizing the seminar format. He is a good speaker and presented his ideas logically. We continued to go to conventions for which he qualified. They were nice, but were usually held in places that were pleasant, but not particularly exciting as the sites always had to include a golf course.

We discovered that there was a Naval Academy Alumni group in town. Jim joined and we found the people fun to be with. At one of the first meetings we went to, Jim excused himself to go to the men's room. When he came back, he had been elected president. He accepted graciously, and ultimately did a great job of revitalizing the organization. There were meetings at our house, luncheons with speakers at the now defunct Petroleum Club, football game viewings at sports clubs when Navy played Army or Air Force and pot luck picnics. It was all enjoyable. Over the years the group also went to Colorado Springs several times to view the Air Force game in the "flesh."

We met some compatible couples, chief among them Kip Paskewich and his wife, Barbara Bradley. Kip was on the Naval Academy football team that was so successful during the early-1960s and that included the legendary, Roger Staubach. Kip is always fun to watch a game with as he knows all the ins and outs. Barbara and I have lunch together every so often and I always look forward to seeing her.

I also discovered a Newcomers club, which I joined (it was primarily for women) and met many extremely interesting people. They had wine tastings to which husbands were invited, so we went to many of those. The monthly luncheons were well attended with good speakers and good food set in pleasant venues. Eventually I met enough other *mah jongg* addicts to have a game every week. One of the players, Gretchen Fanslow, has become a truly good friend. I enjoy her thoroughly.

The city of Albuquerque has a number of excellent museums and an equally excellent zoo. These have given us a great deal of pleasure over the years. Santa Fe, too, has its share of worthwhile museums. My favorite is the Museum of International Folk Art, which is outstanding. It houses all sorts of objects made by everyday people from all over the world. Some of the items are exquisitely made, some crude, but each one obviously comes from the heart. It is all I can do to keep my hands off them.

We got season tickets to the productions at Popejoy Hall, which is the large theatre associated with the university. We thoroughly enjoyed going. However, I must admit that I was quite startled the evening of our first visit. I had dressed in fairly decent clothes and Jim had donned a sports jacket. We had seats in the mezzanine so had to climb stairs to get there. I was totally taken aback to see the man climbing in front of me wearing a very old pair of red sweat pants. They were in tatters. I then realized that I really was in New Mexico.

Just a bit north of Santa Fe there was a flea market. Using the term "flea market" does not do it justice. Dealers came from all over the country to sell their wares. The items for sale ranged from silver jewelry to Mexican pottery to Middle Eastern rugs to unusual clothing to someone there just for the day selling the contents of his garage. It was always entertaining to visit the market even if you did nothing but wander through the aisles gawking at everything. The vendors were talkative and informative about their wares. You always learned something.

One dealer I always enjoyed talking with was a tall, very slender Pakistani woman who sold things, especially small items of furniture and silver tribal jewelry, which she brought back from trips to Pakistan. She confided to me one time that she was tall and thin enough to disguise herself as a man, and that was how she was able to secure the things she sold and get them back to the States. She disappeared some time before the market was closed. I never found out what happened to her. I have always hoped that she stopped selling of her own volition and not because her disguise was penetrated by the Pakistanis.

Another vendor, Merry Elizabeth Foss, sold Mexican items. She was always extremely helpful about explaining to me the ins and outs of the Mexican tourist pottery that I had fallen in love with and had begun collecting. I bought a number of items from her which I continue to enjoy. When the market closed, she moved to Mexico. I hope she is enjoying it.

Merry Elizabeth Foss, a dealer at the flea market just north of Santa Fe, photo taken sometime in the late 1990s.

Unfortunately the market was on Tesuque Indian land which contained a lot of gravel of the type used in road construction. When the highway paralleling the flea market was widened, the Indians closed the market, made everyone leave and sold the gravel to the state for the road project. It took rather a long time to finish the road and by that time many of the local vendors had gone out of business, moved or just lost interest in the market. The ones from out of state just simply didn't return when the market was reopened. It is my understanding that new rules were introduced that put a financial strain on the vendors. We have been to the new market, but it just simply doesn't have the atmosphere and panache of the old one, much to my disappointment and disgust.

The best part of our new lives revolved around our Placitas family. It was so incredibly unreal that they should be so close and that we could see them so often. Alix set her own hours so that she and I were able to get together occasionally during the week and do female things like window shopping and having lunch together. It was also a pleasure to be close when birthdays arrived, school plays were put on, ears were pierced, and holidays came. Our move to Albuquerque was highly successful. Both Jim and I were enjoying ourselves immensely.

Callie totally ecstatic over her third birthday cake, September 1993.

Mark and Cathy moved to Albuquerque, also, as Mark was to go into business with Jim. I thoroughly enjoyed being around the boys, James and Garrett, too. They "helped" Jim in the vegetable garden although they much preferred to be carted around on the riding lawn mower, which was infinitely more exciting.

Jim with grandsons James and Garrett showing off the corn crop, about August 1999.

At Christmas time the cookie-making afternoons were not to be missed. I think there was more flour on the floor than on the table. All the children had so much fun (and so did I) that it was well worth the mess.

On the subject of grandchildren and although totally out of chronological order, I am placing here two pictures I love. One is of Ana at about nine months with a bowl on her head and the other is of Callie at that same age, also with a bowl on her head. Sometimes I wonder why we buy toys. Kitchen utensils are much more fun.

Ana with a kitchen bowl on her head.

Callie with a kitchen bowl on her head.

11

TRAVELING RESUMES

IN OCTOBER AND NOVEMBER OF 1999, I fulfilled a lifelong ambition. Ever since I was aware that my sister's name meant rock and that there was actually an ancient city named Petra, I had wanted to visit it. We finally made it to the "rose-red city half as old as time." It was part of an unforgettable tour to Jordan and return to Syria, a country which we had learned to like very much.

We landed in Amman and stayed in a hotel on the outskirts of the city. Muslims are called to prayer five times a day by the *muezzin*, who climbs the steps to the top of one of the mosque's minarets and announces the fact that it is time to pray in a loud and sometimes grating sing-song voice. In today's world, the call to prayer is primarily prerecorded and broadcast over loudspeakers placed at the tops of the minarets. The sound reproduction is really quite poorly done and quite ugly.

At that time there were two mosques in Amman with calls to prayer that were different from any we had heard before in the Middle East. One of the *muezzins* would start the call. Then a second *muezzin* would follow with another verse. They were not only melodic, they were presented one after the other, never interrupting, never clashing. We, of course, could not understand a single word, but the calls were truly beautiful.

The next day we toured the city briefly (there is not a great deal to see in Amman) and then drove north to Jerash, which is an impressive Roman site that would take a true historian weeks to explore. We were able to visit for only half a day but it was enough time to let us realize how far the Roman power and influence extended. When one hears about the "might of Rome," Jerash certainly exemplifies it. Acre after acre of magnificent ruins—arches, temples, the forum, basilicas, fountains, roads, sculptures all in outstanding condition and yet hundreds of miles from Rome itself. All of which conjures up images of their administrative and management abilities, not to mention their military might.

Madaba was another stop to see the Church of St. George where there was a mosaic floor map of the Holy Land and Lower Egypt as it appeared in the Sixth Century. Although no longer complete, what remains is quite detailed with the Dead Sea, the River Jordan, Jerusalem and the Nile River clearly shown. It, too, was impressive and the workmanship admirable, even though dulled by time.

The next day we went south to the Red Sea staying overnight in Aqaba, which is Jordan's only port, then north again to Wadi Rum, an immense flat sandy area surrounded by red stone mountains. A *wadi* is a dry river bed. During World War I, Lawrence of Arabia trained his Arab allies there, preparing for the attack on Aqaba which would be approached by Lawrence and Prince Faisal from the desert or back side of the city. The attack, led by Lawrence on 6 July 1917, was a masterful bit of military strategy since the guns of Aqaba were positioned to fire toward the sea. Also the route across the desert to the land side of Aqaba is a brutal stretch of terrain and no one suspected an assault from that direction.

The deep red mountains of Wadi Rum have horizontal streaks of caramel colored stone here and there throughout the *wadi*. When they were formed millennia ago, the streaks oozed over the red stone giving the impression of a giant chocolate cake with melted caramel frosting flowing out from between the layers. Breathtaking—you almost wanted to take a bite.

Jordan shares a border with Saudi Arabia which is patrolled by the Jordanian Camel Corps. As evening approached, we drew near a huge black Bedouin tent that had been set up for an official reception of some kind. Many dignitaries were in the tent and the Camel Corps appeared to perform a short drill to impress everyone. They certainly impressed me. The camels were tall, graceful, well fed and well groomed with gleaming white teeth not usually found in camels. Their riders were equally well groomed and handsome with the addition of huge black moustaches.

After the drill I could not help myself and I went closer to the camels. The saddles and bridles were of beautiful leather with bright red and green balls of wool suspended from them which moved with each step the animal took. (I have recently discovered that the balls of wool are amulets designed to keep the Evil Eye away.) Elegant is the only word to describe them. I must have had the wistful expression of a child at Christmas on my face because before I realized it, a member of the elite Corps had made one of the camels kneel and I was helped onto the saddle. The ride didn't last long, but it was completely awesome. Lila on a Jordanian Camel Corps camel riding through the desert sunset in Wadi Rum. I was completely thrilled.

The author about to be helped onto the saddle of a Jordanian Camel Corps camel
for a short ride in Wadi Rum, Jordan, November 1999.

Our hotel in Petra was just outside the entrance to the old city. Close enough that some of the tombs were outside the gates and on hotel property. I must say it was eerie to have our evening cocktails sitting in an ancient burial site with flickering candle light making moving shadows on the rock walls of the tomb. It was almost as though the spirits of the people who had been buried there had come to visit with us.

The next morning we walked through the *Siq*, the narrow, narrow entrance to Petra through a cleft in the rock. It is about a mile long with vertical sides going straight up quite a distance on both sides. High up on the walls of rock were remnants of clay pipes approximately six inches in diameter, which were gently sloped to provide a gravity flow of water since there were few if any sources of water in the city of Petra. When you finally emerge into the city itself, the façade of the Treasury, carved from solid stone, is directly in front of you. It is truly awe inspiring. This is your first impression of what is to come, and perfectly epitomizes the stark beauty of the city of Petra.

Jim and the author in front of the Treasury in Petra, Jordan, November 1999.

So many of the pictures one sees of Petra are limited to the Treasury building. While it *is* magnificent, it is only a small fraction of the many buildings, temples and tombs which were carved from the living rock. Speaking of carving, the stone cutters always started from the top of each structure so that the falling stone fragments would not damage the completed work as would have happened had they started at the bottom.

After exploring the ruins for hours, we took a horse drawn carriage back to the entrance. The driver whipped the horse unmercifully and Jim became furious with him. King Hussein's American wife, Queen Noor, had established a stable for the horses where they were supposed to be taken care of and protected from that sort of cruelty. The drivers were also given some training in the care and handling of horses. Our driver didn't seem to have learned anything. Jim reported him to the authorities, but we have no idea whether or not it did any good.

Before going on our trip to Petra, I had discovered that a professor at the University of Arizona was excavating there at the Temple of the Winged Lion. Jim offered me the chance to go as a paying helper, as is the custom at many digs. We decided not to do anything definite until after we returned from our trip to Petra.

We were not impressed by what we saw of the excavation site, although it is not always easy for the layman to know what has been accomplished just by looking at the site. However, we decided that it would probably be better if I did not go. The decision was clinched when I was told that helpers *walked* the mile through the *Siq* into the ruins, worked hard all day in the sun and then *walked* back at the end of the day. Guess I'm just too much of a sissy.

On the long drive to the Syrian border, we passed several Crusader castles which broke the tedium. To see them loom up on the horizon made you feel as though you were part of a caravan approaching a safe area to stop for the night. It was great to finally arrive in Damascus again as we both have always liked the city immensely. We bought two rugs in a shop on *The Street Called Straight* and then wandered into the bazaar which is always an adventure.

The rug store on *The Street Called Straight* in Damascus, Syria, in November 1999.

We went into another rug shop and started chatting with the owner. Since he was a typical rug merchant, we were invited upstairs where the "better" rugs were kept as well as Indian miniatures, jewelry and other items. The dealer and I were sitting in chairs side by side both holding on to one long side of a rug examining the color, quality of the wool, the knot count and so on. Jim squatted on the floor inspecting the other long side. Suddenly the dealer froze and sat up straight. I also froze and we both stared at a stream of liquid coming out from under Jim's legs and flowing across the slanted floor. Jim saw our reaction and stood up. With great relief we discovered that the plastic bottle Jim had in his pocket had sprung a leak and the stream of liquid was nothing more sinister than water. His kidneys had *not* failed after all. After wandering contentedly around Damascus for another day or two, we drove north stopping in Hama to see the huge wooden water wheels built by the Romans and still in use to carry water from the Orontes River to the surrounding fields.

The huge wooden water wheels in Hama, Syria, in November 1999.

Then on to the Second Century B.C. Roman city of Apamea, which Antony and Cleopatra are said to have visited. The most viewed ruin there is a long double row of fluted columns rising out of the surrounding fields and disappearing into the distance. It gives the almost ethereal impression that if you could follow the road between the columns you would eventually arrive at whatever your idea of Heaven might be.

We then drove on to Homs for the night. Next day we went directly to Palmyra, one of the most incredible cities on earth.

Jim and the author standing
beside a road sign on the way to
Palmyra, November 1999.

Palmyra was founded as a trading center and before the birth of Christ had extended its reach as far as India. The Palmyrans dealt primarily in typical goods carried along the Silk Route. The main street was packed sand rather than stones to keep the feet of the camels from becoming bruised. There is a hotel at the edge of the old city where you can sit in the evenings and have cocktails watching the sun set behind the ruins. The open air lounge is highlighted by tables which are the tops of ancient Corinthian columns. I have asked Jim for a coffee table just like those, but to no avail.

The story of Zenobia, Palmyra's female ruler, is almost like an heroic myth. Unfortunately (as far as I'm concerned), she was subdued by the Romans, again showing their might, and brought to Rome in chains—but at least the chains were made of gold. No one seems to know exactly what happened to her. There is a theory, because of names used several generations later in a certain noble Roman family, that she married a Roman, raised a family and stayed out of politics.

We were also able to see some underground tombs that had recently been discovered by accident when the digging of an oil pipeline caused the collapse of some earth and sand. We crawled under the big pipe, stood up and saw several banks of tombs. The tombs were arranged like cubby holes in a desk, except large enough to have a body inserted feet first. The outside panel of the tomb was a sculpture of a head, either male or female, depending upon who was buried there. I have no idea, of course, whether they were portraits, but they were impeccably carved with distinct individual features and were perfectly lovely. Because they had been underground for so many years, they were in pristine condition. Unbelievable discovery.

The next two days were a dream come true to a ruins buff. I just couldn't get enough. However, we eventually had to leave going further east to the legendary Tigris and Euphrates Rivers. We stopped at a Bedouin *souk* that was primitive and wild. It was one of the most unusual *souks* we had ever been in because it *was* so wild and primitive, even by Mideast standards. There were copper potmakers pounding away, people haggling over vegetables, fly covered meat stalls, knife makers brandishing their wares, Bedouin goat hair tents on display and heaven knows what else. Everyone was clad in colorful local dress which varied slightly from tribe to tribe and, of course, all talking and yelling at the tops of their voices, the women among the most vocal. Did I mention the goats and sheep wandering through the passageways along with the people?

We visited the ruins of the city of Mari, which is about five thousand years old and dates to the Sumerian, Akkadian, Assyrian and Babylonian times. Also saw Duro Europos, another ruined outpost, built by one of Alexander the Great's generals. We collected a huge handful of brightly colored pottery shards which we reluctantly set back on the ground as we left to go on to Aleppo.

Aleppo was great to explore. We more than enjoyed the bazaar although, in our eyes, it didn't measure up to the ones in Istanbul and Damascus. We also visited many of the other sites around the city. However, I'm afraid that they were somewhat overshadowed by the ladies' visit to the *hammam*.

Hammams or bathhouses have been a fixture in the Middle East for centuries. After a while you feel that you simply *have* to try one. There were four women on the tour and in Aleppo we finally had our opportunity.

The entire *hammam* was closed just so we could use it—no men allowed. The building is about six hundred years old and has the usual hot, tepid and cool rooms along with an area where you are scrubbed thoroughly with hot soapy water and brushes stiff enough to be used on an elephant. The floor in this area is constructed of marble slabs worn smooth and satiny by the many bodies that have lain on it to be washed.

We were told to strip to our under pants and sit on the floor all together in the middle of the room. Then a muscular Syrian woman, also clad only in her under pants and very well endowed, approached each of us in turn and proceeded to wash our hair. Then we lay on our backs on the floor while she scrubbed our fronts. The language problem was getting too much for her, especially with four of us, so when it was time to do our backs, she simply took us by the ankles and flipped us over as if we were dead wet fish. It was easy to do on the soapy, slippery floor. What a performance.

Then we rinsed and went through the hot, tepid and cool rooms finally emerging dressed in three big soft towels—one around the head and hair, one around the shoulders and middle, and one around the hips and legs. At that point we were a bit tired and frazzled. However, we were led to an elevated dais near the front entrance where we were served hot very sweet tea.

The management thought at that point they had been closed long enough so they re-opened for business. The first people through the door were a young Syrian man and two women who were tourists from the north. They immediately dashed toward us snapping pictures all the way. Little did I realize when I agreed to go to the *hammam* that pictures of me half clothed would end up in someone else's photo album.

On our way to see Saladin's castle, we passed a section of Roman road which had been exposed down to the foundations by the wind and weather. The construction was somewhat intricate and you could tell that it was time consuming to build. As we clambered over the road, it was impossible not to feel the presence of the soldiers who built it standing beside you waiting for you to express your opinion of their work. The top layer was comprised of large thick slabs of stone, about three feet square each and fitted tightly together. In the next lower layer the stones were not as well dressed, but fit together nicely, also. The bottom several layers were looser and obviously rubble of some sort. The soldiers need not have feared for any criticism—the construction was flawless—even after almost two millennia.

Photo of a Roman road in Syria showing the construction, November 1999.

Saladin's castle is situated above a pine covered ravine in a beautiful setting. Some of the walls have collapsed and the areas between filled with soil blown in by the wind enabling all kinds of wild flowers to take root. We sat among them in the fall sunlight letting our imaginations run wild about what life must have been like there in the Twelfth Century when he was in residence.

From there we went on to see another marvel—the Crak de Chevaliers, which is an incredible crusader castle. It still remains one of Jim's great memories from our travels. After exploring it, we returned to Damascus and had to decide if we wanted to go into Lebanon to see Baalbeck, the ruins of a huge temple complex. There was not much fighting going on at that time and Baalbeck had been another of the sites on my wish list, so we elected to go. The ruins were on a gigantic scale, primarily to impress that part of the world with Rome's might. We thoroughly enjoyed the afternoon poking into all sorts of places. We, too, were impressed with Rome's might as we were so often on this trip. The next day we returned to the States, completely exhausted but also completely happy with our experiences.

Jim and the author in front of a cross section of a fallen column at Baalbek in Lebanon, November 1999.

* * *

Ana's birthday in April of 2000 was her thirteenth, so of course we had to arrange an all-girl trip to London just as we had done for Alix to mark the occasion. We stayed at the Tavistock Hotel were Alix and I had stayed. However, it had gone downhill considerably. The rooms had been cut up to allow for more guests, the baths were tiny and the standard of cleanliness had fallen somewhat. However, we were settled in so we stayed on anyway. Nelli Calame, one of Alix's good friends, came and brought one of her friends, Kathy, with her. I never knew her last name. However, Kathy fit in beautifully and was a pleasure to have her on the trip.

Our first excursion was to Portobello Road, which was as much fun as ever, and then on to a different flea market at Camden Locks. The vendors there were funny, full of backtalk and hilarious to bargain with. Alix and Nelli each bought a wild bright sweater and had more fun doing it than anybody had a right to.

During the next several days we saw the play *Blood Brothers* at the Phoenix Theatre and hired a car to take us around London to get an overview of the city.

Toured the Tower of London (they had moved Henry VIII's suit of armor, so no one was embarrassed by his private parts being prominently protected by the armor as Alix had been years earlier). All of the girls, young and old, looked longingly at the Crown Jewels. Westminster Abbey also impressed each one of us. I do believe that one could visit the Abbey a hundred times and still not see everything.

It was finally time for TEA AT THE RITZ and in everyone's mind it *was* in capital letters. We dressed up, arrived at the hotel and were escorted to a perfectly set table in a corner of the famous pink and gold room. The food was outstanding with Callie falling in love with the tiny salmon sandwiches. Our waiter noticed this and when he replenished the supply of sandwiches, he made sure that there were enough of the salmon to keep her happy. The sweets were totally decadent, too. Frankly, tea at the Ritz can be compared to no other meal anywhere for its pampering and complete spoiling of the spirit.

Our table for Tea at the Ritz, From left to right: Nelli, Kathy, the author, Ana, Callie and Alix, London, April 2000.

Later on that evening we went to a Greek *bazuki* restaurant just as the plate throwing and dancing was reaching its height. Everyone had a grand time. Doing something that is usually forbidden certainly has an allure about it. The girls, as well as the adults, enjoyed the breaking and crashing of the plates immensely. The accumulation of piles of broken crockery was especially satisfying.

Later we experienced an exhilarating day by taking a tour to Henry VIII's Hampton Court Palace with its wonderful gardens. Life there in Henry's time must have been one entertainment after another. It is not exactly clear in my mind how we did it but apparently we boarded a boat to go to Windsor Palace from there. The waterway was full of beautiful swans, ducks and other bird life so the trip was interesting for the girls. Windsor Palace was beautiful, too, with daffodils and other flowers blooming profusely throughout the grounds.

On our return to the hotel, we were too tired to go out, so had snacks in the bar area. Callie seated herself at the bar itself and had a lengthy chat with a woman bartender. I took a picture of them talking away and having what seemed to be a deep conversation about the meaning of life.

Callie and the hotel bartender discussing the meaning of life, London, April 2000.

* * *

September of 2000 saw us on a long postponed trip to China. Fate finally had her way and we were off to China according to the prediction made so long ago by my Chinese *amah*. It was a long anticipated trip and would be taken in a very special Golden Year of the Dragon. However, it didn't start too smoothly.

We wanted to see a good deal of the country, so we scheduled our start in the cities of Kashgar and Urumqi, both very far to the west, almost to the Pakistani border. I must say that my re-introduction to China was about as crude as you can get. After landing, we were hustled to the bus as fast as possible without benefit of a trip to the ladies room. A few miles down the road, the women revolted and the driver stopped at a farm house and asked if we could use the facilities. We went gratefully into a dilapidated and smelly shed. While I was crouched over the business end of the outdoor toilet, a stray sunbeam illuminated the area just below me. I couldn't believe my eyes. The entire pit was filled with writhing, disgusting white maggots.

The hotel in Kashgar was almost as bad. The Chinese government had commandeered all of the better places to house people participating in a meeting of some sort, so we got the dregs. Believe me, they *were* dregs. However, we had a glimpse of magic to make up for some of it. In our decrepit hotel, we watched a Chinese man rapidly paint a series of pictures of donkeys and two humped dromedaries using a black wash on coarse paper. He also painted a little old man atop a donkey. The painter was so fast and so skillful that it really did seem like magic. Needless to say, we bought several.

Our guide was a Chinese Canadian. Frankly, I don't think she spoke Chinese. Neither Jim nor I ever heard her speak any Chinese dialect to any Chinese person the entire time we were on tour. I also think she knew very little about Chinese food. The meals seemed to reflect that. There were twenty of us initially on the tour, so at meals we filled two of the typical round tables for ten quite nicely. However, the tour was in segments with people coming and going as their segment began or ended. Cliques began to form which made most of us uncomfortable and she failed to do anything about it. That is always bad for morale and camaraderie on trips. However, the sites, that were what we came to see, were outstanding.

The Mogao caves, a bit further east, exhibit superb examples of Buddhist art carved on the walls of hollowed out caves cut into the sides of hills. We visited both Xian, with its terra cotta warriors, and Beijing, with its imperial buildings. Saw the Great Wall, the Ming Tombs, and Guilin. Everything was more than expected.

Eventually we boarded our boat for the cruise on the Yangtze which was awesome in some respects and very upsetting in others. Near the site of the high dam the smog was thick and almost roiling, impeding visibility and causing everyone to cough. It reminded you of descriptions of London fogs before they stopped using soft coal for fuel. The dioramas and drawings showing the eventual height of the water level and how many villages would be submerged and people relocated were sad. You wondered privately whether the gains were worth all the suffering as over 1.4 million people were to be displaced by the time the dam was finished.

On the other hand the gorges were indescribable. It was eerie seeing the pathways hewn into the rocky banks of the river that Father had talked about. You could almost see the coolies pulling *Penguin*, Father's gunboat, along over the rapids. My imagination was so vivid that I could see some of them falling into the rapids when the towing lines snapped.

One evening Jim and I went to the stern of the riverboat to get away from all the people. We both became somewhat sentimental and toasted Father with a few tears while we watched the frothy wake as the boat made its way down river.

When the tour arrived in Shanghai, we struck off on our own looking for the things that Mother and Father had talked about. The Bund, a remarkable area on the water front lined with fanciful old buildings, was our first destination. The buildings were not open to the public as they were in a bad state of repair. I believe that today many of them have been renovated and are in use as banks and centers of business again. Even so, their silhouettes lent a certain old fashioned atmosphere to the area.

At one end of the Bund, the Whangpoo River empties into the sea. Whangpoo is the old Westernized spelling. Today it is the Huangpu River. We hired a young man to drive us around for the day. He entered into the spirit of the chase by helping us locate various places. He pointed out the old Russian Consulate Building at the end of the Bund across the river from the Astor Hotel. It was on Huangpu Road, perpendicular to the Bund. The hotel had been a focal point of the expatriate life in Shanghai, which I talked about earlier in this book. We walked boldly up to the front door, opened it and entered.

Across a small lobby you looked directly into a crescent shaped room where the tea dances must have been held. The walls formed little niches where I'm sure small tables had been placed years ago. The center of the room, which had been the dance floor, was now covered with many modern tables on top of which were placed a large number of computers. We were told they were for the buying and selling of stocks, no less.

Someone at the hotel approached us and asked why we were there. After we told them that we were hunting for the past, they took us to the second floor where many, many old photographs of the area and of the hotel hung on the corridor walls. We spent some time there wallowing in the atmosphere before leaving to find the site of the Country Hospital where I was born.

The hospital's address as it appeared on my birth certificate was also Whangpoo Road. However, because of the word "Country" in the name, I thought perhaps it was further out of town. After asking a number of people, some old and some young, we found that the hospital building itself had been torn down, but that it had been located very close to the Astor Hotel. We did find the remains of an old tree that had been on the hospital grounds and I had to content myself with that and a street sign.

Jim and the author in front of the Huangpu Road street sign in Shanghai in
September 2000.

*   *   *

In October of 2000, we decided to see what Mexico's celebration of the
Day of the Dead would be like. Day of the Dead is roughly equivalent to All
Soul's Day with a smattering of Halloween. We had seen this celebration in
Chichicastanango way upcountry in Guatemala a number of years ago, and
wanted to experience it again. So off we went to Oaxaca, Mexico. The celebration
there is not as primitive as Guatemala's, but nevertheless an extremely interesting
blend of pagan and Christian beliefs.

Oaxaca's celebration is different in that there is much more emphasis on death. There are hundreds of items from paperweights to cakes and cookies shaped like skulls and flamboyantly decorated. Skeletons dressed in elaborate costumes are everywhere, especially Katarina, a young woman who died early and personifies death itself. It was interesting to compare the two celebrations.

Each family erects an altar in the home decorated with candles, flowers, little statues, incense and foods that the dead were fond of in life. Marigolds are everywhere. It is eerie and solemn and brings people face to face with the fact that death is always with us.

There was sufficient time to do some other sightseeing, so we hired a car and driver and went to the village where the Tule tree, a 2000 year old cypress, is located along with a beautiful church. The tree stood in the center of a lovely park with flower beds here and there. Growing in one of the beds was a shrub with round hollow papery seed pods somewhat similar to the Chinese lantern plant, except that the pods were yellow in color. I asked Jim if he knew what they were. A heavily accented male voice broke in and told me with a twinkle that they were called "The Bishop's Eggs." I thanked him and we went on with our sightseeing.

Several years later, I saw the same shrub also with seed pods in evidence and said to Jim that we were again in the presence of the Bishop's Eggs. Another passerby, this time a bit more fluent in both colloquial Spanish and English, burst out laughing and told me I was viewing a plant called "The Bishop's Balls." A slight, but important difference.

*   *   *

Even though Jim and I had been to Mexico a number of times, Christmas is always a special time of the year, so we hoped to make it even more special by renting a large house in Oaxaca and going there with the whole family for Christmas of 2001. Alix found a house not too far from the *zocalo* or plaza which would hold not only the six of us, but also had room for Nelli Calame, Alix's good friend, to come for several days, too.

Oaxaca lies in a valley and is surrounded by villages which offer many different kinds of folk art and crafts. There is the rug village, Teotitlan del Valle, where you can buy all kinds of colorful Zapotec tribal weavings. They use natural dyes and will show you how they secure red coloring from a little insect that they have raised on cactus paddles. When they pinch one of the insects it spurts a bright red liquid which they use to dye the wool fibers prior to weaving the rugs.

There is the wild and crazy painted wooden animal village, Arrazola, where you can buy surrealistic small animals that look as though the maker has reproduced his most bizarre drunken nightmares in bright, bright colors. Some of them take your breath away and might even give *you* bad dreams.

And then there is the green pottery village, Atzompa, where the potters have created salt and pepper shakers, sugar bowls, bud vases and all sorts of other things in the most imaginative and fanciful shapes. For example, they attach wings, big ears, pig-like noses and anything else that strikes them at the time. All covered in a medium deep green glaze with great depth. You want to buy them all.

In addition, there are the Zapotec ruins of Monte Alban, which means White Mountain in Spanish. Named because at the time the Spanish discovered the ruins, the mountain was thickly planted with smallish trees covered in white flowers. There are several other ruined temples and villages I haven't talked about. There is truly a great deal to see and do around Oaxaca.

Because it was holiday time, the *zocalo* or town square was packed with people selling everything conceivable. Vendors were groaning from great colorful loads of toys and balloons, baskets of every size and shape and flowers, flowers, flowers.

One evening a Radish Festival was held in the *zocalo*. When I heard about it, I pictured our small round red radishes being carved into flowers and used to decorate mirrors or lamp shades. I was completely wrong. Mexican radishes are an entirely different species of plant. They are a deep brown red and grow into the earth as much as two feet. When they are pulled up, they look something like *gensing* with a number of little branches and roots sticking out from the main stem.

The radish contestant eyes his radish, squinting all the while, conjuring up what it might become if dressed in costume—a dancing girl, a child, a *conquistador*, a dog, or maybe an *iguana*. He dresses his radish in doll-like clothes, and then, along with hundreds of other contestants, enters it in the competition and hopes for the best. To walk among the displays of radishes is an experience in appreciating the incredible imaginative powers of the human race.

Some of the entries in the radish contest in Oaxaca, Mexico, December 2001.

The perimeter of the *zocalo* is occupied by restaurants. Sitting at one of the tables in the cool of the evening sipping a glass of *vino tinto* or red wine is one of life's small, yet wonderful, pleasures. Immediately after we sat down, a familiar flower vendor spotted us and came over to offer one of her fragrant bouquets of gardenias for Jim to buy for me. They had a fine time laughing together while Jim tried to get the price lowered. She stood firm and Jim paid her the ten *pesos* she was due. She never changes the price, but they both enjoy the haggling. The flowers just added to the pleasure.

Susana Trilling, an American living in Oaxaca, is an excellent cooking teacher. We had heard of her reputation, so we signed up for an all-day session. Her four wheel drive vehicle picked us up at the house and headed for Rancho Aurora, her home outside of town. The jolting of the car was severe as the roads were almost nonexistent, but it was fun. We had to ford a stream where women were doing their laundry. Children were splashing in the water having a good time and adding to the confusion.

Susana took us to one of the small local outdoor food markets where we bought the supplies for our lesson. We walked around enjoying the color, the fresh produce, the crafts offered and, most of all, watching the people.

To be honest, I don't remember exactly what we cooked. I do know that it was delicious. I also know that Ana was outside roasting and peeling chilis. She accidentally brushed her hand across her cheeks causing her skin to burn viciously. Susana took her into the kitchen, cut open a tomato and rubbed the pulp on Ana's cheeks. This stopped the burning, but as Ana hated tomatoes, this was almost as bad as the chilis. After Ana's cheeks cooled off, the students, including other people who were attending the class, finished preparing the meal. Then we all sat down and had a delicious, fresh unusual dinner.

On Christmas day itself, we went to what Jim and I refer to as the Restaurant up the Hill. However its real name is *Un Jardin con Restaurante,* which in my halting Spanish, I have translated as "A Garden with a Restaurant." It is situated away from the center of town and really is a cool green garden with all sorts of play equipment to entertain children, brightly feathered birds in cages, as well as an extensive, colorful and delicious buffet. It was a perfect place to have Christmas dinner and a grand finale to our holiday.

Christmas dinner at *Un Jardin con Restaurante* in Oaxaca, Mexico, December 2000: From left to right: The author, Ana, Alix, Callie and Peter.

* * *

If ever a tour cried out to be taken, it was Adventures Abroad's Cooking and Wine Tour of Italy to be led by one of their top guides, Victor Romagnoli in September of 2002. Jim and I fell over each other in our haste to sign up. The tour began in Florence with five days of Italian cooking lessons from two young Italian women who had attended the French Cordon Bleu cooking school. They were good teachers as well as being personable and pleasant. We enjoyed the classes and the resulting food prepared under their guidance was truly outstanding.

Jim cooking with one of the teachers in Florence, Italy, September 2002.

The author cooking with one of the teachers in Florence, Italy, September 2002.

Victor was also most personable and pleasant. In addition, he knew Italian cuisine, wines, the country and the best inns and restaurants to patronize. We went to some first rate places. Since the cooking classes ended at one o'clock, we had the afternoons free.

Victor arranged for wine tastings on two of those afternoons. One was with a young woman and one with a young man, each a licensed Sommelier. The adjectives used to describe the flavors and nuances of the various wines were off the wall—hay, straw, leather, marmalade, herbs, clove, cinnamon, chocolate, coffee, smoke, tar and others that shouldn't be used in polite company. We also learned about legs, rings and tannin. At that point my brain stopped working and I just went with whatever red wine was available.

Another of the afternoons we drove out to Montalcino to sample their *Brunello* wine and look at their cellar. That was another instance of going with the flow. The wines were divine. I really don't know how it is possible to have so many wines available and have them all taste absolutely perfect. Jim and I succumbed to the temptation and had a case shipped back to Albuquerque. What luxury.

Jim and the author in front of the entrance to the Montalcino Winery near Florence, Italy, in September 2002.

The last afternoon we were taken to Volpaia for an olive oil tasting and a tour of an olive farm. The family was welcoming and gracious, showing us around very proudly. I didn't realize that olives could be cured in so many ways. I liked the black olives best. Some of the black olives had been made into a jam, which was somewhat unexpected but very tasty.

We had managed some free time to wander around Florence on our own admiring the famous Ghiberti baptistery doors, the unusual architecture and absorbing the feel of the city. The Ghiberti doors seemed as perfect as they had been when Eileen and I were in Florence years ago, even though we learned that they were reproductions that had been set in place in 1990 when the originals were removed for preservation and safekeeping.

Jim and the author in front of the fake, although beautiful, Ghiberti baptistery doors in Florence, Italy, in September 2002

We were told about a leather school at the back of the Church of Santa Croce. Our visit there was incredible and I walked away with a magnificent black leather coat that is still one of my favorite possessions. The scent of the leather alone is enough to make you caress it. And the cut is so classic I think it will never go out of style. (At least I hope not.)

The next day we drove to Lucca, an old, old town, closely associated with Puccini. We went to a house he had lived in and found it enormous and somewhat cold. While the house was a bit sterile, they did play music from his operas during the entire visit. Since we both are very fond of Puccini's music, it made the house a little warmer and certainly entertained us while we looked around.

Lucca is still surrounded by its ancient city walls, which are quite wide with a pathway on top so are a perfect place to walk to get a bird's eye view of the city. Several times we went to a particular bar that was located near the base of the wall. Each time there were twenty-one different mouthwatering small *antipasti* or appetizers offered by the house for you to munch on as you sipped your wine. It was, in the modern vernacular, awesome.

As we drove throughout Italy, we were allowed into the kitchens of many restaurants and inns to watch master chefs at work. They rarely measured anything, doing it all by feel and appearance. It was like watching a conjuring show. One minute only flour, water and raw spinach were on the counter. The next minute there were beautiful green *ravioli* or dumplings ready for the pot.

We stopped in Modena to see balsamic vinegar being made. It is an extremely simple but hideously time consuming process. They do not start with wine, but with fresh grape juice that is put into small wooden barrels. The barrels lie on their sides and have square openings on the top. A clean linen cloth is placed over the opening to allow for evaporation and keep dust from entering. In some miraculous fashion, after years of aging, it becomes what we know as balsamic vinegar. The longer it is aged and the more liquid evaporates, the thicker and more syrupy it is, and, of course, more expensive. We bought a very small bottle (130 ml) of twenty-five-year-old vinegar for $75 and have treasured it. Some of its uses are strange, wild and fun—dribbled over strawberries, on small pieces of Parmesan cheese, on fish, smoked salmon, eggs or custard. My favorite, and strangest of all, is over vanilla ice cream. Totally extravagant and totally elegant.

The author examining the kegs of balsamic vinegar in Modena, Italy, September 2002.

Since the vinegar is so expensive and time consuming to make, the areas where it is stored during this aging process are wired with burglar alarms as if the crown jewels were being protected. I guess in a way they are as the families usually start a batch for each child when it is born. Rather like an annuity

During our stay in the city of Parma we had another food surprise. We went to a factory where Parmesan cheese was made. The equipment was immaculate. Huge cauldrons of milk were being churned in heated containers. They were carefully watched over by workers who again seemed to do things by sight and feel rather than time. I guess you would really call it instinct and experience.

Eventually part of the mixture in the cauldrons became thick and was pronounced ready. The thick part (curds) was put into molds (two from each cauldron) and rested for a while. Then the molds were opened and the huge wheels of cheese-to-be were immersed in a salt water bath where they would stay for a month. Then they would be stacked in a curing room. The one we were shown held wheels sixteen shelves high. It ages there for a minimum of twenty-four months before it can be sold. Up to a point, the longer the better. Victor bought a piece of the cheese that had been aged for four years. He gave Jim a small piece which Jim describes as nectar of the gods. We bought some two year old cheese and it was not at all bad.

Jim and the author standing between wheels of curing Parmesan cheese in Parma, Italy, September 2002.

The whey left in the cauldron is not thrown away. We went behind the factory to see how it was disposed of and found ourselves face to face with very clean, very intelligent looking white pigs. They happily lapped up the whey and in turn became the famous Parma ham.

Victor had bought 100 grams of white truffles for 150 Euros at one of the restaurants. He would surprise us every now and then by sprinkling truffle shavings over our dinner pasta with great ceremony. When you convert the 100 grams to 3 ½ ounces and the 150 Euros to $185, the truffles turned out to cost $845.73 per pound. No wonder he carried them around carefully and dispensed them sparingly. The taste of the white truffle is very different from the taste of a black truffle. We all truly appreciated and enjoyed our excursion into the rarified atmosphere of genuine "gourmet" food.

We finally arrived in Alba for the White Truffle Festival and found it extremely odd and quite different. Perhaps not as interesting as all of the cooking and eating had been, but interesting in the sense that dozens of grown men were going berserk over ugly little nodules of fungus. These nodules had been located where they were growing wild in the forests by dogs, not pigs, as the pigs would have eaten them. All transactions at the sale were in cash. The scales used were jeweler's scales, so valuable was the fungus. At over $845 per pound, a few grams here and there were significant.

A dealer at the white truffle sale in Alba, Italy, with his jeweler's scale nearby, September 2002.

As a finale, we had a full day in *Barolo* wine country just absorbing views of the glorious countryside, drinking the wine and having a huge lunch Victor described as "late and long." It was a perfect trip.

*   *   *

Making trips with the whole family is always an enjoyable undertaking. We decided to do just that during the holiday season of December 2002 and January 2003. We chose a tour of Egypt which included several nights on a *felucca*, one of those wonderful Nile sail boats that look like giant butterflies hovering over the water. The tour was offered by Adventures Abroad and we met our favorite guide of all time, Yvette Haakmeester, She is a lovely tall blond Canadian who is caring, knowledgeable, funny and has great rapport with touring people of all ages.

Yvette Haakmeester in Egypt
aboard a *felucca* on the Nile, Egypt,
Christmas 2002-2003.

Of course, we started in Cairo by going to the museum, viewing King Tut's regalia, checking out Ahkenaton and Nefertiti, and looking at innumerable mummies. (Ana and Callie's reactions to the mummies were a combination of morbid curiosity interspersed with many "yucks." Or at least that's what I thought. They may tell me differently.) We explored Coptic Cairo, went to Memphis and Sakkara, saw the Sphinx and pyramids and actually did an "Egyptian" dance on the first level of the stones of one of the pyramids. Then it was time to board the train for Aswan.

Callie and Ana with one of the great pyramids in the background, Egypt,
Christmas 2002-2003.

Callie, Alix, Ana and Peter doing an "Egyptian" dance near the base of one of the great pyramids, Giza, Egypt, Christmas 2002-2003.

In Aswan, Sara, one of the children of another family on the tour, had a birthday, so there was a big celebration in a tent with all the waiters in local garb. They performed some native dances that were extremely energetic. Sara had a birthday cake, too, so she had the best of both worlds. She was obviously delighted.

We rode camels to an old monastery, St. Simeon's, and had a fine time clambering over the ruined walls and looking into various nooks and crannies. Then it was time to visit Abu Simbel.

The author teaching the other tour members how not to ride a camel, Egypt, Christmas 2002-2003.

After a short flight south, we were driven to Abu Simbel. It is an enormous temple which was built by one of the most famous of the pharaohs, Ramses II. It would have been flooded and under water when the Aswan Dam across the Nile was finished. However, donations came in from all over the world, thanks in part to UNESCO. In an incredibly ingenious feat of engineering, the temple was dismantled and moved to high ground. The dust, generated when the stone blocks were sawed apart, was saved. It was used in the mortar when the blocks were put back together so the color matches. When looking at the temple, it is almost impossible to believe that it had been cut into a large number of blocks, moved and reassembled. A remarkable achievement.

Jim and the author at Abu Simbel temple in Upper Egypt, Christmas 2002-2003.

The Cataract Hotel is to Aswan what the Ritz is to London. It has been famous for years. If you are not a guest at the hotel, you cannot just walk in for dinner. Yvette seemed to have extensive contacts, for she arranged for us to go there for dinner one evening even though we weren't staying at the hotel. I will grant you it wasn't at a fashionable dinner hour and the dining room was somewhat empty, but we were there and that was enough.

Now that the obligatory sightseeing preliminaries were over, it was time to board our *felucca*. A *felucca* is a small wooden boat propelled by sail. It has no cabin, just an open space with planks for sitting. For our trip, more wooden boards were placed across the boat from gunwale to gunwale arching slightly in the center creating a relatively stable area. Thin pads were placed on top and that is where we sat, played games, talked, watched the passing scenery and slept for the next three days. There was, of course, no toilet, no running water and no privacy whatsoever. Toward the forward part of the vessel there were no boards across the boat and that is where the cook/captain had his old Coleman stove and prepared the meals. The actual sailing of the boat was done from an area closer to the stern by other members of the crew. They slept in that area, too.

Four feluccas sailing on the Nile, Egypt, Christmas, 2002-2003.

Boarding the feluccas on the Nile, Egypt, Christmas, 2002-2003.

Fortunately everyone on the tour was easy going and cooperative. There were two families and a couple. Each family had its own *felucca* as did the couple, who shared their area with Yvette. At night the three vessels were tied together for meals and sleeping. Washing, tooth brushing, retreating behind bushes, and so on, were carried out in as dignified a manner as possible. Speaking of meals, it was surprising the delicious food that the captain of the *felucca* could turn out considering his meager equipment.

Activities on board: Callie in the middle with two of the other children playing chess, on the Nile, Egypt, Christmas 2002-2003.

More on board activities: switching to cards, on the Nile, Egypt, Christmas 2002-2003.

As we sailed along, we visited the temples of Kom Ombu and Edfu, which were still awe inspiring to me in spite of my having visited them previously. Our family seemed to agree as necks were craned and many appreciative comments were made. We disembarked at Edfu and drove to Luxor.

Jim and the author at the temple of Edfu, near the Nile, Egypt, Christmas 2002-2003.

Yvette wanted to make sure that our Christmas dinner was classic, so she had the hotel dining room prepare turkey, stuffing, sweet potatoes and all the trimmings just for us. They did a pretty bad job of it. We sat munching our bland mess, while the rest of the people in the dining room feasted on especially appetizing looking Egyptian dishes. We couldn't fault Yvette as her heart was completely in the right place, but we did eye the Egyptian buffet with longing.

We toured the Valley of the Kings, took a donkey ride to Queen Hatshepsut's Dier al-Bahari temple and generally soaked up more of Egypt's entrancing ancient culture. On a more modern note, we went to the Winter Palace (where Jim and I had stayed so many years ago) for cocktails. The girls loved the Luxor *souk* as well as the Temple of Luxor. On New Year's Eve, Yvette arranged for entertainment by a troop of Dervishes. How they could whirl around and around in their huge colorful skirts without making themselves sick to their stomachs was beyond my comprehension. However, they were great to watch and I was glad they were the ones doing the whirling and not me.

Whirling dervishes at our New Year party, Luxor, Egypt, Christmas 2002-2003.

We returned to Cairo and visited the Citadel. By that time, school was reconvening and it was necessary to go back home again. I hope that everyone else had as much fun as I did.

* * *

Manny, our invaluable helper and jack-of-all-trades, had diabetes. In 2003, he got an infection in his foot and, unfortunately had to have part of it amputated. He was fitted with a prosthesis that seemed to work well. However, the doctors discovered a heart problem that he hadn't known about and it frightened him. He could handle diabetes, but heart trouble really upset him. The upshot was that he felt he could no longer work for us. We tried several of his relatives, other people who were recommended to us and companies that specialized in yard care. None of them worked, and Jim and I simply couldn't do it all. As a result, we started house hunting.

Briefly, in late 2003 we bought a house in an area called Shadow Hills near the crossroads of Montgomery and Tramway. If you are familiar with the layout of Albuquerque, that is a long, long way from the North Valley in distance as well as in atmosphere. The house was relatively inexpensive as it needed a great deal of work. The community looked pleasant and we hoped to meet neighbors and enjoy being in a neighborhood again as long as we had to sell the house on Rio Grande. We were wrong. However, we didn't realize that until after we had bought the house, renovated it and moved in.

We had a new kitchen installed and both bathrooms totally redone utilizing brightly colored Mexican tiles. The dreadful carpeting was replaced with Saltillo tiles, which are big twelve inch tannish Mexican floor tiles from the city of Saltillo. The new flooring made our haphazard collection of Middle Eastern rugs look really special. Other things were also replaced, but I won't go into that. We moved in April of 2004.

We discovered that there were several community rules that we were unintentionally disobeying from the beginning. The garages were small as the house was thirty years old and cars were smaller when the houses were built. Therefore, we couldn't put two cars plus a garbage can into the garage. They simply wouldn't fit. We thought that we had neatly solved the problem by putting our garbage can behind an extremely large and extremely ugly bush in the small front yard. The can was only visible for a nanosecond as you were either coming or going down the street, and even then, you had to crane your neck to look for it. I will admit that it was visible to our immediate neighbors when they left their houses.

After all kinds of nastiness, we ultimately had to have a handyman build an alcove for the can in a corner of our front wall. By doing so, we hid the can, lost two big pots for growing herbs and spent eight hundred dollars unnecessarily. Peace was restored to the neighborhood. However, a bad taste was left in our mouths, especially mine, and it had taken me a while to get over it. In the meantime several people have moved, with younger more affable people taking their places, so I am looking forward to the future.

* * *

The year 2004 marked Callie's thirteenth birthday. Even though her birthday is not until September, we went in April, a great time of year in London. This trip everyone rebelled at the thought of the Tavistock Hotel, so I reluctantly agreed to one on Gloucester Road. It turned out to be acceptable and was within walking distance of a tube stop. Sally Blanton, a friend of Alix's from Placitas, came with us. We met Nelli Calame in London as she was working in India for Intel and flew in from the east. Our first excursion was to Portobello Road, of course, to initiate Sally into the flea market scene.

The next day we went to Stonehenge. The weather couldn't have been more perfect for viewing old and mysterious ruins. Even though it was April, the weather was cold and bleak and windy with low grey clouds hovering over the landscape. You could almost see the ancient people getting ready to perform their rites. It made the usual chills go up and down my spine.

From left to right: the author, Nelli Calame, Callie, Ana, and Sally Blanton at Stonehenge, England, April 2004.

Our next day trip was to the city of Bath with its Roman ruins. The girls seemed to like the experience. The hot springs were steamy and smelled of sulfur; the models of "the way it was" were interesting; and the later English spa facilities were quite modern in some respects. Frankly, I don't think I would mind getting into the water itself even though it smelled pretty bad, but I really don't think I could have drunk as much of it as the ancients did, cure or no cure.

So as not to make everything "a learning experience," we went to Harrod's, the enormous and legendary department store on Brompton Road. The Food Halls were at their magnificent best with virtually every edible food in the world on display, and then some. The offerings included *paté*, cheeses, meat, fish, seafood, game, (including boned quail.), pastries, Indian food, and many other edibles with all of the displays done perfectly and enticingly. You wanted to buy and eat everything. There were also potted flowering plants, cut flowers and arrangements. I saw an exotic yellow orchid wrapped and labeled for delivery to "The Duchess of Cornwall" so I guess everybody shops there.

We wandered through the clothing sections of the store and ultimately arrived at the hat department. English garden parties in the spring are "the thing" with the Queen's garden party at the top of the list. Naturally, those typical big brimmed hats are the featured article of clothing for female attendees and Harrod's had a tasteful and very ladylike display. Naturally we wanted to try some on, but the clerk wouldn't let us pick them up and put them on our own heads. She had to handle the hats wearing white gloves, no less. However, since she was willing to help us, we had a wonderful time trying them on. The only other drawback was that she wouldn't let us photograph each other wearing the hats. After we looked at a few price tags, we discovered why. Most of them were hideously expensive with some of them running as much as three thousand English pounds.

Harrod's is a London landmark. I forgot to mention an amusing thing that happened to Jim years ago when he and I were at the store. He was wearing a necktie with maroon and navy blue slanting stripes. (This was in the days when one dressed decently when traveling.) It was actually the necktie chosen by his broker/dealer's "honor" group—the people who had sold the most for the company. While I wandered the store, Jim went to a lower level where there was a bar to have a beer while he waited for me. As he walked in, one of three elderly British men spoke coldly to him asking "Are you qualified?" Jim didn't have the foggiest notion what the man was talking about. He soon discovered that the tie was the regimental tie of the Queen's Own Regiment and therefore only members of that regiment should wear it. They talked for a while. Jim explained that he had been in the U.S. Navy and had served in Vietnam. To shorten the story, they not only forgave him, but bought him a beer and "chatted him up" until it was time for him to meet me.

Jim couldn't stand being out of the loop on Callie's trip, so he arrived in London at the Ritz just as we were sitting down for tea. He couldn't have timed it better. Tea was delightful as it always is. We stuffed ourselves with everything including the salmon sandwiches, which were replenished regularly as they had been before. Somehow everything tastes especially good in that setting—the candles shimmering, the pink and gold decor shining softly, the exquisite table appointments and especially the feeling of serenity and peace.

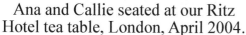

Ana and Callie seated at our Ritz Hotel tea table, London, April 2004.

Callie standing near the Ritz Hotel's exit door, London, April 2004.

After tea, we decided that it was time for a cocktail. We asked our waiter where we should go. He recommended the Stafford Hotel, which he said was around the corner. We found the hotel, went into the American Bar and Jim and I fell in love with it instantaneously. It is an old hotel. The bar was a regular gathering place for American officers on duty in Britain during World War II. There is a tremendous amount of U.S. wartime memorabilia attached to walls and ceilings including many photographs, letters, plaques, small flags, insignia and so forth. It is very warm and homey, yet formal, with good drinks and impeccable service. We have since been welcomed as old friends, as each subsequent trip to London has definitely required a visit to the Stafford.

The British Museum was on our "to do" list and we all enjoyed it. Ana saw the Elgin marbles from the Parthenon. She seemed very impressed. Our play this visit was Agatha Christie's *The Mouse Trap*, which is always very entertaining with its surprise ending you are not supposed to reveal. I can't remember how long it had been running, but well over fifty years as I recall. We went back to the Greek *bazuki* restaurant also, but arrived too early for much activity. However, the owner brought out some plates for us, so we had our own small party throwing them on the floor with much enthusiasm.

Everyone returned to the States except Jim and me. We stayed on for a few days and visited Kew Gardens, Warwick Castle, Shakespeare's Globe Theatre, the Cotswolds, and went to a great play, *Anything Goes.* On a more sober note, we visited Churchill's grave. We also visited the "War Rooms," which are the underground bunkers where Churchill and certain members of the government monitored and directed the progress of World War II. There were bedrooms (very small), bathrooms (also small), and many offices and conference rooms. Mrs. Churchill had her own room which was minute. It held a bed and small dresser. The entire complex had been left as of the day of surrender—maps in place, telephones handy, pencils and paper on the tables and so on. To anyone who remembers the war and the incredible sacrifices that were made, it is a pilgrimage rather than a visit.

*   *   *

In September of 2004, we decided to take a trip to Cambodia to see Angkor Wat, which both of us had always wanted to visit. (While living in Thailand, we had tried twice to make the trip. One time the Thais and the Cambodians were having an armed border dispute. The other time Mark had measles.) We traveled to Siem Reap via Hong Kong and Singapore with a few days stopover in each city. It had been a fairly long time since our last visits to those cities, and truthfully, we were startled by the changes in both. Hong Kong had now been returned to China after the British lease of ninety-nine years expired. The British had left and with them much of the orderliness and politeness of the city. We found the people rude, in a constant hurry and if you didn't keep up with them you were summarily pushed aside. Literally.

Worst of all, our favorite hotel, the Luk Kwok, had been torn down and another building erected on the site. The owners were the same, but the whole philosophy was different. Gone was the second floor dining room with its *dim sum* and *mah jongg*, with the clicking of the tiles and the shouts of the people. You could still order *dim sum*, of course, but it came directly from the kitchen—no pushcarts. The dining room was exceedingly sedate with white tablecloths and crystal and could have been anywhere in the world. The street markets had virtually disappeared as had the street vendors. Everything seemed sanitized and somewhat uninteresting.

In Singapore the situation was similar. A new government had taken over and their motto seemed to be "Cleanliness is Next to Godliness"—only more so. The baggage carousel at the airport was immaculate. The metal spoke-like things that revolve to move the luggage were polished so brightly that they made your eyes ache. The flat upper part of the carousel was thickly crowned by dozens of yellow orchid plants in full bloom, each one perfect. There were a number of people sweeping the floor looking in vain for any discarded litter.

The taxi ride to the hotel revealed even more cleanliness. There was absolutely no trash at the sides of any of the roads, which had been repaved and planted with superb tropical flowers and trees along the verges. It was quite attractive, I must admit, but could have been anywhere.

When we checked in at the hotel we found out about all the no-nos and taboos that were in effect throughout Singapore. The following list is a partial one that was printed on a tee shirt I bought:

> No crossing streets in prohibited area—fine $500 Singapore dollars
> No urinating in elevators—fine $500 Singapore dollars
> No littering in public areas—fine $500 Singapore dollars
> No importing of chewing gum—fine $1000 Singapore dollars
> Forgetting to flush in a public toilet—fine $500 Singapore dollars
> No picking of flowers in public gardens—fine $500 Singapore dollars
> No smoking in prohibited areas—fine $500 Singapore dollars
> No vandalism in public areas—fine $2000 Singapore dollars
> No spitting in public areas—Fine $500 Singapore dollars

I was almost quaking in my proverbial boots when I discovered that I had brought in illegal chewing gum. Their punishments can range from fines to jail time to public caning even though the tee shirt listed fines only. I don't remember the exchange rate in 2004 to give you the exact equivalent of $500 Singapore dollars, but in 2009 it was 1.4 Singapore dollars to one American dollar, so you can see that the fines were pretty severe for the local population.

Also banned by the government were the outdoor food markets on Orchard Road that Jim and I had so dearly loved. The food vendors were now housed in modern sterile buildings with the servers wearing aprons and plastic gloves and with sneeze guards in place over the food.

The shop houses had also been systematically demolished until someone pointed out that they were part of the city's heritage, so they stopped. However, not until there were only two or three blocks of houses left.

One of the few remaining areas
of shop houses in Singapore,
September 2004.

The red light district had also disappeared as well as the transvestite area on Bougis Street. Chinatown and the Indian section were cleaned up beyond recognition. Worst of all was that the *riijstafel* restaurants were gone and nobody seemed to care.

We checked out the Raffles Hotel, as usual, and found that the famous Long Bar had been moved from its original spot on the main floor, to a second story location at the rear of the hotel. It was almost criminal—everything was new, shiny and awful. Somerset Maugham was surely doing cartwheels in his grave.

We did have a bit of fun dressing up in Chinese costumes for our photo to be taken. We were posed in a Chinese room decorated quite authentically, as far as I could see. Even our feet were positioned the "right" way so that we really did look Chinese until you came to our faces. We used the picture as our Christmas card that year.

Sometimes I think we're spending too much time in the Orient:
Jim and the author, Singapore, September 2004.

Only the fact that chili crab was still available in the Changi beach area kept us from weeping as at the death of a loved one. Even so, the crabs had been fished out in the Singapore area and had to be imported live from Sri Lanka. Nevertheless, they were fantastic and we enjoyed them immensely.

Our waiter holding the crab we had selected at the restaurant at Changi Beach, Singapore, September 2004.

The author eating the crab with great relish. Jim is not far behind her, Changi Beach, Singapore, September 2004.

To be frank, we enjoyed the crab, mourned the changes to the city and were glad to be on our way.

*   *   *

Cambodia was everything it was supposed to be. The photographs one sees of that country are magnificent, but do not do it justice in any way. We were completely awed and entranced. We were able to spend four days in the Siem Reap area staying in an opulent modern hotel and taking day trips to the various temples and ruins. It was a dream.

There was also a shop where tourists could buy local products at fair prices. It was housed in a lovely teak building that in itself was pleasing to visit. I bought several handmade tin gourds and birds, which are true works of art.

They are stylized and are unmistakably gourds and birds, but have a certain flair that makes you chuckle when you see them.

One of the sad things we saw, which bothered both of us, was the fact that there were so many land mines still in the ground around the temples and in the fields nearby. We were told not to wander off the pathways into fields or jungle. When we exited the temples, we had to walk back to our car passing groups of men playing various musical instruments in what seemed to be small orchestras. On closer look, each man was injured—no hands, a leg gone, an arm gone, and so on. We were told that most of the injuries came from the land mines which had been put in place during their long civil war. These men were earning what money they could from the donations of the people passing by. The government, as well as volunteer organizations, was trying to locate and remove the mines, but it is a slow and tedious process. I wish them every success.

Angkor Wat is an imposing structure. It is awe inspiring from almost every point of view—the engineering, the water management, and the art. All come together to make it one of the most truly magnificent places on earth. Seeing it at sunset or sunrise is thrilling. The spires against the colors of the sky are spectacular. The temple was dedicated to the Hindu god Vishnu by King Suryavarman II, who reigned between 1131 AD and 1150 AD. It was built over a period of thirty years and has incredible examples of Khmer and Hindu art. It has the longest continuous bas-relief in the world. It runs along the outer gallery walls and narrates stories from Hindu mythology.

Jim and the author in front of Angkor Wat in Cambodia, September, 2004.

In addition to the large temple complex of Angkor, which is the highlight of the area, there are innumerable other temples. Each one is slightly different from the others, but nevertheless impressive. Ta Prohm is an area which has been kept uncleared of jungle vegetation so that you can see the damage the big fig trees can do and how most of the monuments would have looked when first rediscovered.

Ta Prohm, an area near Angkor Wat left uncleared of jungle vegetation, Cambodia, September 2004.

In driving from one temple complex to the next, we naturally passed through local villages and small markets. The high temperature and humidity made us thirsty. However, as usual, care had to be taken when selecting one's drink in order to avoid the Asian version of "turista." My favorite was always a fresh young coconut that had been refrigerated until very cold. The milk of a young coconut is clear and only slightly sweet. Just right for quenching thirst. Right in front of you the vendor whacks off the top with an enormous knife, inserts a clean straw into the coconut and hands you the most refreshing drink you could possibly ask for.

We went to a number of the outlying temples, enjoying each one. My favorite was Banteay Srei, which seemed to have been built with a much more feminine outlook. The stone filigree work is delicate and lacy, making you feel less in awe of the gods, but no less religious. It is a delightful sight.

The author drinking the milk from a fresh young coconut the most refreshing beverage in the world, Cambodia, September 2004.

The delicate carving of Banteay Srei near Angkor Wat, Cambodia, September 2004.

All in all Cambodia was a great experience. After the misery of the last years, I sincerely hope that they are on the way to a happier future.

12

NEW BEGINNINGS AND MORE TRAVEL

I N AUGUST OF 2005, AFTER divorcing Peter, Alix married Bernie Linnartz in a beautiful outdoor ceremony at Bernie's house in Placitas. Bernie's birthday was the day before the wedding, so there were two days of celebrations. For the birthday, I was assigned the task of picking up a number of cakes from a bakery and a large amount of beef tenderloin. I was so concerned with the cakes and getting them to Placitas intact that I completely forgot to buy the beef. When I arrived at the house Bernie got the cakes out of the car. Then he came up to me and casually asked if there were anything else in the car he could bring in. I told him no, and then suddenly realized that I had failed to buy the beef. In a great rush, Bernie's son, Benjamin, accompanied me to the only market in the area. Fortunately, they were open at that strange hour and they also had enough filet. The day was saved.

The marriage ceremony the next day was also held outside in the early evening and was quite lovely. Although there was a huge drop in temperature as rain clouds moved in, everything went well until a huge downpour started. However, the mood was festive so no one minded being crowded inside the house and under the *portal*. It somehow added informality and spontaneity to the event.

Alix and Bernie just after their wedding ceremony, Placitas, New Mexico, August 2005.

Alix and Bernie continued to live in Placitas for a while but eventually decided to move farther north to Taos. They ultimately bought a charming home with a large yard unfortunately infested with a small colony of prairie dogs. They also acquired a semi-wild part coyote dog named Sadie who is handsome but so reserved that she has yet to allow me to touch her. However, the prairie dog problem was solved.

* * *

The rest of the first decade of the twenty-first century became a virtual frenzy of trip taking. We went to many of the countries on our ever-lengthening "Wish List" and had a thoroughly good time doing it. I haven't described all of them here, but rest assured—there were lots of them. We both had a wonderful time, enjoying every minute.

* * *

Earlier in the year, in May of 2005, we met Bernie, Alix and the girls in Turkey. We wanted especially to have the girls see something of that country and its culture. However, Jim and I went ahead so that we could see a few things in Eastern Turkey before joining them. He and I had already been to the western part of Turkey visiting Troy, Ephesus and the other sites available on that coast, including the Grand Bazaar in Istanbul. One of the things we looked forward to seeing in the east was Nemrud Dag, a huge manmade mountain with the grave of Antiochus II at the summit. There are also huge heads with pointed hats scattered here and there that are the "signature" of the area. I'm sure you've seen pictures of them. There are also statues of lions and other creatures.

Jim and the author standing near a statue of a lion at the top of Nemrud Dag in Eastern Turkey, in May 2005.

The day we went to Nemrud Dag was grey and misty making the mountain hideously slippery. Part way up the mountain we hired donkeys to take us the rest of the way to the top. My donkey liked to walk at the very edge of the pathway giving me a view 1000 feet down of exceedingly sharp boulders to fall on should he make one misstep. I didn't like that idea, so I kept pulling extremely hard on the pommel of the saddle, especially with my right arm, to make him move back from the edge. My efforts made me feel better, but the donkey basically ignored me and walked exactly where he wanted to. We finally made it to the top. It was worth it. In spite of the mist, the view was stunning and the big heads and lions even more stunning.

The sides of the mountain were too steep to ride the donkey down, so we had to walk, slipping and sliding over the sharp rocks because a slight drizzle had begun. When we finally reached the bottom safely, I don't think I have ever been as relieved in my life. However, my right arm kept hurting for the rest of the trip, but not enough for me to give in and go home. (Later, back in Albuquerque, I went to an orthopedic surgeon and discovered that I had broken my own rotator cuff by pulling on the donkey's pommel too hard and had to have an operation to repair it.) The rest of the trip was great, except for the guide. But then, that's another story.

We met the others in Istanbul and toured the city with them seeing all the magnificent sights of that magnificent city. Of course, the Grand Bazaar held everyone's attention for hours. I do believe that a person would have to be one of the walking dead not to find the bazaar utterly enthralling.

We flew to Cappadocia area to see the eerie landscape of fairy chimneys carved by the wind and rain from a volcanic rock called *tufa*. Over the centuries people have hollowed out the centers of the chimneys and actually live in them. They are very comfortable.

Bernie and Alix near some *tufa* formations in Cappadocia, Turkey, in May 2005.

After more sightseeing and driving, we boarded a *gulet*, which is a smallish wooden coastal boat. Many of them have been fitted out to carry tourists along the coast of southern Turkey. They, too, are exceedingly comfortable. Our time on the *gulet* went by quickly.

Photo of our *gulet* at anchor off the Turquoise Coast of Turkey, May 2005.

The girls, as well as Bernie and Alix were able to kayak and swim, which all of them thoroughly enjoyed.

From left to right: Alix, Ana and Bernie swimming, with Callie in the kayak, all having a good time on the Turquoise Coast of Turkey, May 2005.

I enjoyed sitting comfortably in the stern watching it all in my newly purchased red tee shirt that matched the red Turkish flag.

The author relaxing in the stern of the *gulet* on the Turquoise Coast of Turkey, May 2005.

We put into several ports along the way. One of them was Myra, St. Nicholas' home. The church there was old and serene with thick, thick walls. It seemed odd to be in a place where the Santa Claus story started along with the whole Christmas bit. It seemed even odder to think that it happened in Turkey rather than the North Pole.

Eventually it all ended and we had to go home. It had been a grand tour.

*   *   *

Tunisia and Malta had been "wish list" destinations, so in May of 2006 when we discovered that Yvette was going to lead an ElderTreks tour to Tunisia and we could go on our own very conveniently

309

afterwards to Malta, we promptly signed up. As usual, Yvette had everything well organized. Tunisia is a beautiful country as well as being exceedingly interesting. The people are delightful and we felt right at home. The ruins of Carthage are probably the most famous. However, the Romans really "did unto" the Carthaginians when they finally defeated them after so many years of war, so there is really not much left of Carthage to see. Yvette made everything "come alive," however, so we couldn't complain too much about the damage the Romans did so many years ago.

Since Tunisia is not too large, we were able to make a circle around the country visiting all sorts of places—Bulla Regia, with ruins of Roman houses built underground to avoid the heat, but complete with Roman mosaic floors and fountains; Dougga and Sbeitla with their spectacular ruins; several desert oases; but, best of all, a lavish picnic in the ruins of El Jem, an amphitheater almost as large as the Coliseum in Rome. I expected gladiatorial bouts to begin any minute. It was a great, great trip.

Jim trying on a hat in a Tunisian market, May 2006.

I'm afraid that Malta did not quite come up to our expectations. It has a rather forlorn air about it and the suffocating presence of a militant Catholic church is everywhere. We were surprised to learn that divorce is against *civil* law. In addition, we were told that priests even investigate the building permits filed with the government for additions to houses, and so forth. When they discover a permit, they actually go to the homeowners and convince them under threat of dire consequences once they die (Hell) unless they give the money to the church and forget the addition to the house. The technique seems to work.

One of my main reasons for wanting to go to Malta was to see a large well known cave thousands of years old. However, I learned to my disappointment that tickets had to be secured weeks in advance, so we weren't able to see it. Even so, we were both glad that we had had a wonderful tour of Tunisia with Yvette, so all was not lost.

*   *   *

Both Jim and I have always been fascinated by the British institution known as the "pub." It is a short nickname for "Public House," which in itself doesn't mean much to Americans, but is the British name for a tavern. Pubs date back very far in British history—some to the twelfth and thirteenth centuries. The very old ones are treasures with dark wood, worn tables and innumerable legends and stories built up around them.

Jim and the author in front of a pub called Black Bull in Paradise, Great Britain, September 2006.

The author viewing the interior of a typical pub, Great Britain, September 2006.

In September of 2006, when we discovered a company that offered *An Archaeological Pub Crawl of Great Britain* we signed up immediately. (Jim says that it was for the sake of science that we made the trip.) It turned out to be more of a tour around southern Scotland and England visiting historic sites rather than a true pub crawl visiting ancient taverns only. Most of the hotels we stayed in were also old and beautiful, including The Lord Crewe Arms Hotel in Blanchland.

The sign of The Lord Crewe Arms Hotel in Blanchland, Great Britain, September 2006.

Because there were just three of us on the tour, the guide (a personable and knowledgeable young American who had just gotten his doctorate at Glasgow University), was able to cater to our desires to go off the beaten track here and there, if we all agreed.

After visiting Edinburgh Castle, we traveled to the Antonine Wall, which the Romans under the emperor Antonius Pius built across southern Scotland in 142 AD starting at the Firth of Forth on the east and going clear across the country. It is an earthen wall. By that I mean that the Roman soldiers dug deep into the ground throwing up the earth close to the edge of the lengthy pit they were creating along the boundary line. If you were to cut a cross-section, it would be shaped like the letter "S" standing on its side. I don't remember the final height of the wall, but it was quite high. Every so often pits were dug on the far side of the wall with huge sharpened stakes put in them vertically to deter horse soldiers. It is constructed far differently from Hadrian's Wall, which we saw later.

The weather that day was misty and foggy. The section of the wall we visited was somewhat isolated far out into the country side. Over the centuries, trees had grown up in the area, some of them now quite large. As we approached, we walked through tall grass dripping with moisture. The silence was eerie. I swear that there were Roman soldiers standing guard there waiting for us to make one false move. If I turned my head quickly, I could almost see the soldiers retreating behind the trees. After the hair on the back of my neck calmed down and my goose bumps subsided, it was splendid.

Hadrian's Wall was built in 122 AD. This wall is constructed of stones. It snakes across Britain south of the Antonine Wall. It has become a favorite destination of true trekkers who follow the wall from one end to the other. There are many ruins of small forts, turrets, living quarters and so on, alongside the wall itself.

The author standing alongside Hadrian's Wall near the remains of a fort, Great Britain. September 2006.

The author examining Hadrian's Wall more closely, Great Britain, September 2006.

A few years ago at the base of the wall, archaeologists discovered some letters written in Latin which were sent to and from various Roman officers' wives inviting each other to birthday celebrations, and so forth, sounding very much like modern young matrons. There were also some ledgers and accounting information as well as inventories. All of these were written on pieces of wood and were preserved by the action of the acidic soil. We were fortunate to see a large number of these relics at the British Museum on a later trip to London.

The rest of the tour included many ruins of Catholic churches, abbeys and monasteries that had been destroyed by Henry VIII. They were exceedingly impressive. You could quite understand why Henry wanted the clerics' wealth, not to mention obliterating their power, thus enabling him to marry as often as he pleased. We stayed in more old hotels and inns, which oozed charm and also visited innumerable castles, including Linlithgow where Mary, Queen of Scots was born and lived off and on. Cambridge University, the Uffington White Horse, the henge at Avebury and the Viking city of York were among the other sites. All in all, it was a good tour, but the two Roman walls were the best part.

*   *   *

We had been to India several times, but couldn't resist the lure of a forty-day trip which included much of the south which we hadn't seen, as well as Sikkim, Darjeeling and the Pushkar Camel Fair. Therefore, in October of 2006, we flew to New Delhi and then caught a local flight to Kolkata (Calcutta), where we met the rest of the group, then flying to Darjeeling to spend three days in an incredibly beautiful mountain environment. Every morning, before the clouds appeared, we had a magnificent view of the Himalayas.

The night before our departure from Darjeeling, a young man was murdered (seven stab wounds in the back), so the locals decided to blockade the main road out of Darjeeling until the murder had been solved. Mobs are definitely to be avoided if at all possible. Our bus was stopped and surrounded by the local crazies before we could get out of town. We ultimately escaped them. Fortunately our local guide was very familiar with the area and knew of the only other road out of town which went to Gangtok, Sikkim, our next destination.

Jim describes the alternative road as a "hemorrhoid packer," which, although not very ladylike, does describe it pretty accurately. Although a two-way road, it was so narrow that we were passing oncoming vehicles, including elephants, by at about one inch on either side. One of the sides being rocks. Although the road itself was ghastly, it was scenic as we were driving through hundreds of acres of tea plantations. At one of the plantations three men were standing on the side of the road near the tea plants urinating into them. As Jim said, it gives new meaning to the words "Orange Pekoe."

Our Gangtok guide was left behind when we headed for Kalimpong. We now had the services of a young Canadian man from the tour company. He was a very nice person, but simply did not have the wherewithal to be a tour leader as he tended to read to us in a monotonous voice from guide books as we were driving along. Not quite my idea of what a good tour guide should do. (He suffered badly when compared to Yvette.)

My further recounting of the places we visited is not in order as we backtracked quite a bit. The Ajanta Caves are filled with Buddhist religious carvings and many paintings which are really murals on the living rock walls. Both the carvings and the paintings are breathtaking. The only problem is that they are somewhat difficult to get to once you get off the bus. Some wonderful soul thought of sedan chairs. So Jim and I were carried up in great style.

The author being carried to the Ajanta Caves in a sedan chair, India, October 2006.

Jim being carried to the Ajanta Caves in a sedan chair, India, October 2006.

The author gaping at the Ellora Caves, India, October 2006.

The Ellora Caves are primarily religious carvings hewn out of the living rock and are equally breathtaking. Jim tells me that we had a local guide for both the Ajanta and Ellora Caves. Looking back I don't remember the guide at either location. I think I was just simply overwhelmed by both awesome sites and was too busy looking on my own to pay attention to a guide.

We also spent time in Goa, a former Portuguese enclave. It is on the coast in an area of white sand beaches and clear water. It reminded me of Hawaii—same trees and plants, burned red bodies, tall sweet drinks and holiday atmosphere. Our hotel was more than satisfactory. Our stay was topped off by a sublime lobster curry with a great bottle of Chilean wine.

Speaking of wine, whenever I think of it, I am amused by our wine experience in Bangalore. We ordered a bottle of Kendall Jackson red wine (surprised to see an American wine listed on the menu) at dinner one night, not really looking carefully at the menu and thinking in terms of US prices. We were astounded when we found out that the cost was $105. We had left the restaurant early, leaving our guide to pay the bill, which he had volunteered to do. The next day, he stuck to Jim like a leech until Jim went to an ATM, secured some cash and paid him for the wine.

Varanasi (the old name was Benares) is the holiest of Hindu cities. It dates from at least the Sixth Century BC and is located on the Ganges River. The river is lined with temples and pavilions, as well as booths which sell an assortment of flower "necklaces" for the pilgrims to drape over holy objects and places. Most of the flowers are jasmine and smell divine

The flower necklace seller in his both in Varanasi, India, October 2006.

Itinerant storytellers and musicians abound. Jim took a picture of an amazing man with brightly colored clothing, a white, wavy beard sporting a fairly unusual turban in a shade of brilliant orange-yellow. He was a delight to the eye.

An itinerant musician in Varanasi, India, October 2006.

There is a huge series of steps down to the river. Observers board small boats, going out into the river itself to face the devout on the steps.

The devout on the steps beside the Ganges River in Varanasi, India, October, 2006.

When we visited, it was the day that the people worshiped the rising sun. When the sun was finally visible, everyone cheered and began bathing in the river. It sounds somewhat mundane, but they were so sincere and intent on what they were doing that it was really a moving experience to watch.

Jim and the author in a boat on the Ganges River in order to watch the Ceremony of the Rising Sun, Varanasi, India, October 2006.

Khajuraho, Udaipur, Mumbai (Bombay). Bangalore, Agra and many other cities were also on the itinerary. One of them was Sarnath, where we saw remains of a temple where Lord Buddha had sat in meditation under a *po* tree and then preached his first sermon. It is said that the tree growing in the courtyard is a modern day descendant of that tree by means of cuttings taken over the years.

Jim is leaning on the ruins of a temple where Lord Buddha is said to have sat in meditation and then preached his first sermon, Sarnath, India, October 2006.

A sign inside one of the airports really made us aware that we were in India. We couldn't resist a picture in front of it.

Jim and the author standing in front of a sign in an airport
that brought home the fact that we really were in India, October 2006.

Security at that airport was a mess but the best part was a huge sign listing those who did *not* have to frisked or clear security. It included the President, various ministers and the Dalai Lama. Unfortunately my name wasn't on it, so I was frisked by a woman in a khaki uniform *sari* or typical Indian women's dress, complete with epaulets. She was quite lovely and most dignified. She and her friend thought my painted fingernails were all right, too.

Sign directing the author to the Ladies Frisking Booth at airport security, somewhere in India, October 2006.

Speaking of fingernails and hands, I succumbed and let a woman in one of the markets paint the palm of my hand with henna. As well as being skillful and entertaining to watch, she did a beautiful job. The dye lasted about a week. The design and the "omm" letter in the palm of my hand made me feel quite exotic.

The author showing her henna painted hand, somewhere in India, October 2006.

The author's exotic henna painted hand up close, somewhere in India, October 2006.

I'm not at all sure how he managed it, but our Canadian guide had us arrive at the Pushkar Camel Fair (one of the main reasons for the trip, as it is held only once a year) a day late so that we missed the most impressive part of the Fair. In addition to that, at the end of the tour in south India in Kochi (Cochin) when we were to cruise on a river, rest and recover ourselves before returning home, he got the dirtiest and most squalid of the houseboats for our use. However, with true "tourist spirit," we made do with what we had and basically enjoyed it all. (Well, most of it.)

* * *

Overseas Adventure Travel's catalogue increasingly tantalized us about the virtues of a trip to Costa Rica and Nicaragua, especially with teen agers. We invited Ana and Callie to go with us and headed south in June of 2007. There would be white water rafting, hiking, mud bathing, sailing through the forest canopy on zip lines, walking on rickety rope and wood bridges high among the trees and any number of other dangerous but highly desirable pursuits—desirable at least as far as the girls were concerned. I was also impressed by the fact that Costa Rica had dismantled its army in 1948 and seemed to do beautifully without it.

Our guide, Victor, (a different Victor) met us even though we emerged from customs late. We had been talking with the baggage people because Jim's bag was missing. Victor had a helper whose job was to take care of just such happenings. (Ominous) He seemed to think it was a "piece of cake," so we felt better. Just when we thought we were somewhat off the beaten path in a third world country, the hotel turned out to be a Marriott Courtyard and there was actually a Hooter's across the street.

The next morning we had a quick tour of San Jose including the Opera House which had been built in 1897. We had not been able to get into that building on our previous trip to Costa Rica as it had suffered some damage from an earthquake and was closed. It is extremely ornate in the Victorian style, but luxurious and comfy. It holds only about one thousand people.

We then got on our way to our next hotel, stopping en route at a "knock off" shop so that Jim could buy some clothing to wear when white water rafting since his suitcase was still missing. All the tour members were scrabbling around in boxes in the store looking for bargains, too. When we ultimately arrived at the hotel we found that it consisted of somewhat large round buildings scattered here and there around the grounds. The interiors were cut like a pie so that each room was a big triangle. It was awkward but efficient in an odd way.

Up early the next morning for the white water rafting. Jim, dressed in his new shorts (black, knee length), new shoes (velcro sandals) and my tee shirt (Tecate beer), was an awe inspiring sight.

Callie, Jim and Ana white water rafting with two other members of the tour in Costa Rica, June 2007.

Off the party went while I took a hike with Roberto, who showed me some of the flora and fauna of the area. There were tiny poisonous frogs that were red on the front half and blue on the back half. They were known as "blue jeans." Great name. In another part of the country we saw a "Jesus Christ" lizard—it can walk on water.

After the rafting, we went directly to a pineapple plantation. The tour was extremely informative and included all of the farming areas plus the packing and shipping area. For some reason they made bald headed Jim wear a huge coarse black hairnet. There he was in his slightly wet black baggy shorts, the tee shirt hanging about him in huge folds and his shiny bald head covered with a totally outlandish hairnet. He was gorgeous.

The pineapple plantation was in the process of "going organic," so we had a chance to taste an organic pineapple side by side with one grown in the normal manner. All of us were stunned. There was a huge difference in taste with the organic pineapple winning hands down. Victor, the guide, instructed Jim exactly how to pick out a pineapple in the grocery store. Since our trip and his newly acquired knowledge, he has brought home some beauties.

Victor had great rapport with the young people on the tour. He had three children himself and was a single dad. He bragged about his avocado *guacamole* and made a huge batch of it for us all the while wearing a chef's white hat and chattering away about how good it would be. He put on quite a show. The *guacamole* truly *was* good and we cleaned the plate.

There were three other young girls on the trip. There began to be a friendly rivalry between Victor and all of the girls that he could stand up against the five of them in a game of soccer and win. They, of course, challenged him. At one of our overnight camps there was a field big enough to see who was right. The field was located near a dormitory which housed the young men who took care of the camp. The game began. Gradually the young Costa Rican men emerged from their dorm to watch the proceedings. Soon there were a large number of people on the field playing for both sides and ogling the girls. I don't think anybody really won, but they all had a good time.

On one of the drives between hotels, we had a rest stop at a building clinging to the side of a mountain. There was a large window with a wide sill looking out over a valley filled with trees. A number of hummingbird feeders hung in the window with many, many varieties of hummingbirds enjoying lunch. They were so intent on feeding that they ignored us. You could therefore get very near to them and examine them closely, all the while listening to the whirr of their wings. Their iridescent feathers were glorious.

Another activity we all loved (except Jim) was zip lining. Permanent wire lines were strung between trees way up in the canopy. At the end of each "leg" of your ride there was a small landing platform where you transferred from line to line. The landing platform was against the trunk of the tree, so you really *did* want to be able to stop and not hit it going full speed. However, the braking was done by pulling very hard on a handle that went along the line with you. The girls were confident enough to zip on their own.

Ana, the author and Callie after zip lining in Costa Rica, June 2007. Can you tell that Callie enjoyed it?

I was afraid I wasn't strong enough to stop the contraption before I banged into the tree at the far end of each segment knocking myself silly. I, therefore, sat on the lap of one of the attendants and let *him* worry about how to stop. It was much better that way.

The author zip lining with someone to brake for her in Costa Rica, June 2007.

Our tour concluded with a flight to Managua, Nicaragua, which was interesting but extremely depressing. The contrast between Costa Rica and Nicaragua was marked. The Nicaraguan government is so corrupt that they are sucking the financial life out of the entire country. It unfortunately left us somewhat upset. Even the area hit by the 1972 earthquake was still rubble. I sincerely hope that at some point the country gets back on its feet. Unfortunately that will not happen until the corruption which permeates the country is overcome.

The only bright light was that Jim got his suitcase back.

*   *   *

We were still longing to get to Burma, so in October of 2007, we decided to try again. This time there was a tour to Laos and Vietnam included. The Evil Eye was still hovering over us and for the umpteenth time we were frustrated in our efforts to get there, as rioting broke out in Burma yet again. However, the tour company made very acceptable adjustments. We had flown from the States to Bangkok, as that airport is a big Far Eastern hub. Bangkok was a mass of elevated roads, flyovers and tracks for a sky train. The city was a huge mish-mash of high rises, gardens, bridges, slums, back alleys and peddlers. It seemed to me that there had been no central planning whatsoever. We did visit Suan Pakkad Palace and found it a rather cold museum now rather than the lived-in home we remembered. Our hotel was on the outskirts of the city, so we didn't see how bad things really were until we took a trip to Thailand a few years later.

After a day or two in Bangkok and learning more about the Burmese fiasco, we were told that the tour company had decided what it would do for us in lieu of our segment to Burma. The solution was a complete surprise and a very welcome substitute. We were to go to one of the large islands that make up part of Malaysia. The island included Sabah, Sarawak, Borneo and the separate Sultanate of Brunei.

We first flew to the city of Kuching, which is in the Malayan part of the island of Borneo. Then we went on to Kota Kinabalu, a city further along the north coast of the huge island in the area called Sabah. We enjoyed our expeditions into the jungle seeing all sorts of wild animals and, of course, the "wild man of Borneo" otherwise known as the *orangutan*. (In the local language *orang* means man and *utan* means tree.) The primates are incredibly human in appearance and truly seem to be men swinging from tree to tree. Easy to see how the confusion arose.

We had to get to our lodge by boat as there were no roads. The trip was punctuated by many animal sightings, including large elephants, crocodiles, orangutans and so forth. It was like being in a cageless zoo. But then we *were* in Borneo.

We were surprised and fascinated when we saw some movement in the jungle next to the river bank. What appeared, to our delight, was a fully grown pigmy elephant approximately four feet tall. He obviously wanted to go for a swim, so he jumped off the river bank, swam a short distance, blew water from his trunk and in general put on a fine show.

The orangutans are becoming somewhat endangered as more and more land is appropriated to grow a certain species of palm for its oil. We went to a rescue mission and, of course, "adopted" a baby orangutan to support while she was being raised and trained to return to the wild. Her name is SogoSogo. She made great progress and has been off on her own in the jungle for a few months now. We have adopted another, a very young female with the improbable name of Michelle. We hope she does as well as SogoSogo. Her pictures are adorable, if you can call an orangutan adorable.

At feeding time we saw an eleven year old male orangutan come to the platform for bananas. His coat was a beautiful reddish brown rather like the dyed hair of Spanish women, who will not tolerate being grey, so they dye their hair that particular shade of red, but are really not fooling anyone. He glistened in the sun as does the hair of the Spanish women.

Touring the Sultanate of Brunei as a mere outsider and a tourist was somewhat disappointing. We were told about the social programs, the educational opportunities, the lack of taxes, and so on. However, we saw nothing of the palace or other royal enclosures since the buildings are located at some distance away from the road and behind trees and other tropical plants. Not to mention the high walls patrolled by armed guards. Nor, of course, did we see the helicopters Dale Hardy sold to the Sultan. It was still somewhat shocking to realize we were quite near the richest man in the world.

We took a Royal Brunei Airlines plane from the sultanate to Kuala Lumpur. The stewardesses wore strange white caps somewhat like headdresses. They removed them during takeoff and then put them back on again. Before the safety talk, an *imam* or holy man blessed the flight while the TV monitor showed photos of mosques. I correctly assumed that we would be quite safe on that leg of our journey.

After Malaysia, we flew to Laos, a country filled with the gentlest of people with a very easygoing attitude toward life. I could understand our servant, Daeng's, personality and why nothing ever bothered her. It was peaceful and serene in Vientiane. Most Laotians speak Thai in addition to their own language. Jim's Thai was resurrected from the very depths of his soul and he had a splendid time talking with people, especially the children, with whom he liked to bargain and tease. Somehow in spite of Jim's bargaining with three little girls who were selling trinkets outside the gate to their house, he ended up paying their asking price after at least fifteen minutes of spirited discussion. They were really tough.

We also visited the famous Plain of Jars, which is an area covered by huge clay jars. No one knows what they were used for, but many theories exist—everything from brewing casks to burial urns. The area is startling to see and well worth the extra effort to get there.

The mysterious Plain of Jars in Laos, October 2007.

We then went on to Vietnam to the northern city of Dien Bien Phu where the French suffered their final defeat by the *Viet Minh* or Communist forces in a battle which lasted from 13 March to 7 April 1954. Although the museum was somewhat primitive, they had an exceptional display that showed the progress of the battle utilizing red lights for one side and green lights for the other. A voice with an American accent recounted the battle in English, while the lights darkened showing the outlying posts being overcome one by one. It was an exceedingly graphic illustration, well done and easy to understand, but horrifying.

From there we went on to Hanoi, which is a beautiful city with a small lake at its center. Of course we went to the infamous "Hanoi Hilton," which was the prison where many shot-down pilots were imprisoned under brutal conditions for so many years. The actual cell where John McCain, probably the most famous prisoner, was held is no longer there as part of the prison complex. It was demolished to make way for a real hotel. However, there were enough cells left for us to draw our own conclusions. John's flight suit, parachute and shoes were on display. He was picked up, badly injured, after he landed in the lake in the middle of Hanoi. Because of the time frame of the Vietnam War, many of the shot-down pilots were classmates, friends or acquaintances of Jim's from the Naval Academy. John had been in Jim's company at the Academy, although two years behind him with the Class of 1958. This made the visit to the prison even more personal and upsetting.

After the high drama of Hanoi, we went to Ha Long Bay, one of the most spectacular natural areas in the world. It is stunning. Huge rocky pinnacles of karst crowned with small twisted trees rise sharply from the blue water; wooden junks hover like big brown birds over the bay; fishermen with their exotic nets add an otherworldly note to the scene. I could have stayed there for weeks.

Eventually we arrived in Saigon or Ho Chi Minh City, as it is now called. The new name hasn't really stuck. Even the locals were still referring to it as Saigon. Jim showed me around the city pointing out many of the landmarks familiar to him. We had a drink on the rooftop lounge of the Majestic Hotel where he had watched a firefight across the river so many years before. We tried to find the house he had shared with some other officers and the parking lot where he had had the nasty experience with the plastic bomb in his jeep—all without success. However, our time there did give me a sense of the city for which I was grateful.

We moved on to Hoi An, passing an area which had been heavily mined and somewhat barren when Jim was there. It was now a resort.

Hoi An was a shopping Mecca of the first order. It was all I could do to restrain myself. But then how many walls can you cover with pictures? (I did get several primitive folk art prints.) And how much fabric can you buy? (I resisted.) Actually it was a pleasure just to walk into the shops and see what was available, even if you purchased nothing.

In spite of not getting to Burma, it was a superb trip. A great deal of the success was due to the fact that it was led by Alistair Smith, another of Adventures Abroad's top guides. We had gone to Spain earlier with Alistair and thought him particularly adept at his job. He had lived in Spain for several years as a teenager, so he knew places to take us that were not included in the published itinerary, which is always fun. It makes tourists feel special. We appreciated his expertise and patience on this trip, too. Not the least of which was his ability to select excellent and unusual menus with strange but tasty dishes for us to try.

* * *

In January of 2008, the spring semester of her junior year, Ana was awarded an internship in Washington in the office of one of New Mexico's Representatives, Heather Wilson. Naturally we were all *very* proud of her. Since Alix was fairly new at her job and couldn't take time from work, Jim and I escorted Ana back to Washington and got her settled in her living space.

Before we left Albuquerque, she and I had a great time buying new "East Coast" clothes and generally getting ready for the adventure. I must admit I took a lot of vicarious pleasure in doing this. It reminded me of getting ready to go to Germany years ago.

We arrived in Washington the Friday of the Martin Luther King holiday weekend, rented a car and started out to find the hotel where Jim had made a reservation. No luck. Between one-way streets, the cordoned off area around the White House, our lack of familiarity with the city after the passing of the years, and so on, we were just plain lost. Jim eventually spied a Hilton. They had two rooms available, so we took them, called the other hotel to cancel, and gratefully settled in.

After eating a great dinner in the bar, Jim and I casually ordered "a brandy." Then Jim had a second. When we got the bill, we saw to our horror that the waiter had given us the very best and they were $30 apiece. Shocking, but very tasty and a good way to celebrate Ana's scholastic coup in getting the internship. (You would have thought that the wine experience in India would have taught us to pay more attention. Apparently not)

The next day we set out to find the place where Ana was to live. Again getting lost frequently. We finally located it, left her luggage and headed toward Annapolis and our aerie above Chick and Ruth's Delly on Main Street and home away from home. During the next two days we ate crab, saw Petie and Jim, ate crab, showed Ana the Naval Academy, ate crab, ate crab and more crab.

On Tuesday we returned to Washington, took Ana to her lodgings and attempted to return the rental car and find the airport, finally succeeding in doing so. Then we were off to Albuquerque leaving Ana to her grand adventure. According to her, it *was* a grand adventure. She had many anecdotes to tell us. She apparently enjoyed her time in Washington and liked the responsibility she had. What a great experience for a young woman.

*   *   *

In 2008, Colonel Gaddafi of Libya began to see the error of his ways in not allowing American tourists into his country to spend money and boost the economy. When we found out that he had relented, we quickly reserved a place on a tour in March of that year. Not missing a beat, Gaddafi upped the visa fees, so we had to ante up an additional $500 each for the privilege of visiting Libya. Would you call these extra fees bribes?

There are a number of UNESCO World Heritage sites in Libya. We were to visit five of them and be given the "expert advice" of an American archaeologist who was excavating at Cyrene, one of those sites. It all sounded great.

When we stepped off the plane, we were immediately met and stopped by the local guide. He took our passports and replaced the Arabic translation of the visa with a more "correct" one. We were lucky as one participant had landed, had his visa examined and was promptly deported to Milan at his own expense. He never did join the group. A second person, the representative of our American tour company, was sent to Malta. She, however, did eventually join us. The Libyan Government assigned a "Tourist Policeman" to our group. His name was Hakim. He went everywhere with us. Although he did not speak very much English and we could not communicate with him as we would have liked, he turned out to be an exceedingly straightforward and nice person. In the end, he saved us some tense moments.

Before leaving for the desert, we visited a newly discovered Phoenician tomb on the outskirts of the city. It was small and truly exquisite. The walls were cream with delicate frescos depicting animals, winged humans, arena fighters dragging in wild animals by long chains, and flowers, flowers, flowers. There were places for two bodies—a perfect place to spend eternity.

The peaceful and serene Phoenician tomb outside of Tripoli, Libya, March 2008.

Our first UNESCO site was the huge desert area called the Akakas in southern Libya. Ten thousand years ago the climate had been moist and tropical. There were crocodiles, hippos, fish and other water loving animals living there at that time. Images of these creatures had been carved into the rocks by the early people forming primitive, but very graphic, petroglyphs. Of course, now the area is desert.

Petroglyph of a crocodile-type animal carved into the rock beside a river thousands of years ago in the Akakas Desert, Libya, March 2008.

It took thousands of years of natural global warming to change this area from jungle to desert. This change was an evolutionary process, not caused by automobiles and manmade pollution generating factories. It makes you wonder why people in today's world can't realize that automobiles and factories do not cause global warming.

Also in the area were red pictographs painted on the vertical flat surfaces of many of the huge rocks. The paint was made by grinding a particular red rock having a high iron content and then mixing the dust with urine. The dry, dry air had kept them intact for centuries until some European tourists began to pour water on them to bring out the color so that they would photograph better. The pictographs then began to dissolve and melt. What a tragedy.

Pictograph of a giraffe and another animal painted thousands of years ago on the rock cliffs of the Akakas Desert, Libya, March 2008.

We camped out in the desert in one-man tents for several nights. The tents were surprisingly comfortable and warm, which was really appreciated as it gets extremely cold in the desert when the sun goes down.

There were, of course, no baths and so on, but it was fun, in a way. You washed your face with water from one of the bottles of drinking water and when you brushed your teeth, you just spit into the sand. The helpers erected a portable toilet in the evenings when they put up the tents. I must say that it really made you appreciate modern plumbing.

Jim and I had our own jeep and driver. The vehicle was in dreadful condition but Mohammed seemed to know its quirks and kept it running smoothly. The group was accompanied by a truck which held the tents, food, and other equipment. It usually went on ahead to the next camp site and had things under control before we arrived. I must say that having a cook along was almost laughable. Most noon meals consisted of little piles of canned legumes of various types, drained and then set on a round tray with *hummus* or *tahine* (combinations of chick peas and olive oil) in the middle. The legumes were usually plain kidney beans, chickpeas, pinto beans, black beans and mushy peas. One time we were exceedingly lucky and got yellow corn kernels. Some sort of hard, dry bread was also served. It took hours to chew. The evening meals were not much better. However, we did get *couscous,* a Moroccan pasta, every once in a while served with a watery stew.

Our bathroom facilities while driving during the day were primitive to say the least. The ground was completely covered with small boulders or large rocks; whichever way you want to describe them. Therefore whenever I saw a scraggly bush or a decent size pile of rocks, Mohammed would stop, I would partially disappear behind the rocks, and then we would resume our incredibly rough, bumpy drive.

The author emerging from behind one of the better rest stops in the Akakas Desert, Libya, March 2008.

We left the desert a day early, much to everyone's delight, and were told we were going to a hotel. We arrived and found that it was more or less a hostel with hard beds, little hot water, thin worn out towels and everything rather second, if not third, rate. We also eagerly anticipated some decent food. Our hopes were dashed when we were told that lunch was being served in an area out the back door. Off we trotted and found ourselves in the *parking lot* surrounded by cars, eating off a makeshift table and being served the same canned bean lunch that had haunted us for a week. So much for that tour company.

Tuareg nomadic tribes roam this area of Libya. I was immediately captivated by the insignia of the various tribes. These have been reproduced in a silver colored metal (you never know how much actual silver is used) by local craftsmen. The shapes are unusual and can be said to resemble crosses, star formations or anything else your imagination devises. Jim bought me several that I had strung with black onyx and silver beads making quite tailored and striking looking necklaces. I also have one strung with black and red-colored coral which is outstanding.

After the Akakas Desert, we went on to the underground city of Ghadames. To escape from the heat, the people dug down into the ground where the temperatures were cooler. They had complete dwelling places below the surface which even included areas that were planted with a few crops. Those areas were open to the sun, but most of the rooms themselves were covered over with a roof. The rooms were whitewashed and decorated with red and orange designs. The red "paint" was made from pomegranate blossoms, while the orange came from the peel of the fruit itself. The designs were executed by the teenage daughters of the families and are light, airy and charming.

The houses usually have three to four stories. Women can go from house to house without going outside. In addition to the farming plots, there are mosques, baths, markets and schools all within the underground towns.

When we returned to Tripoli, we were housed in a hotel near Tripoli's famous Marcus Aurelius arch, named for one of the Roman emperors. The arch is a number of feet below the present level of the ground and therefore rather interesting to investigate. The hotel was delightful. They had a pet turtle that crawled around the lobby and occasionally ate some lettuce and a few houseplant leaves. We were upgraded to a "suite"—Jim got the huge hard double bed with hardly any access to the room itself. I got the small hard single bed in the living room. However, after the desert, everybody was happy.

We ate in some odd restaurants. Jim snapped a picture of me at one of the "better" ones as I was entering some information in my journal.

The author catching up in her journal at one of the outdoor restaurants in Tripoli, Libya, March 2008.

Back on the Mediterranean Coast, we visited Sabratha, and Leptis Magna. Both are ruins of magnificent ancient Roman cities. Leptis Magna was the "home town" of Lucius Septimius Severus, one of the more famous Roman emperors. His arch, which was erected in his honor in 203 AD, is extremely impressive and forms the entrance to the city. It is also situated on one of the two main cross streets which are standard in important Roman cities.

The Arch of Septimius Severus in the ruins of Leptis Magna, an ancient Roman city in Libya, March 2008.

The city must have intimidated newcomers the minute they set eyes on it. Leptis Magna has been partially reconstructed and is really worth going out of your way to see. It must have been like putting together a really difficult three dimensional jigsaw puzzle with many of the pieces missing. On second thought, most archaeology is exactly that.

Cyrene was another Roman site although it had not been uncovered to the point where you could conjure up a true city in your imagination. Our "expert" had been in charge of the excavations at Cyrene and really didn't bother to explain things properly to mere tourists. I, at least, failed to see what had actually been accomplished, although in fairness I should say that the site had been idle for a number of years during the time foreigners were banned from Libya and was only at the time of our trip going to be worked on again.

Our final "adventure" took place on the bus ride to the airport to go home. One of the unthinking women on the tour took a number of photographs through the bus window of the walls of one of Gaddafi's compounds. About a mile down the road we were stopped by the police who were intent on arresting the photographer. Someone had been spotted using a camera by their surveillance equipment. The Libyans have a theory that if they can't find the culprit, then they just arrest everyone and haul them *all* off to jail.

Fortunately, by this time, Hakim, our tourist policeman, realized that we were harmless. The woman had a digital camera. He took the camera, jumped off the bus and huddled with the police for what to us seemed hours. Eventually he returned, gave her the camera, and explained that he had extricated us from our problem by having all the offending pictures deleted. God bless modern cameras as well as Hakim.

*   *   *

As everyone already knows, I am a flower nut and Jim is equally bad about vegetables, so in the spring of 2008 we decided to go to London to see the famed Chelsea Flower Show. It was everything it was supposed to be and then some. We attended the show itself on only one day and found it completely absorbing. It was difficult to see how so many plants could be forced to maturity and full bloom totally outside of their normal season.

One of the display gardens at the entrance to the Chelsea Flower Show, London, Spring 2008.

The displays were exceedingly well done. Some of them were so elaborate it was hard to believe that they were temporary and would be dismantled in a few days. Many items were offered for sale, including seeds, plants, vases, and other garden items including fountains.

Charming fountain adorned with a statue of an elf offered for sale at the Chelsea Flower Show, London, Spring 2008.

In addition to the flower show itself, we were taken to Wisley, Hever, Great Dixter and Sissinghurst. These are all famous English estates with superb gardens and had long been on my wish list. They truly lived up to their reputations. All, of course, were impeccably maintained. Each garden was completely free of weeds, perfectly mulched and blooming profusely. The wide stretches of lawn were always a uniform shade of green, again without weeds or any yellow spots. We also went to the great public gardens at Kew, which always make me think of that Alfred Noyes poem with the refrain "Go down to Kew in lilac time, in lilac time, in lilac time." It was peaceful and serene.

We had dinner on our own several times in good restaurants and went to a performance of the musical, *Billy Eliot,* that wonderful show about a young boy who longs to become a dancer against his working class father's wishes. Somehow the story of his ultimate success in the dance world, as well as his father's conversion to his way of thinking, is quite heartwarming. It is much like a male Cinderella story. Everybody loves it. England again fulfilled its mission as one of our favorite destinations.

*　　*　　*

In 2009 during Callie's senior year at Taos High school, she and three boys from her Culinary Arts class entered the state cooking competition. They were under the tutelage of Benjie Apodaca, an instructor at their school. They had to devise a menu and create recipes for a three course meal which was to include an appetizer, a main course and dessert. At the competition, which was held in Albuquerque, they had to prepare two servings of each offering. The first was for display to show the plating of the food and its visual appeal. The second was for the judges to taste. All of this had to be completed within one hour. Their equipment was somewhat limited as they had only two heat sources. There were high standards of cleanliness, technique and, of course, appearance and taste.

The judging was carried out by men and women walking around the hall looking extremely serious, not talking and making occasional notes on their clipboards. We were told that they were professional chefs. We in the audience were not permitted to talk with the competitors or judges. We were to remain as still as possible so as not to distract anyone.

Callie created the dessert. It really was a masterpiece. Truly appetizing. Finally it was over, the appearance plates were put on display and we had only to wait for the judges to make their decisions and announce them later.

The first course was an eggplant and goat cheese tart, the entree was lamb, and the dessert an almond crepe shell filled with fruit coulis and garnished with decorations made with white as well as dark chocolate. All the dishes looked picture perfect. Jim overheard one of the tasting judges say to another, "Taste this." referring to Callie's dessert. Just his tone of voice gave Jim hope. He wasn't wrong. When the winners were announced Taos came in first and would be going to San Diego for the nationals. Everybody cheered and cried. We were *very* proud of them.

Callie and her team hard at work at the cooking competition, Albuquerque, 2009.

Callie holding her prize winning dessert, Albuquerque, 2009.

*   *   *

In April that year, we went to the cooking nationals in San Diego to be with Callie when her team competed. There were teams from all fifty states, plus Puerto Rico and Guam. The atmosphere was very professional and completely intimidating. I'm afraid that the pressure was too much for everyone and the Taos team did not place in the top ten. However, the experience was wonderful for the four young people and we, as well as the city of Taos, were very proud and pleased for them.

*   *   *

In June of 2010, Jim and I decided to take a trip to Israel, staying over in both New York and London, coming as well as going, to make it a bit easier on ourselves, as we were beginning to have the usual aches and pains brought on by the passing of the years. It had been fifty years since we were last in Jerusalem and things do change. We wanted to see what was happening to Israel in today's world.

Our flight to Tel Aviv from London aboard British Air was somewhat strange. The plane was packed. Every seat was taken. Service was not up to their usual standards because of a cabin crew strike. Ground and other crewmembers pitched in so the flights could go as scheduled. It was rather odd to see a man with captain's stripes on his uniform serving coffee and tea to passengers. (He did a creditable job.) Surprisingly, lunch was extremely good—a tasty Indian chicken curry.

New York, London and the first few days in Tel Aviv were great. We arrived a few days ahead of the other tour members. Our hotel was a converted old movie theatre and quite strange. There were old cameras and other film equipment scattered around the public rooms. All were in deplorable condition and, to my eyes, exceedingly unattractive. Also the whole building curved following the lines of an amphitheater. It was odd.

We enjoyed going to the flea market in the Old Jaffa area where we bought two bronze fish that the proprietor of one of the shops had brought from Syria when he emigrated. Fish also keep away the Evil Eye, so I was told that they were very good for "lucking." (Jim describes this purchase as typical of me when on a trip—heavy and expensive.) We found a bar and restaurant around the corner from the hotel called the Amelia Earhart, named for the famous American woman aviator. It had good food, the people were nice and the outdoor patio in the evenings was cool and breezy. It was also a great people-watching place. It had the added attraction of a "duty" cat that made the rounds of the tables regularly each evening to scrounge for food. He was adorable and I wished, as always with cats, that I could take him home with me.

After the other tour participants arrived, the pace became a little more hectic. The people joining us were all delightful and fun to be with. We toured Jerusalem seeing the Western Wall with the area in front of it divided so that men and women visited different parts.

The Western Wall clearly showing the segregated male and female visiting areas, Jerusalem, June 2010.

The older part of Jerusalem was a weird combination of many religions. Following the Stations of the Cross was a very sobering experience and one not soon forgotten. The stations are marked by ceramic plaques inserted into walls and buildings which tell what happened there and direct you to the next station.

One of the streets showing two of the Stations of the Cross plaques embedded into the wall of a building at the left of the photo, Jerusalem, June 2010.

We re-visited the Church of the Holy Sepulcher and found that the exterior had been repaired, but the interior was still divided among squabbling Christian sects. Of all places for that sort of thing to go on, that particular church was not it.

Our tour guide, Ya'Ara, (whose name means "honeysuckle" in Hebrew) was superb. We set off the next day driving up the coast to the Lebanese border. It took several days as we stopped in Haifa, Caesarea and several other places, including a stay at a *kibbutz* or collective farm. We went into the Golan Heights (where we visited a winery and had lunch with a Druze woman) and then down to the Sea of Galilee eventually reaching Herodium, the pleasure palace King Herod had constructed for himself on top of a mountain which also later held his tomb. Also ran into herds of camels. Guess you can't escape them in the Middle East. Camels are feisty animals, but with enough exposure to them, you can become very fond of them in a way.

Camels we met along the way, Israel, June 2010.

This was near the beginning of the trip and I blithely assumed that I could climb to the top of Herodium with very little effort. Besides, I wanted to see it. After I had reached the point of no return on the mountain, which kept growing larger and larger, my fellow travelers took pity on me and pushed, pulled and dragged me to the top. They were very kind. The temperature was 104 degrees Fahrenheit. Frankly, I don't know how we all made it.

We were also able to go to Masada, the mountain fortress held by the Jews after the rebellion against the Romans in 69 AD. Masada finally fell to the Romans in 74 AD. Fortunately there was a tram which took you to the top of the mountain. We therefore arrived in one piece and were able to look at everything without too much panting. Before the tram was installed, the only way to the top was by a precarious path about two feet wide and bordering on straight up. The temperature that day was also over 104 degrees Fahrenheit which didn't help much.

The new entrance to Masada, Israel, June 2010.

As we were walking at the top to the entrance of Masada, a group of young students asked Jim if he had climbed the path rather than using the tram. Short of breath and perspiring profusely, Jim's response was "Of course I climbed the path. I also walk on water."

It was incredible to see the storerooms, the living quarters and other parts of the small city-like area. When defeat by the Romans was inevitable, the remaining people committed suicide. Israeli soldiers today take an oath that "Masada shall not fall again."

Legend has it that two women and three children did not commit suicide and survived. Before we toured the top of Masada, Ya'Ara dressed herself in suitable attire and pretended to be one of the women dramatically recounting what happened in the last hours. She did a fine job as an amateur actress. All of us were impressed and applauded vigorously.

As we drove near Mt. Sodom we were told that it is the "highest lowest mountain or the lowest highest mountain" in Israel. Its base is way below sea level in the lowest place on the planet, but the summit is above sea level. Everything in that area seems to have a very high salt content, compliments of Lot's wife, I suppose.

Jerusalem, Bethlehem, Jericho, and a number of other cities were also visited including Ramallah were we saw Yasser Arafat's tomb. It was stark, modern and bristling with well-armed soldiers, most of them young enough to be our grandchildren.

As the trip went on, the churches began to blur into each other and one town looked very much like another. All in all, the excessive heat, climbing up or down long slippery flights of steps, eating repetitious, nasty food and keeping up a pace that left little time for recouping at the end of the day took its toll. We made a vow that in the future we would go in the cool season to tropical countries and find tours a little less strenuous. Since there are a large number of those available, we weren't too depressed.

Here and there around the country, we saw coffee shops called "Stars and Bucks." If you looked closely you could see that the font the logo was printed in, the insignia, and almost everything else was curiously similar to a certain American chain although not an exact copy. I would love to know if it was copyright infringement or if the American company went to Israel and simply changed the name slightly. However, the coffee was excellent.

The front of one of the Stars and Bucks coffee shops, Israel, 2010.

There were some funny uses of English by the locals which occurred during the trip. They always made me smile although my own forays into other languages are certainly dismal enough. At lunch one afternoon the menu mentioned a number of Middle Eastern specialties listed separately—*kibbe, tabouli, shish kabob*, etc. Just under the list, the restaurant announced that if you wanted more variety, you could have a plate with "all of the up."

(My use of the word "separately" in the paragraph above triggered memories of one of my language lapses. We were in Mexico in a hotel where it was deemed safe to eat raw green salad. I chose one that had a number of ingredients—lettuce, tomatoes, green and red sweet peppers, and so on. I wanted my dressing on the side, so I asked for the salad "separado." My jaw dropped when I was served each salad ingredient separately. There must have been ten plates set in front of me. However, I *did* get my dressing on the side, so all was well. I still don't know how to get my dressing on the side in Spanish, but hope to one day.)

Another funny example occurred one morning when we came down for breakfast in Tel Aviv. Jim asked one of the waiters if he could find him a banana for his cereal. The waiter disappeared into the galley while Jim stood at the door awaiting his return. Another waiter appeared, approached Jim and asked, "Do you have a puzzle?" After traveling for so many years, Jim, almost by second nature translated the phrase into: "Is there a problem?"—"May I help you?"—"Is something wrong?" Since none of these translations applied, Jim said no, and waited patiently for the other waiter to bring his banana. Puzzle solved.

Another time Ya'Ara was telling the story about Elijah running away. She said that he was "on the flee." Later the Palestinian guide called out to one of the people on the bus who was walking in the aisle while the bus was moving, "Sit down. If he make brakes, you will fall." I also like the guide throwing stale or "expired" bread to fish in a pond.

However, the best one of all occurred when we were about to enter the tunnels under the Western Wall in Jerusalem. Jim doesn't like confined spaces, so he questioned the guide on the height of the tunnels. He was told that it was not a problem and that he could walk "erected."

One evening before dinner several of us were in the bar of the hotel having cocktails. One of the Jewish women on the tour whose family had patronized the resorts and shows in the Catskills for years started telling jokes. Her accent was perfect, her timing impeccable and the jokes were hilarious. She was so quick with them and everyone was laughing so hard, that I don't think that anyone remembered a single joke. It was one of the best "shows" I have ever been to.

* * *

The political situation in Israel is surreal—like something from a Salvadore Dali painting. Nothing is what it seems. The Israelis "won" the 1967 war, but are still without a united country. They are compounding the problem, I think, by not assimilating the Palestinians, but actually physically segregating them in ghettos with huge walls and checkpoints, as *they* were segregated in Europe before World War II. Palestinians cannot go into Israeli areas but the Israeli army can go into Palestinian areas anytime it wants to check people at random. The Palestinians have no passports, the schools are inferior, the housing is inferior and life in general in the Palestinian areas is inferior. The infrastructure is sometimes non-existent—imagine no garbage collection throughout the Palestinian areas. However, we were told that after the huge walls were constructed between the two areas that the number of terrorist attacks by Palestinians on Israelis declined dramatically.

On the other hand, it does seem to me that the Palestinians have enough room to have their own landfills for garbage, and can somehow come up with the initiative and ability to construct some of the things they need. However, as an outsider, I will never know what it is like to live on either side of the big walls. Each side has its problems.

We met with a large number of Palestinian and Israeli people, both men and women from all walks of life, listening to their stories and points of view. The discussions were very open and truly represented the opinions of the speakers. We realized that our government is naïve and unthinking when it tries to broker a peace settlement in an area of the world that has been at loggerheads for thousands of years. The only conclusion we could possibly arrive at was that memories are too long, situations too peculiar and Israel, the Holy Land, will never truly be at peace with itself and the rest of the world. A genuine pity. I hope I am wrong.

13

RETURN TO THAILAND

J IM FINALLY GOT HIS WISH and we booked another trip to Burma (Myanmar) and Thailand in February of 2011. There were no uprisings, riots, or border disputes to interfere with the smooth operation of the tour, so we were "off and running." Bangkok was the city where the tour was to begin, so we reserved a room at the same hotel the tour would be using a few days early in order to explore some of our favorite places on our own. We also splurged on Frequent Flyer miles and flew First Class on Cathay Pacific. It was a somewhat strange experience in that the seats are so isolated that you have no one to talk to. Even Jim and I were separated and couldn't talk to one another unless we made a point of getting up and walking to the other's cubicle. I guess that a tired businessman on his way home would appreciate the peace and quiet, but I found it somewhat disconcerting, as well as the constant inquiring by the attendants as to whether or not I needed or wanted anything.

As our plane approached Bangkok, we could see that the skyline had changed dramatically. There were a large number of high rise buildings, office complexes and hotels that were new. The network of highways and bridges was formidable. (Again, I was extremely thankful that I wasn't going to be doing any driving.) I couldn't spot any *klongs*. However, we did discover later that a few are left.

The hotel was on Surawong Road and was more than comfortable. Jim Thompson's silk shop was a short walk from the hotel. We hurried down to see it and were more appalled than we had been on our first visit after he disappeared. It was totally "Europeanized." The items offered for sale were bland, colorless and so expensive as to be ridiculous. A small café had been set up on the second floor (of all things), so we had a cup of tea while we tried to recover. Both of us were in shock. Mr. Uthai's area behind the store was long gone and nobody seemed to remember him.

At the hotel, we ran into a couple we had met on a previous tour. They had just finished touring Burma and Thailand and were leaving the next day to return home. We were sorry as we enjoyed them and would have liked sharing dinner. However, Bob's descriptions of the Buddhas he had seen in both Burma and Thailand did make us laugh. He claimed that he had seen sitting, standing, reclining, golden, walking, praying, resisting evil, smiling, pointing, protecting, earth touching and subduing Mara Buddhas and really did not need to see any more. In a way, I can see his point.

We had lunch several times on the terrace of the Oriental Hotel overlooking the river. The food and service were up to their old standards, so that made us feel somewhat better. The lobby was beautifully decorated with hundreds of orchids formed into large vertical arrangements which hung down from the high ceiling. The hotel shops were extremely upscale with the prices even more upscale and shocking. Even so, it was fun to see.

We went to a large shopping mall only to discover that it, too, was filled with a number of upscale European brand stores. Strangely they were very well patronized. We were told later that Thailand is one of the favorite destinations of wealthy mainland Chinese, and they are the people who do the shopping in the malls.

The tallest building in town (eighty stories) has a restaurant on the top floor. We thought that it would be a nice place to have dinner and look out over the city. We tried to make reservations, but they were completely booked. However, they recommended their restaurant on the seventieth floor, which was a little less formal and a little less expensive. We accepted and they made a reservation for us. When we emerged from the elevator we were led to our table, seated and given menus. The view was indeed spectacular, the temperature balmy and the menu enticing—until you looked at the prices. For a very simple meal and medium quality wine, the charge for the two of us would have been about $450. We thanked them and left. However, we now knew of another destination of the wealthy mainland Chinese.

One odd note struck us. Even though the price of gasoline was high, it was possible to hire a taxi using a meter, and travel miles extremely inexpensively. It didn't seem to make sense to either of us, but we were grateful. We were also struck by the large number of Thais in service jobs in the hotel, the shops, and so on, who had a fairly good command of English. When we had lived in Bangkok, English speaking Thais were few and far between. Eventually the rest of the tour participants arrived. We then set off for Burma.

*　　*　　*

Yangon (Rangoon) is the capital and the site of the most famous of the temples, the Shwedagon Pagoda. It is enormous, exotic and awesome in the true meaning of that word. It is said that so much gold has been applied to the *stupa* or spire that it probably weighs about ninety tons. The grounds had been cleaned up since I was there, and everything seemed a bit sterile. (No red betel nut spit to slip in.) However, the complex is quite large and as you walk around looking at the statues, the small chapels and noticing the people with their reverent attitude toward it, you realize how important it is in their lives.

Jim and the author in front of the main Shwedagon Pagoda, Rangoon, Burma, February 2011. (Yangon, Myanmar)

Jim and the author near a protective lion in the Shwedagon Pagoda compound
in Rangoon, Burma, February 2011. (Yangon, Myanmar)

The tour went on to Mandalay and several other cities, including Bagan, with
its plain of ancient temples. It reminded us of Ayutthaya in Thailand. Everything
seemed a little run down. Even the famous *wats* and other ruins were rather sad
and forlorn. However, enough was left to give us a glimpse of what it was like
years ago.

The ruins of Bagan in Burma, February 2011 (Myanmar)

We stayed in a hotel on the shore of the Irrawaddy River somewhere upcountry. I'm not exactly sure of the location, but the site was magnificent. There was a large outdoor dining area shaded by several mature trees that spread their branches over the tables and gave just the right amount of shade. Huge glossy black birds hovered in the lower branches ready to pounce on any crumbs that might fall to the ground. Their cries were raucous and reflected their aggressive attitude toward life. They were survivors.

*   *   *

I don't know whether the poor food supply caused the Burmese to eat a certain variety of rat or whether it had been done for years. We were invited to try "long tail chicken" which turned out to be a very large rat fried until crisp. Then the diners pulled the meat bit by bit from the carcass. I am usually fairly willing to try most anything in the way of food, but this one stopped me. It still had its tail and whiskers in place.

We were surprised by the Burmese people. However, it was a mistake on our part to have expected them to be as outgoing and smiling as the Laotians and Thais. They have been under a repressive government for years and it is showing in the faces of the people. Jim compares them to a mistreated animal that retreats and won't look you in the eye. I think he may be right. However, after all the attempts to get to Burma, it was something of a triumph to actually be there. It was well worth all the time and trouble.

After flying back to Bangkok, we went north to both Chiang Rai and Chiang Mai via Sukothai. We had not been to Chiang Rai before, so couldn't compare. However, today's Chiang Mai bears little resemblance to the city we visited so many years ago with Sangob and Krishna. We were startled and somewhat dismayed.

However, on our earlier trip to Chiang Mai we had not visited any elephant refuges. This time we did and found the experience truly delightful. The best part was watching Suda, a five year old female paint a picture. Yes, that's what I said—paint a picture. Her trainer set up and easel for her which held a large piece of stiff white paper. He then handed her a paint brush loaded with paint. She grasped the brush with the tip of her trunk and started to work. When she ran out of paint, or wanted a different color, the trainer supplied her needs. Her painting eventually showed two black elephants in a blue river with green banks and a bright red flower. It was fantastic. We bought it (funds going to help support the refuge), brought it home, and had it framed. It is now hanging in our office next to four photos Jim took of Suda while the work was in progress. Great inspiration.

Suda, the elephant in the process of painting a picture at the elephant refuge near Chiang Mai, Thailand, February 2011.

Suda's completed picture, which hangs on our office wall, painted at the elephant refuge near Chiang Mai, Thailand, February 2011.

* * *

This trip was not one of the best, but it taught us a lot about what the passage of time can do to both one's memories and reality. It was worth taking. However, it did indeed underscore that the old saying "You can't go back" is very true.

POSTSCRIPT ONE

THE PASSAGE OF TIME ALSO changes the dynamics within families, creating problems no one envisions. When Mark and Cathy moved to Albuquerque, Jim began training Mark to eventually take over his insurance and investment business. However, that didn't happen quite the way we had imagined it.

We had always thought that Dickey was an acceptable surname. However, it was not acceptable to Cathy. Mark and Cathy's last names as well as the last names of their two boys were changed from Dickey to Richards without our knowledge. In fact it was almost six months before we were aware of the change.

Had we known, it might have been a warning of things to come. When we returned from a trip, we found that Mark had planned a hostile take-over of the business. This action precipitated a legal conflict which basically destroyed twenty-seven years of Jim's work. It also culminated in our disavowing and disinheriting Mark and his family. We no longer have contact with them. The entire affair was unfortunate, unnecessary and extremely upsetting.

*   *   *

As bad as it was, the old saying about making lemonade out of lemons came into play. Without the responsibilities of the business to take our time and energies, we have been able to travel extensively and frequently. Retirement has given us the opportunity to visit many places we would not have been able to see otherwise, although at great emotional cost.

POSTSCRIPT TWO

ANA GRADUATED FROM THE UNIVERSITY of New Mexico in December of 2009 at the end of the fall semester. We were very proud of her as she had worked during her entire college career and still earned top grades.

Ana holding her diploma,
Albuquerque, December 2009.

She and her roommate, Dani Bauer, continued to work for a month or two but then decided that they needed a bit of adventure. Dani is from Alaska and wanted to return. Ana decided to go with her to see what the "Last Frontier" was all about. She bought a Small Utility Vehicle (SUV) more suitable for Alaska. In April, they packed up their automobiles and started the long trip to Anchorage driving in tandem. Their route took them inland through Calgary and Edmonton.

They found a small apartment they could share and settled in comfortably. Ana eventually secured a job with a firm that rents heavy equipment to drilling companies, and does other things I'm not really conversant with. She loves it and has been given increasing responsibility, including the planning of the company's Christmas party with a budget of $10,000. A hostess's dream. Dani seems to be equally happy.

*   *   *

Callie is a junior at the University of New Mexico. She is majoring in business and marketing. She also works in the office for the Executive Masters Program for business students on campus to help with her finances. Between classes, homework and long hours on the job, she has a heavy schedule. She would like to take advantage of a year abroad, preferably France. However, she will wait a while for that. In spite of her tight schedule, I'm sure she finds some time for "fun." I know she enjoys soccer.

Callie dressed for soccer, Albuquerque, December 2011.

POSTSCRIPT THREE

TRAVELING CONTINUES TO CONSTITUTE AN extremely large part of Jim's and my lives, our time and our interests even though upcoming trips will not be as strenuous as previous ones. We tried to instill in our children, and then our grandchildren, the fascination we felt for travel and the witnessing of everyday life, as well as the history, of other parts of the world. I hope, in some small way, that we succeeded.

In today's world, customs and habits change swiftly. The internet, cell phones and television have all contributed their share to the homogenization of world culture. Who knows what new electronic devices will be invented and further contribute to this. I am indeed grateful to have seen a number of places and countries before they were overrun by "modern civilization."

I also believe that it is time to stop comparing and enjoy things as they come.

THE END

ACKNOWLEDGEMENTS

THERE ARE A NUMBER OF people to whom I am extremely grateful for help with this book. I sincerely thank them for their contributions of time and effort.

First, I would like to thank my husband, Jim, who read, re-read and then re-read the manuscripts again, each time helping me remember details of various incidents and jogging my memory of others I had completely forgotten. Many times when we were chatting in the evenings or went out for dinner, something would come back to one or the other of us. I would then borrow his trusty pen and fill a paper napkin with notes. Some evenings my purse was stuffed with napkins.

His skills as a photographer are also greatly appreciated. Even some of the photos he himself is in were arranged according to his photographer's "eye."

Second, Alexis Powers, who felt that I had some ability to put words to paper, and encouraged me to start writing. We'll see if she is right.

Third, Paula Froman, who took time from her busy life to proofread the manuscript offering many suggestions as to better wording, punctuation and so on. She was also very helpful in determining if I had laid enough groundwork in previous chapters so that the reader would be able to follow what they were then reading.

Fourth, my sister, Petra Evans (Petie), who reminisced and giggled along with me as we recalled events of the past.

Fifth, Trianne Freese. widow of Jim's cousin, Ralph Freese, who sent many photographs and much information on the Parker side of the family, which was quite useful and helpful.

Sixth, Dennis Claude, my cousin, who regaled me with all sorts of family stories, some printable and some not.

Seventh, Jeff Howard who works at "Picture Perfect," a photography store in Albuquerque. He was able to perform miracles on the old photos to make them usable.